ESSENTIALS OF
PUBLIC POLICY
FOR
MANAGEMENT

Rogene A. Buchholz
University of Texas at Dallas

PRENTICE HALL, INC., ENGLEWOOD CLIFFS, N.J. 07632

Library of Congress Cataloging in Publication Data
BUCHHOLZ, ROGENE A. (date)
    Essentials of public policy for management.

    (Prentice-Hall essentials of management series)
    Includes bibliographies and index.
    1. Industry and state—United States.   2. Business
and politics—United States.   3. Industry—Social
aspects—United States.   I. Title.   II. Series.
HD3616.U47B762 1985   338.973′0024658   84-11627
ISBN 0-13-286824-5
ISBN 0-13-286816-4 (pbk.)

Prentice-Hall Essentials of Management Series
Stephen P. Robbins, **editor**

Editorial/Production supervision: Fay Ahuja and Diana Drew
Interior and cover design: Christine Gadekar
Buyer: Edward O'Dougherty

10   9   8   7   6   5   4   3   2   1

Printed in the United States of America

Prentice-Hall International, Inc., *London*
Prentice-Hall of Australia Pty. Limited, *Sydney*
Editora Prentice-Hall do Brasil, Ltda., *Rio de Janeiro*
Prentice-Hall Canada Inc., *Toronto*
Prentice-Hall of India Private Limited, *New Delhi*
Prentice-Hall of Japan, Inc., *Tokyo*
Prentice-Hall of Southeast Asia Pte. Ltd., *Singapore*
Whitehall Books Limited, *Wellington, New Zealand*

CONTENTS

3

HISTORICAL DEVELOPMENTS

IN PUBLIC POLICY

4

ORIGINS OF PUBLIC POLICY

5

THE PUBLIC POLICY PROCESS

6

THE IMPACTS OF PUBLIC POLICY

ON BUSINESS AND MANAGEMENT

Contents

7

PUBLIC ISSUES MANAGEMENT   177

8

CORPORATE POLITICAL ACTIVITIES   219

9

THE FUTURE OF PUBLIC POLICY

AS A NEW DIMENSION OF MANAGEMENT   260

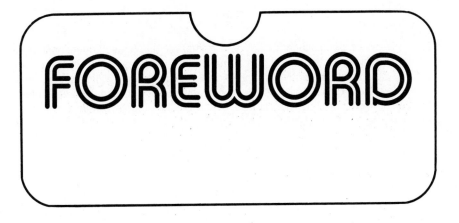

FOREWORD

With the rapid growth in recent years of courses in such areas as personnel, organizational behavior, production, decision science, labor relations, and small business management, there has developed an increased need for a viable alternative to the standard 500- or 600-page, casebound textbook. The Essentials of Management Series has been designed to fill that need. The Series consists of brief, survey books covering major content areas within the management discipline.

Each book in the Series provides a concise treatment of the key concepts and issues within a major content area, written in a highly readable style, balancing theory with practical applications, and offering a clarity of presentation that is often missing in standard, full-length textbooks. I have selected authors both for their academic expertise and their ability to identify, organize, and articulate the essential elements of their subject. So, for example, you will find that the books in this Series avoid unnecessary jargon, use a conversational writing style, include extensive examples and interesting illustrations of concepts, and have the focus of a rifle rather than that of an encyclopedic shotgun.

The books in this Series will prove useful to a wide variety of readers. Since each covers the essential body of knowledge in a major area of management. they can be used alone for introductory survey courses in colleges and universities or for management development and in-house educational programs. Additionally, their short format makes them an ideal vehicle to be combined with cases, readings, and/or experiential materials by instructors who desire to mold a course to meet unique objectives. The books in this Series offer the flexibility that is either not feasible or too costly to achieve with a standard textbook.

Stephen P. Robbins
Series Editor

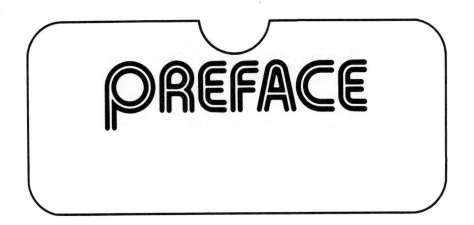

PREFACE

The importance of public policy to business executives can hardly be overestimated. Indeed, it seems fair to say that the total environment in which business operates is more a function of public policy than it is of traditional free market forces. The aggregate economic conditions that a company faces as far as employment and income levels are concerned are largely determined by the fiscal and monetary policies of government. Specific industries are affected by protectionist measures, environmental regulation, subsidies, and tax policies. Beyond the industry level, the fate of individual companies is oftentimes in the hands of government due to the necessity of winning a government contract or the need for a guaranteed loan from the government.

The foregoing are merely illustrations of the way in which public policy can affect business organizations. Since public policy is so important, it is necessary for business executives and business students to have some knowledge of what public policy is all about and how it is formulated. Knowledge of how public policy shapes the business environment is important in order to analyze the impact specific measures might have on a particular company, industry, or the entire business sector. The public policy process must be understood so business executives can know how and when to appropriately and effectively participate in public policy formulation. To abdicate this role is to leave the fate of business up to government officials, public interest group leaders, and other participants in the public policy process. This hardly seems to be a wise position for corporate management to take in view of its responsibility to stockholders, employees, consumers, and the public at large.

Public policy is too important to be left up to government or interest groups alone. Many of the adverse consequences of government regulation formulated in the 1960s and 1970s might have been avoided if business had been more active in its formulation. Business has a responsibility to participate in the public policy process and help solve the nation's economic and social problems. In the words of John Dunlop, former Secretary of Labor and a leading advocate of public policy for business:

> The absence of effective leadership for the business community on many public policy questions—in consensus building and in dealing with other groups and governments—means that business enterprises forfeit almost entirely to politicians. The rapid expansion of government regulations in recent years and

specifically government's penchant for rigid, bureaucratic "command and control" regulations, even when ineffective and counterproductive, have arisen in part from a lack of coherence and consensus within the business community about more constructive choices for achieving social purposes.[1]

This book is designed for use by business executives and students in schools of business and management. It is hoped that the book will find a market in the trade, both for reading by individual executives and in executive development programs. In academia, the book should be useful in a business and society course as well as a traditional business policy course where environmental influences on business policy are considered. It should also be useful for executive development programs sponsored by schools of business and management.

Various topics related to public policy that are of importance to business managers and students are discussed in the book. The evolution of the public policy concept as a new dimension of management is discussed in the first chapter. In the second chapter, some definitional and conceptual material related to public policy is discussed to provide some intellectual foundations for subsequent material. An historical overview of major developments in public policy and business is presented in chapter three. The origins of public policy are discussed to give the reader an idea of how public issues, which originate in our society, may become formal public policy. The process by which public policy is formalized is discussed next. This discussion covers the way the federal government operates. Impacts of public policy on business include changes in corporate structure and behavior that public policy has brought about. The process of public issues management is discussed and analyzed in chapter seven. This will familiarize the reader with an evolving function within corporations, through which management's response to public issues that affect the corporation is formalized. This function is an emerging one that involves various roles within the corporate organization. The strategies that can be adopted for public policy participation are the subject of chapter eight. These strategies are discussed in a framework that corresponds with the stages of public policy formulation. Finally, a word is said about the future of business and public policy.

Thanks are due to many people who were influential in the writing of this book. William C. Frederick of the University of Pittsburgh is owed a great debt of personal gratitude for introducing me to the field of business environment and public policy, and serving as my mentor during my years of study at that institution. Lee E. Preston and James E. Post deserve credit for introducing me to the concept of public policy in their book, *Private Management and Public Policy,* which was very influential in shaping my thinking. Equally influential was Murray L. Weidenbaum, whom I worked with for three years at the Center for the Study of American Business (CSAB) at Washington University in St. Louis, Missouri. This association made me aware of the impacts public policy has on business. My work with the American Assembly of Collegiate Schools of Business, which along with the CSAB sponsored the study of the business environ-

[1]John T. Dunlop, "The Concerns: Business and Public Policy," *Harvard Business Review,* vol. 57, no. 6 (November–December 1979), p. 86.

ment/public policy field that I conducted, acquainted me with many aspects of the public policy dimension of management. James E. Post and Stephen P. Robbins, the series editor, also deserve thanks for reviewing the book at an early stage and making many suggestions for improvement. The people at Prentice-Hall with whom I worked provided a great deal of assistance and encouragement at every step of the process. Their interest in this project is greatly appreciated. Finally, my wife deserves no end of credit, not only for her understanding and support in writing the book, which took time away from family responsibilities, but also for her help in typing the manuscript.

Rogene A. Buchholz

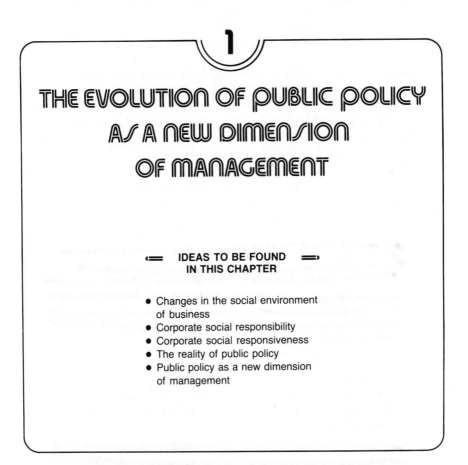

THE EVOLUTION OF PUBLIC POLICY AS A NEW DIMENSION OF MANAGEMENT

⟸ **IDEAS TO BE FOUND** ⟹
IN THIS CHAPTER

- Changes in the social environment of business
- Corporate social responsibility
- Corporate social responsiveness
- The reality of public policy
- Public policy as a new dimension of management

Management education underwent a period of concentrated self-examination in the late 1950s and early 1960s with the publication of two comprehensive studies that were widely discussed throughout the business and academic communities.[1] A third study followed which summarized the above reports and offered a series of recommendations for the improvement of management education.[2]

Among other things, these reports stressed the importance of including "environmental" courses in the curriculum of business schools and of promoting research into environmental issues and problems. It was clear from references to the business environment that these reports were concerned not only with the more traditional economic and legal environments, but with the social and political environments as well. For example, one

[1] Frank C. Pierson, *The Education of American Businessmen* (New York: McGraw-Hill, 1959); Robert A. Gordon and James E. Howell, *Higher Education for Business* (New York: Columbia University Press, 1959).

[2] Committee for Economic Development, *Educating Tomorrow's Managers* (New York: CED, 1964).

author stressed the need for "the manager of tomorrow to understand, and be sensitive to, the entire economic, political, and social environment in which we will live and in which his business will operate and be judged."[3]

While not necessarily introducing the issue of the environment to business educators and management practitioners, the reports at least reawakened interest in a broad range of environmental influences on business as part of a professional business education. A narrow vocationalism, the reports stressed, that ignores these environmental influences, is not appropriate for preparing managers for today's world. The importance of the environment to business is described in the following quote:

> There are two points to stress about the relations between business firms and their environment. One is the fact of mutual interaction. The environment helps to determine the alternatives on the basis of which business decisions are made and also affects the value systems which supply the criteria for choosing among these alternatives. At the same time, business firms, individually and particularly collectively, react upon their environment. It is this fact that makes it so important for businessmen to bring a keen sense of social responsibility to their jobs. More than economic effects ensue from their decisions. Business activity affects government policy in a variety of ways. It helps to determine the conditions of community living; it has been largely responsible for the kind of urban civilization in which we live; it helps to shape the intellectual and moral tone of the times.
>
> Another important aspect of the interrelations between business and its environment is that these relations are continuously changing, evolving out of the past into a future that can be but vaguely foreseen. Change and uncertainty are the very essence of the businessman's life. It is a truism that the world which today's students will have to manage a generation hence will be much different from the world which they and their teachers know at present. Businessmen clearly have to be equipped to deal with unforeseen change, to have some idea of the sources of change in their environment, and, so far as this is possible, to anticipate change.[4]

CHANGES IN THE SOCIAL ENVIRONMENT OF BUSINESS

The last paragraph could not have been more prophetic. The decade of the 1960s was one of sweeping social change that affected business organizations in ways that are still not fully understood and accepted. The focus on civil rights for minorities, equal rights for women, protection of the physical

---

[3] Pierson, *Education*, p. 323.

[4] Gordon and Howell, *Higher Education*, p. 65.

environment, safety and health in the workplace, and a broad array of consumer issues has had far-reaching and long-lasting impacts on business organizations and on the management of these organizations. The long-term effect of this social change is a dramatic change in the "rules of the game" by which business is expected to operate.

While social movements have appeared at various times throughout American history, they seemed to proliferate in the 1960s. The decade began with the civil rights movement based on the dissatisfaction of blacks with their status in American society. Pressures for change had been building for several years. In 1955 a black woman, Rosa Parks, had refused to move to the rear of a city bus in Birmingham, Alabama, a customary practice in southern states with Jim Crow laws. This refusal led to her arrest and ignited a social movement throughout the South in support of civil rights for blacks. Boycotts of buses and white merchants, and nonviolent demonstrations and marches were used with great success to influence public opinion. The result of this movement was the passage of new federal laws relating to civil rights that attempted to provide equal opportunity for blacks and other minorities to pursue their interests in all areas of American society.

Soon after the civil rights movement began to have a major impact on American society, many women began to express dissatisfaction with their lot in society. They complained about the lack of equal opportunity in the workplace: being paid less than men for performing essentially the same job, being denied an opportunity to move into higher-paying jobs in management and the professions, and a host of other problems. Outside the workplace they complained about being stereotyped as housewives and mothers, being treated as sex objects, and being treated unfairly when applying for credit. Thus began a feminist movement to pursue equal status for women in American society. The movement also used the tactics of boycotts and demonstrations to influence public opinion, and pressed for legislation and even a constitutional amendment, which was subsequently defeated, to assure equal rights for women in all areas of American life.

The consumer movement resulted from dissatisfaction with the quality of products available on the marketplace, the inadequate response of companies to consumer complaints, the meaninglessness of warranties, the number of accidents related to consumer products, and similar problems. The consumer movement was concerned with a variety of issues that grew out of a technologically sophisticated and complex marketplace coupled with a highly affluent and educated population that had high aspirations and expectations regarding the quality of life it wanted for itself. The dramatic event which sparked the movement was the publication in 1965 of Ralph Nader's *Unsafe at Any Speed*, a book that was critical of the Corvair automobile and indicted the producer, General Motors, for a lack of concern about automobile safety. The response of General Motors to this book catapulted Nader into a leadership position in the consumer movement. The primary tactic used by the consumer movement to pursue its goals was one of working within the political system to pass an enormous amount of consumer legislation.

The ecology movement sprang up almost overnight, helped by books that focused on DDT and other alleged evils which were being perpetuated by business and causing environmental problems. During the latter years of the 1960s, many of the energies that had gone into the civil rights movement were channeled into the environmental movement as the former matured. Public consciousness about pollution of the environment increased rapidly. The result was a major public policy effort to control pollution and correct for the deficiencies of the market system in controlling the amount and types of waste discharged into the environment.

> Fifteen or so years ago, pollution and ecology were two terms rarely found in the lexicon of business. Today environmental survival and pollution abatement are major topics of the times and receive prominent exposure in the literature of business and economics. If any one issue provided the initial sustenance for social responsibility proponents, that issue was the effect of business operations and practices on the physical environment. Probably more words have been written on this subject than on most others of a business and social problems context.[5]

Other social changes that were taking place in the 1960s and the 1970s had to do with the growth of entitlement programs (social security, medicare, medicaid, food stamps, etc.) that captured an ever-increasing share of the federal budget. The energy, safety, and health consciousness of the population spilled over into a concern about safety and health in the workplace, where a crisis atmosphere was created that led to a comprehensive federal law dealing with occupational safety and health. Concern about the ethical standards of business emerged out of the Watergate experience and the foreign payments controversy.

It is clear that a major social revolution took place during the 1960s and 1970s that had major impacts on business. There was a change of values throughout society evidenced by a concern about the social impacts of business, a change of personal attitudes as business received more criticism, and a change of social organization as more and more interest groups emerged to institutionalize these social concerns.

There are many reasons for this unprecedented amount of social change. The educational level of society increased after World War II, which may have increased the aspirations and expectations of many people for a higher quality of life than they were presently experiencing. Television and

---

[5] Arthur Elkins and Dennis W. Callaghan, *A Managerial Odyssey: Problems in Business and Its Environment*, 2nd ed. (Reading, Mass.: Addison-Wesley, 1978), p. 173.

other media had an enormous impact on the amount of information flowing throughout society, making people aware of problems and events instantaneously, and influencing public opinion in support of emerging social movements. There was also a general euphoria throughout American society in the 1960s that the great society could be created by eliminating poverty, cleaning up pollution, and solving all our social problems, while providing an ever-increasing standard of living for all citizens.

Perhaps society can also be thought of in the familiar model developed by Abraham Maslow with respect to individual development. During the 1950s, many people became relatively affluent and moved into a middle-class or even upper-class status. They were blessed with new products that made life easier and more interesting. Thus a large part of society may have felt that its basic economic or lower-order needs were satisfied, and attention could be turned towards fulfillment of higher-order needs such as pollution control, respect for the basic rights of all citizens, increasing the safety and health aspects of the workplace and marketplace, and providing more economic resources for the less fortunate members of society.

CORPORATE SOCIAL RESPONSIBILITY

Given this kind of a social revolution, it is not surprising that the social environment was given increasing attention during the 1960s and 1970s by business corporations and schools of business and management. While some scholars suggest that the concept of corporate social responsibility may have had its origins in the 1930s, the concept really came into its own during the 1960s as a response to the changing social values of society.[6] Executives began to talk about the social responsibilities of business and develop specific social programs in response to problems of a social, rather than economic, nature. Schools of business and management implemented new courses in business and society or in the social responsibilities of business.

There are many definitions of social responsibility, but in general it means that a private corporation has responsibilities to society that go beyond the production of goods and services at a profit—that a corporation has a broader constituency to serve than that of stockholders alone. Corporations relate to society through more than just the marketplace and serve a wider range of human values than the traditional economic values implied when the corporation is viewed solely as an economic institution. Corporate social responsibility means that corporations have a responsibility to help society solve some of its most pressing social problems (many of which the

[6] William C. Frederick, "From CSR$_1$ to CSR$_2$: The Maturing of Business and Society Thought," Graduate School of Business, University of Pittsburgh, 1978, Working Paper No. 279, p. 1.

corporation helped to cause) by devoting some of its resources—human, financial, capital—to the solution of these problems.

The concept of social responsibility received increasing attention during the 1960s because of the need for corporations to respond to the changing social environment of business. This change was often described as a change in the terms of the contract between business and society that reflected changing expectations regarding the social performance of business.[7] The old contract between business and society was based on the view that economic growth was the source of all progress, social as well as economic. The engine providing this economic growth was considered to be the drive for profits by competitive private enterprise. The basic mission of business was thus to produce goods and services at a profit, and in doing this business was making its maximum contribution to society and, in fact, being socially responsible.[8]

The new contract between business and society was based on the view that the single-minded pursuit of economic growth produced some detrimental side effects that imposed social costs on certain segments of society or on society as a whole. The pursuit of economic growth, it was believed, did not necessarily lead automatically to social progress. In many cases it led instead to a deteriorating physical environment, an unsafe workplace, needless exposure to toxic substances on the part of workers and consumers, discrimination against certain groups in society, urban decay, and other social problems. This new contract between business and society involved the reduction of these social costs of business through impressing upon business the idea that it has an obligation to work for social betterment. The new contract does not invalidate the old contract—it simply adds new terms or additional clauses to that contract (Figure 1.1) and includes a responsibility for both economic and social impacts.

> Today it is clear that the terms of the contract between society and business are, in fact, changing in substantial and important ways. Business is being asked to assume broader responsibilities to society than ever before and to serve a wider range of human values. Business enterprises, in effect, are being asked to contribute more to the quality of American life than just supplying quantities of goods and services.[9]

The debate about social responsibility was extensive. The supporters of social responsibility argued the following:

[7] Melvin Anshen, *Managing the Socially Responsible Corporation* (New York: Macmillan, 1974).

[8] Milton Friedman, "The Social Responsibility of Business Is To Increase Its Profits," *New York Times Magazine*, Sept. 13, 1970, pp. 122–26.

[9] Committee for Economic Development, *Social Responsibility of Business Corporations* (New York: CED, 1972), p. 12.

```
┌─────────────────────────────────────────────────────────────────────┐
│                          NEW CONTRACT                                 │
│   ┌───────────────────────────────────────────────────────────────┐  │
│   │                       OLD CONTRACT                            │  │
│   │                                          ┌───┐                 │  │
│   │   Economic Inputs                        │   │  Economic Outputs│ │
│   │    ● Capital Goods                       │ B │   ● Goods and Services│
│   │    ● Raw Materials                       │ U │   ● Jobs and Income   │
│   │    ● Human Resources                     │ S │   ● Dividends and Interest│
│   │                                          │ I │                 │  │
│   │                                          │ N │                 │  │
│   │                                          │ E │                 │  │
│   │   Social Inputs                          │ S │  Social Outputs │  │
│   │    ● Air and Water                       │ S │   ● Pollution    │  │
│   │    ● Quality of Work Force               │   │   ● Injuries and Illness│
│   │    ● Composition of Work Force           └───┘   ● Discrimination and Poverty│
│   └───────────────────────────────────────────────────────────────┘  │
└─────────────────────────────────────────────────────────────────────┘
```

Figure 1.1
The Contract between Business and Society

Source: Rogene A. Buchholz. *Business Environment and Public Policy: Implications for Management*, © 1982, p.414. Reprinted by permission of Prentice-Hall, Inc., Englewood Cliffs, N.J.

1. Business must accommodate itself to social change if it expects to survive.
2. Business must take a long-run or enlightened view of self-interest and help solve social problems to create a better environment for itself.
3. Business can gain a better public image by being socially responsible.
4. Government regulation can be avoided if business can meet changing social expectations before issues become politicized.
5. Business has enormous resources that would be useful in solving social problems.
6. Social problems can be turned into profitable business opportunities.
7. Business has a moral obligation to help solve social problems that it has created or perpetuated.

The opponents of social responsibility pointed out the following:

1. Social responsibility provides no mechanism for accountability as to the use of corporate resources.
2. Managers are legally and ethically bound to earn the highest possible rate of return on the stockholder's investment in the company they manage.[10]
3. Social responsibility poses a threat to the pluralistic nature of our society.[11]

---

[10] Friedman, "Social Responsibility."

[11] Theodore Levitt, "The Dangers of Social Responsibility," *Harvard Business Review*, vol. 36, no. 5 (September-October 1958), pp. 41–50.

4. Business executives have little experience and incentive to solve social problems.[12]

5. Social responsibility is fundamentally a subversive doctrine that would undermine the foundations of a free enterprise system.[13]

After the smoke began to clear from this debate, it was clear to both proponents and opponents of corporate social responsibility that there were certain key issues that had not, and perhaps could not, be settled. One key issue concerned the operational definition of social responsibility. How shall a corporation's resources be allocated to help solve social problems? With what specific problems shall a given corporation concern itself? What priorities shall be established? Does social responsibility refer to company actions taken to comply with the law or only to those voluntary actions that go beyond legal requirements? What goals or standards of performance are adequate? What measures shall be used to determine if a corporation is socially responsible or socially irresponsible?

The traditional marketplace provided little or no information to the manager that would be useful in making decisions about solving social problems. The concept of social responsibility provided no clearer guidelines for managerial behavior. S. Prakash Sethi wrote that social responsibility "has been used in so many different contexts that it has lost all meaning. Devoid of an internal structure and content, it has come to mean all things to all people."[14] Given this lack of precision, corporate executives who wanted to be socially responsible were left to follow their own values and interests or some rather vague generalizations about changing social values and new public expectations.

Another key problem was that the concept of social responsibility did not take into account the competitive environment in which corporations function. Many advocates of social responsibility treated the corporation as an isolated entity that had unlimited ability to engage in unilateral social action. But it came to be increasingly recognized that corporations are severely limited in their ability to respond to social problems. If a firm unilaterally engages in social action that increases its costs and prices, it places itself at a competitive disadvantage relative to other firms in the industry that may not be concerned about being socially responsible. Concerted action to solve social problems is not feasible in a competitive system unless all competitors pursue roughly the same policy on the same prob-

---

[12] Gerald D. Keim and Roger E. Meiners, "Corporate Social Responsibility: Private Means for Public Wants?" *Policy Review*, no. 5 (Summer 1978), p. 83.

[13] Milton Friedman, *Capitalism and Freedom* (Chicago: University of Chicago Press, 1962), p. 133.

[14] S. Prakash Sethi, "Dimensions of Corporate Social Responsibility," *California Management Review*, vol. 17, no. 3 (Spring 1975), p. 58.

lems. Since collusion among competitors is illegal, the only way such concerted action can occur is when some other institution, such as government, makes all competitors engage in the same activity and pursue the same policy.

> . . . every business . . . is, in effect, "trapped" in the business system that it has helped to create. It is incapable, as an individual unit, of transcending that system . . . the dream of the socially responsible corporation that, replicated over and over again can transform our society is illusory . . . Because their aggregate power is not unified, not truly collective, not organized, they [corporations] have no way, even if they wished, of redirecting that power to meet the most pressing needs of society . . . Such redirection could only occur through the intermediate agency of government rewriting the rules under which all corporations operate.[15]

The debate about social responsibility never took this institutional context of corporations seriously. Yet all the while the debate about social responsibility was continuing and corporate executives were asking for a definition of their social responsibilities, government was in fact rewriting the rules under which all corporations operate through a vast amount of legislation and regulation pertaining to the physical environment, occupational safety and health, equal opportunity, and consumer concerns.

The last issue that remained unresolved in the debate about social responsibility concerns the moral underpinnings of the notion. The term responsibility is a moral term that implies an obligation to someone or something. It is clear that business has an economic responsibility to produce goods and services and perform other economic functions for society. But why does business have social responsibilities as well? The debate about social responsibility produced no clear and generally-accepted moral principle that would impose upon business an obligation to work for social betterment.[16] To impose this obligation various moral strictures such as business survival, enlightened self-interest, responsible use of power, corporate citizenship and similar moralistic generalizations were used. The opponents of social responsibility fared no better in this regard raising the specter of an end to free enterprise, declining productivity, increased government interference in private decisions, and all the rest. Such moralistic debate generates a good deal of heat but little light. The absence of a clear moral principle supporting the notion of corporate social responsibility is perhaps the most fundamental problem with the concept.

---

[15] Neil W. Chamberlain, *The Limits of Corporate Responsibility* (New York: Basic Books, 1973), pp. 4, 6.

[16] Frederick, "From CSR$_1$ to CSR$_2$," p. 5.

CORPORATE SOCIAL RESPONSIVENESS

The intractability of these issues, according to one author, "posed the dreadful possibilities that the debate over corporate social responsibility would continue indefinitely with little prospect of final resolution or that it would simply exhaust itself and collapse as a viable legitimate question."[17] But beginning in the 1970s, a theoretical and conceptual reorientation began to take place regarding corporate response to the social environment. This new approach was labeled corporate social responsiveness, and while initially it appeared that only semantics was involved, it gradually became clear that the shift from responsibility to responsiveness was much more substantive. This shift represented an attempt to escape the unresolved dilemmas that emerged from the social responsibility debate. The concept of corporate social responsiveness was defined by one author as follows:

> Corporate social responsiveness refers to the capacity of a corporation to respond to social pressures. The literal act of responding, or of achieving a generally responsive posture, to society is the focus of corporate social responsiveness . . . One searches the organization for mechanisms, procedures, arrangements, and behavioral patterns that, taken collectively, would mark the organization as more or less capable of responding to social pressures. It then becomes evident that organizational design and managerial competence play important roles in how extensively and how well a company responds to social demands and needs.[18]

Research in corporate social responsiveness focused on internal corporate responsiveness to social problems. For example, Ackerman and Bauer[19] developed a conceptual model that outlined three stages of the internal response process of corporations: awareness, commitment, and implementation (Exhibit 1.1). In the first stage, the chief executive officer recognizes a social problem to be important. This awareness is marked by several activities. Initially, the chief executive officer may begin to speak out on the issue at meetings of industry and trade associations, stockholders, and civic groups. He or she may also commit corporate resources to special projects, such as ghetto plants, waste recovery facilities, and training centers. Finally, the CEO perceives the need for an up-to-date company policy, which is then communicated to all managers in the organization. However, responsibility for implementing the policy is assigned as a matter of course to the operating units as part of their customary tasks performed in running the business. While this approach fails to provoke acceptable action or achievement with

[17] *Ibid.*, p. 5.

[18] *Ibid.*, p. 6.

[19] Robert W. Ackerman and Raymond A. Bauer, *Corporate Social Responsiveness* (Reston, Va.: Reston, 1976).

EXHIBIT 1.1
Ackerman/Bauer Model of Corporate Responsiveness
Phases of Organizational Involvement

Organizational Level	Phase 1	Phase 2	Phase 3
Chief Executive	Issue: Policy problem	Obtain knowledge	Obtain organizational commitment
	Action: Write and communicate policy	Add staff specialists	Change performance expectations
	Outcome: Enriched purpose, increased awareness		
Staff Specialists		Issue: Technical problem	Provoke response from operating units
		Action: Design data system and interpret environment	Apply data system to performance measurement
		Outcome: Technical and administrative learning	
Division Management			Issue: Management problem
			Action: Commit resources and modify procedures
			Outcome: Increased responsiveness

* Phase 1—social concerns exist but are not specifically directed at the corporation.
* Phase 2—broad implications for the corporation become clear but enforcement is weak or even nonexistent.
* Phase 3—expectations for corporate action become more specific and sanctions (governmental or otherwise) become plausible threats.

From R. Ackerman and R. Bauer, *Corporate Social Responsiveness: The Modern Dilemma* (Reston, Va.: Reston Publishing Co., 1976), p. 128. Reprinted with permission of Reston Publishing Co., Inc., a Prentice-Hall Co.

respect to the problem in most cases, the major outcome of this phase is at least a sense of enriched purpose and an increased awareness of social problems.[20]

The key event heralding the beginning of the second phase is the appointment of a staff specialist reporting to the chief executive officer or to the senior staff. The staff specialist coordinates the corporation's activities in response to a social problem, helps the chief executive officer perform his or her public duties, and ensures that the corporation's response to the problem is implemented throughout the organization. The specialist begins to gather more systematic information on the company's activities relating to the problem and matches this data with his or her assessment of environmental demands. This is the beginning of an internal data system and a systematic manner of assessing and interpreting the environment to management. The specialist also mediates between operating divisions and external organizations, including government agencies that are pressuring the corporation.[21]

Eventually, however, it is discovered that the appointment of a staff specialist still fails to elicit the corporate response envisaged in corporate policy. The staff specialist's attempts to force action on the corporation are alien to the decentralized mode of decision-making within most corporate organizations. The staff specialist becomes overburdened with moderating conflict within the organization and crisis-by-crisis involvement. But at least a good deal of technical and administrative learning is accomplished in this phase.[22]

In the third phase, top management sees the organizational rigidities to be more serious than previously acknowledged. They cannot be waved away with a policy statement nor can they be overcome with a staff specialist. Instead, the whole organizational apparatus has to become involved. In this phase, the CEO attempts to make the achievement of a social policy objective a goal for all managers in the organization by institutionalizing the policy. This attempt involves modifying procedures of the company related to the setting of objectives, reward systems, performance measurement, and similar procedures.[23]

This initial research by Ackerman and Bauer triggered other models of the corporate response process. For example S. Prakash Sethi[24] also developed a three-stage model that defined corporate behavior as social obligation, social responsibility, and social responsiveness (Exhibit 1.2). In

---

[20] Robert W. Ackerman, "How Companies Respond To Social Demands," *Harvard Business Review*, vol. 51, no. 4 (July-August 1973), p. 92.

[21] *Ibid.*, pp. 92–93.

[22] *Ibid.*, pp. 93.

[23] *Ibid.*, pp. 93–95.

[24] Sethi, "Dimensions," pp. 58–64.

the first stage, social obligation, the corporation seeks legitimacy by meeting legal and economic criteria only. The corporation believes it is accountable only to its stockholders and strongly resists any regulation of its activities. In the second stage, social responsibility, the corporation searches for legitimacy by recognizing the limited relevance of meeting only legal and economic criteria, and accepts a broader set of criteria for measuring corporate performance that includes a social dimension. Management considers groups other than stockholders that might be affected by its actions and is willing to work with these outside groups for good environmental legislation. In the third stage, social responsiveness, the corporation accepts its role as defined by the social system, and recognizes that this role is subject to change over time. Furthermore, it is willing to account for its actions to other groups, even those not directly affected by its actions, and assists legislative bodies in developing better legislation. Thus business becomes an active supporter as well as promoter of environmental and social concerns.

From these examples, it can be seen that corporate social responsiveness deals with how corporations respond to social problems. The important questions in this philosophy are not moral, related to whether a corporation should respond to a social problem out of a sense of responsibility, but are more pragmatic and action-oriented, dealing with the ability of a corporation to respond and what changes are necessary to enable it to respond more effectively.

One of the advantages of the social responsiveness philosophy is its managerial orientation. The concept ignores the philosophical debate about responsibility and obligation and focuses on the problems and prospects of making corporations more socially responsive. One of the reasons for research into corporate response patterns is to discover those responses that have proven to be most effective in dealing with social problems.

The corporate social responsiveness approach also lends itself to more rigorous analytical research to discover patterns of response and focuses on specific techniques, such as environmental scanning or the social audit, to improve the response process. Such research can also discover how management can best institutionalize social policy throughout the organization. One can investigate which organizational structures are most appropriate, whether top management commitment is crucial, what changes in the reward structure improve the corporation's response to social problems, what role the public affairs departments should play in the response process, and how social policy can be best formulated for the organization as a whole.[25]

Given these advantages, however, the concept of corporate social responsiveness still faces the same key problems that plague the social responsibility concept. The concept of social responsiveness does not clarify

[25] Frederick, "From CSR_1 to CSR_2," pp. 12–13.

EXHIBIT 1.2
A Three-State Schema for Classifying Corporate Behavior

Dimensions of Behavior	State One: Social Obligation Proscriptive	State Two: Social Responsibility Prescriptive	State Three: Social Responsiveness Anticipatory and Preventive
Search for legitimacy	Confines legitimacy to legal and economic criteria only; does not violate laws; equates profitable operations with fulfilling social expectations.	Accepts the reality of limited relevance of legal and market criteria of legitimacy in actual practice. Willing to consider and accept broader—extralegal and extramarket—criteria for measuring corporate performance and social role.	Accepts its role as defined by the social system and therefore subject to change, recognizes importance of profitable operations but includes other criteria.
Ethical norms	Considers business value-neutral; managers expected to behave according to their own ethical standards.	Defines norms in community-related terms, i.e., good corporate citizen. Avoids taking normal stand on issues which may harm its economic interests or go against prevailing social norms (majority views).	Takes definite stand on issues of public concern; advocates institutional ethical norms even though they may be detrimental to its immediate economic interest or prevailing social norms.
Social accountability for corporate actions	Construes narrowly as limited to stockholders, jealously guards its prerogatives against outsiders.	Construes narrowly for legal purposes, but broadened to include groups affected by its actions; management more outward looking.	Willing to account for its actions to other groups, even those not directly affected by its actions.
Operating strategy	Exploitative and defensive adaptation. Maximum externalization of costs.	Reactive adaptation. Where identifiable internalize previously external costs. Maintain current standards of physical and social environment. Compensate victims of pollution and other corporate-related activities even in the absence of clearly established legal grounds. Develop industry-wide standards.	Proactive adaptation. Takes lead in developing and adapting new technology for environmental protectors. Evaluates side effects of corporate actions and eliminates them prior to the action's being taken. Anticipates future social changes and develops internal structures to cope with them.

Response to social pressures	Maintains low public profile, but if attacked, uses PR methods to upgrade its public image; denies any deficiencies; blames public dissatisfaction on ignorance or failure to understand corporate functions; discloses information only where legally required.	Accepts responsibility for solving current problems; will admit deficiencies in former practices and attempt to persuade public that its current practices meet social norms; attitude toward critics conciliatory; freer information disclosures than state one.	Willingly discusses activities with outside groups; makes information freely available to public; accepts formal and informal inputs from outside groups in decision making. Is willing to be publicly evaluated for its various activities.
Activities pertaining to governmental actions	Strongly resists any regulation of its activities except when it needs help to protect its market position; avoids contact; resists any demands for information beyond that legally required.	Preserves management discretion in corporate decisions, but cooperates with government in research to improve industry-wide standards; participates in political processes and encourages employees to do likewise.	Openly communicates with government; assists in enforcing existing laws and developing evaluations of business practices; objects publicly to governmental activities that it feels are detrimental to the public good.
Legislative and political activities	Seeks to maintain status quo; actively opposes laws that would internalize any previously externalized costs; seeks to keep lobbying activities secret.	Willing to work with outside groups for good environmental laws; concedes need for change in some status quo laws; less secrecy in lobbying than state one.	Avoids meddling in politics and does not pursue special-interest laws; assists legislative bodies in developing better laws where relevant; promotes honesty and openness in government and in its own lobbying activities.
Philanthropy	Contributes only when direct benefit to it clearly shown; otherwise, views contributions as responsibility of individual employees.	Contributes to noncontroversial and established causes; matches employee contributions.	Activities of state two, *plus* support and contributions to new, controversial groups whose needs it sees as unfulfilled and increasingly important.

S. Prakash Sethi, "Dimensions of Corporate Social Responsibility." Copyright © 1975 by the Regents of the University of California. Reprinted from *California Management Review*, Volume XVII, No. 3, p. 63, only by permission of the Regents.

how corporate resources shall be allocated for the solution of social problems. Companies respond to different problems in different ways and to varying degrees. But there is no clear idea as to which pattern of responsiveness will produce the greatest amount of social betterment. The philosophy of responsiveness does not help the company decide what problems to get involved in and what priorities to establish. Thus it provides no better guidance to management than does social responsibility on the best strategies or policies to be adopted to produce social betterment. The concept seems to suggest that management, by determining the degree of social responsiveness and the problems it will respond to, decides the meaning of social responsiveness and what social goods and services shall be produced.

The concept of social responsiveness does not take the institutional context of business any more seriously than did social responsibility. Research has not dealt very thoroughly with the impact government regulation made on the corporation and how the corporation responded to this change in the political environment. Individual institutions were again treated as rather isolated phenomena that could choose a response pattern irrespective of the institutional context in which that corporation operated.

Finally, the question of an underlying moral principle is ignored. Social pressures are assumed to exist and it is believed that business must respond to them. This places business in a passive role of simply responding to social change. The concept of social responsiveness provides no moral reason for business to get involved in social problems. It contains no explicit value theory and advocates no specific set of values for business to follow in making social responses.[26]

THE REALITY OF PUBLIC POLICY

In the mid-1970s, academics and businessmen began to realize that a fundamental change was taking place in the political environment of business—that government was engaged in shaping business behavior and making business respond to a wide array of social problems by passing an unprecedented amount of legislation and writing new regulations pertaining to these problems. The political system responded to the social revolution of the 1960s by enacting over one hundred new laws regulating business activity (Exhibit 1.3). New regulatory agencies were created or new responsibilities were assigned to old agencies. These agencies issued thousands of rules and procedural requirements during the 1960s and 1970s. The number of pages in the Federal Register grew from 20,036 in 1970 to 42,422 in 1974. In March 1979, the Office of the Federal Register reported that 61,000 pages of government regulations had been issued, a 305 percent increase in eight years.

[26] *Ibid.*, pp. 14–16.

This regulatory role of government continued to expand until the 1980 election of Ronald Reagan. The new type of social regulation, as it came to be called, affected virtually every department or functional area within the corporation and every level of management. This growth of regulation was referred to as a second managerial revolution. Decision-making power and control over the corporation was shifting from the managers of corporations to a vast cadre of government regulators who were influencing—and in many cases controlling—managerial decisions in the typical business corporation.[27] In 1976, for example, a total of eighty-three federal agencies were regulating business in one or another aspect. The types of decisions which were becoming increasingly subject to government influence and control were basic to the operation of a business organization. According to Murray Weidenbaum, former chairman of the Council of Economic Advisors during the Reagan administration and one of the leading regulation experts in the United States, these decisions included the following:

What lines of business to go into?
What products can be produced?
What investments can be financed?
Under what conditions can products be produced?
Where can they be made?
How can they be marketed?
What prices can be charged?
What profit can be kept?[28]

During the late seventies, more and more attention was paid to the changing political environment of business. Books were written that provided a comprehensive overview of the impact government regulation was making on business.[29] Studies were completed that attempted to measure the costs of social regulation to the private sector.[30] This activity drew attention to the political environment of business and indicated that this environment, largely hostile to business, was giving rise to legislation and regulation that interfered with the ability of business to perform its basic economic mission. Social regulation was costly, it had negative impacts on productivity, it contributed to inflation, and it diverted management attention from the basic task of running the business.

[27] Murray L. Weidenbaum, *Business, Government and the Public* (Englewood Cliffs, N.J.: Prentice-Hall, 1977), p. 285.

[28] Murray L. Weidenbaum, *The Future of Business Regulation* (New York: AMACOM, 1979), p. 34.

[29] *Ibid.*.

[30] See Murray L. Weidenbaum and Robert DeFina, *The Cost of Federal Regulation of Economic Activity* (Washington, D.C.: American Enterprise Institute, 1978); Arthur Anderson, *Cost of Government Regulation* (New York: The Business Roundtable, 1979).

EXHIBIT 1.3
Significant Regulatory Legislation, 1960-1979

Civil Rights Act of 1960

Federal Hazardous Substances Labeling Act of 1960

Fair Labor Standards Amendments of 1961, 1966 and 1974

Federal Water Pollution Control Act Amendments of 1961

Oil Pollution Act of 1961 and Amendments of 1973

Food and Agriculture Act of 1962

Air Pollution Control Act of 1962

Antitrust Civil Process Act of 1962

Drug Amendments of 1962

Clean Air Act of 1963 and Amendments of 1966 and 1970

Equal Pay Act of 1963

Civil Rights Act of 1964

Food Stamp Act of 1964

Automotive Products Trade Act of 1965

Federal Cigarette Labeling and Advertising Act of 1965

Water Quality Act of 1965

Clean Water Restoration Act of 1966

Fair Packaging and Labeling Act of 1966

Federal Coal Mine Safety Act Amendments of 1966

Financial Institutions Supervisory Act of 1966

Oil Pollution of the Sea Act of 1966

Age Discrimination in Employment Act of 1967

Air Quality Act of 1967

Wholesome Meal Act of 1967

Agricultural Fair Practices Act of 1968

Consumer Credit Protection Act of 1968

Natural Gas Pipeline Safety Act of 1968

Radiation Control for Health and Safety Act of 1968

Cigarette Smoking Act of 1969

Child Protection and Toy Safety Act of 1969

Federal Coal Mine Health and Safety Act of 1969

Tax Reform Act of 1969

National Environmental Policy Act of 1970

Bank Holding Act Amendments of 1970

Bank Records and Foreign Transactions Act of 1970

Economic Stabilization Act of 1970 and Amendments of 1971 and 1973

Environmental Quality Improvement Act of 1970

Fair Credit Reporting Act of 1970

Investment Company Amendments of 1970

Noise Pollution and Abatement Act of 1970

Occupational Safety and Health Act of 1970

Securities Investor Protection Act of 1970

Water and Environmental Quality Improvement Act of 1970

Export Administration Finance Act of 1971

Consumer Product Safety Act of 1972

Equal Employment Opportunity Act of 1972

Federal Environmental Pesticide Control Act of 1972

Noise Control Act of 1972

Agriculture and Consumers Protection Act of 1973

Emergency Petroleum Act of 1973

Highway Safety Act of 1973

Water Resources Development Act of 1974

Energy Policy and Conservation Act of 1975

Toxic Substances Control Act of 1976

Resource Conservation and Recovery Act of 1976

Clean Air Act Amendments of 1977

Water Pollution Control Act Amendments of 1977

Endangered Species Act Amendments of 1978

Amendments to the Age Discrimination in Employment Act of 1978

Emergency Energy Conservation Act of 1979

Safe Drinking Water Act Amendments of 1979

Source: Rogene A. Buchholz, *Business Environment and Public Policy: Implications for Management,* © 1982, p. 158. Reprinted by permission of Prentice-Hall, Inc., Englewood Cliffs, N.J.

Management educators began to take public policy seriously during the same time period. Two conferences of business school deans were held, one in 1976 and the other in 1977, that dealt with regulatory reform and public policy respectively. At both meetings many deans expressed the conviction that something new was happening with respect to the role of business in society that deserved attention in course offerings of schools of business and management. Out of these meetings came the idea for a comprehensive study of what was called the business environment/public policy area, a study that was co-sponsored by the American Assembly of Collegiate Schools of Business and the Center for the Study of American Business at Washington University in St. Louis, Missouri.[31] The purpose of this study was to assess the state of the art in the field and make recommendations for improvement of teaching and research. Many management educators expressed the belief that there was a strong need for improved curriculum in this area if schools were to adequately prepare future managers for the world in which they would be working.

The theoretical and conceptual foundations for this public policy approach were laid a few years earlier by Preston and Post who attempted to define the functions of organizational management within the specific context of public policy.[32] They stated that public policy is, along with the market mechanism, the source of guidelines and criteria for managerial behavior. The public policy process is the means by which society as a whole articulates its goals and objectives, and directs and stimulates individuals and organizations to contribute to and cooperate with them. Appropriate guidelines for managerial behavior are to be found in the larger society, not in the personal vision of managers or in the special interest of groups. Thus a business organization should analyze and evaluate pressures and stimuli coming from public policy in the same way it analyzes and evaluates market experience and opportunity.

Thus began a serious concern with public policy as a new dimension of management. Many business leaders have since recognized the importance of public policy to business and are advocating that business managers become more active in the political process and work more closely with government and other groups to help shape public policy. Acceptance of this view involves acceptance of a public as well as a private role for management in society. Typical of such attitudes on the part of business leaders are the following quotes.

Executives are realizing that the day is gone when the spot at the top of

---

[31] Rogene A. Buchholz, *Business Environment/Public Policy: A Study of Teaching and Research in Schools of Business and Management* (St. Louis: Center for the Study of American Business, Washington University, 1979).

[32] Lee E. Preston and James E. Post, *Private Management and Public Policy* (Englewood Cliffs, N.J.: Prentice-Hall, 1975).

an organization chart permitted a private life style. A generation or two in the past, you could get by in business by following four rules: stick to business, stay out of trouble, join the right clubs, and don't talk to reporters. Some of us may yearn for that bygone era, but we have to take life as it comes—and today's executive is more often in the midst of the fray. CEO's are now to be found tramping through the corridors of Washington and the state capitals, testifying, talking with elected representatives and administrative aides, pleading cases in the agency offices and occasionally in the White House. Reporters are learning the names of businessmen and finding that many more of them have their doors open.[33]

. . . I want to add my own conviction that business executives must participate personally in the formation of public policy. This is not something we can delegate to our trade associations. We must study the issues, develop constructive positions, and then speak out—in public forums, in Congressional testimony, in personal contacts with our representatives in government. This is an unavoidable responsibility of business leadership today, for companies large and small.[34]

I think we must put behind us the low-profile stance that so many in business have adopted. Too many of us have left the responsibility for government to others. We've had the attitude of "We're too busy with our jobs." I feel that if we want to maintain our jobs and if we want to restore growth and vitality to our businesses, we must participate in the governmental process. We must join in the public policy debate . . . a debate that holds our future in its resolution.[35]

The motivation for this concern with public policy is clear. If the rules of the game for business are being rewritten through the public policy process and business is being forced to respond to social values through complying with laws and regulations, then it behooves business to learn more about the public policy process and become involved in helping to write the rules by which it is going to have to live. Rather than fighting change, which proved to be a losing battle in many instances, or simply accommodating itself to change, business has now, by and large, adopted a more sophisticated approach to social change. This approach has been called the pro-active stance, which means that business attempts to influence change by becoming involved in the public policy process. Thus business

[33] Irving S. Shapiro, "The Process: Business and Public Policy," *Harvard Business Review*, vol. 57, no. 6 (November-December 1979), p. 100.

[34] Reginald Jones, "The Legitimacy of the Business Corporation," General Electric Company, An Executive Speech Reprint, 1977, p. 4.

[35] Robert L. Mitchell, "Reason and Participation: The Road to Better Government-Business Interaction," remarks to the 3rd International Conference of the National Petroleum Refiners Association, San Antonio, Texas, April 3, 1978, p. 11.

attempts to influence public opinion with respect to specific social issues or with regard to the free-enterprise system in general, and attempts to influence the legislative and regulatory process with regard to specific laws and regulations.

To coordinate and direct these efforts to influence public policy, a new function has emerged within corporations called public issues management. This function helps the corporation effectively respond to a public issue that may affect its behavior. Public issues management involves anticipating issues that may affect the corporation, researching those issues to develop a position, and developing strategies to assure the corporation will have maximum impact on the outcome of the public policy process.

Academia has responded to this public policy focus by putting more public policy content into its old business and society or business and government courses. New courses have been instituted that focus explicitly on the public policy process, government regulation of business or public issues management. Research has focused on regulatory reform, political action committees, advocacy advertising, executive liability, lobbying activities, and environmental forecasting and strategic planning.

The public policy focus has some distinct advantages over the corporate social responsibility and corporate social responsiveness concepts discussed earlier. For the most part, there is no question about the nature and extent of management's social responsibilities. Once regulations are approved, these responsibilities are spelled out in excruciating detail. The government gets involved in specifying technology, labeling requirements, safety equipment, and the like. Where questions arise about the legality or feasibility of regulations, the court system is available to resolve the issue. Specific health and safety standards, for example, are either struck down or upheld by the courts. Affirmative action programs are supported or struck down according the court's interpretation of civil rights legislation.

Obviously, the public policy focus treats business in its institutional context and advocates that managers learn more about government and the public policy process so managers can appropriately influence the process. Government is recognized as the appropriate body to formalize and formulate public policy for the society as a whole. Some form of response by government to most social issues is believed to be inevitable, and no amount of corporate reform along the lines of corporate social responsibility or corporate social responsiveness is going to eliminate some form of government involvement. Government has a legitimate right to formulate public policy for corporations in response to changing public expectations.

> Society can choose to allocate its resources any way it wants and on the basis of any criteria it deems relevant. If society wants to enhance the quality of air and water, it can choose to allocate resources for the production of these goods and put constraints on business in the form of

standards . . . These nonmarket decisions are made by those who participate in the public policy process and represent their views of what is best for themselves and society as a whole . . . It is up to the body politic to determine which market outcomes are and are not appropriate. If market outcomes are not to be taken as normative, a form of regulation which requires public participation is the only alternative. The social responsibility of business is not operational and certainly not to be trusted. When business acts contrary to the normal pressures of the marketplace, only public policy can replace the dictates of the market.[36]

There is also, at least on the surface, no need for a moral underpinning for a business obligation to produce social betterment. Society makes decisions about the allocation of resources through the public policy process based on its notions about social betterment. The result is legislation and regulation that directly impinges on business behavior. Business, then, has a moral obligation to obey the law as a good citizen. Failure to do so subjects business and its executives to all sorts of penalties, monetary and otherwise. The social responsibility of business is thus to follow the directives of society at large as expressed in and through the public policy process.

PUBLIC POLICY AS A NEW DIMENSION OF MANAGEMENT

Throughout most of its history, the corporation has been viewed solely as an economic institution with only economic responsibilities. These responsibilities include producing goods and services to meet consumer needs, providing employment for much of the nation's work force, paying dividends to shareholders, and making provision for future growth. If these economic responsibilities were fulfilled, business was considered to have discharged its obligations to society and made its maximum contribution to society's wealth.

As briefly described in this chapter, the last twenty years have seen a dramatic change in the environment in which business operates. The economic functions of business are no longer as dominant as they traditionally have been and must be seen in relation to the social and political roles business has been asked to assume. The business institution has been reshaped to meet these new responsibilities as government through the public policy process has defined new roles for business to perform in society.

This changing role of business in society has, of course, made an impact on the managerial task within corporations. Managers have had to incorporate social and political concerns into their decision making. These concerns

---

[36] Rogene A. Buchholz, "An Alternative to Social Responsibility," pp. 12–16, *MSU Business Topics*, Summer 1977. Reprinted by permission of the publisher, Graduate School of Business Administration, Michigan State University.

have become a part of routine business operations in many corporations as managers spend more and more of their time dealing with public policy matters.

This new dimension of management was foreseen some years ago by Walter G. Held, formerly director of Advanced Management Programs for the Brookings Institution.[37] Held stated that management theory at that time revealed a striking penchant toward introspection with relatively little attention being paid to the world in which business was challenged to survive and grow. That external world involved a changing relationship between business and government. Many of the major problems confronting a business executive, Held asserted, were becoming more societal in one or another of their aspects, and increasingly, societal problems were becoming governmental in nature.

Thus, in addition to technical, administrative, and human relations skills, the manager of a modern corporation must also learn and develop skills that are relevant to the public policy dimension of the manager's task. Research is needed, Held said, to define more precisely the nature of these skills and the proficiency required in them. At a minimum the manager must be "sensitized to the importance of public policy, the processes by which it is made, and the factors that are relevant to public policy issues and their impact on business."[38]

More recently, Henry Tombari, assistant professor of Management Sciences at the California State University at Hayward, has described the role of management in modern society as "politico-economic" in nature. Such a role requires management to become involved in the public policy process as well as the market process. Management must reshape the nation's primary economic institution, the corporation, into one that is politico-economic and fits with society's values and its political system.[39]

Fran Steckmest, former Public Affairs Consultant for Shell Oil Company, calls an executive who is skilled in the public policy process a "public policy corporate executive."[40] This type of executive deals effectively with the public policy dimension of business as an integral factor in managing the corporation. The public policy corporate executive recognizes that the day of the cloistered executive has passed and has the knowledge, skills, experience, and attitudes for this new role. Steckmest describes the qualifications that are needed to operate effectively in the public policy arena as follows:

[37] Walter G. Held, "Executive Skills: The Repertoire Needs Enlarging," *Columbia Journal of World Business*, vol. 2, no. 2 (March-April 1967), pp. 81–87.

[38] *Ibid.*, p. 85.

[39] Henry A. Tombari, "The New Role of Business Management," *The Collegiate Forum*, (Fall 1979), p. 12.

[40] F. W. Steckmest, "Career Development of the Public Policy Corporate Executive," *Public Affairs Review*, 1981, pp. 71–87.

Knowledge: A basic understanding of the U.S. social, economic, and political systems, including history, structure, institutions, and processes; an understanding of current and emerging social, economic, and political issues impacting corporations and society; familiarity with the principles and techniques for public policy analysis; and an understanding of basic attitudes and viewpoints of the leadership of significant insitutions and interest groups.

Skill: Ability to apply the foregoing knowledge in planning, day-to-day decision-making, and particularly in communicating effectively under the varying circumstances required in the public policy process; e.g., person-to-person, small meetings, speeches, legislative testimony, and press, television and radio interviews.

Experience: Participation in the public policy process; e.g., analysis of public policy issues and formulation of corporate positions; explaining public issues and positions by speeches, legislative testimony and TV/radio appearances; and interaction with counterparts in government, the media, academia, unions and public interest groups. Participation in the political process; e.g., activity on behalf of a political party or advocacy group; election campaign work, or service as an elected or appointed official.

Attitude: Personal commitment to sustain and improve the U.S. system of political democracy and capitalist economy. Also, as William S. Sneath, Chairman of the Union Carbide Corporation advises: "Corporate participation in the public policy process requires conduct which engenders credibility and trust; recognition that there is no perfect public policy; and understanding that the process works by balancing interests and the corporate goal must be to strengthen—not dominate—the system."[41]

Underscoring the need for this type of executive, Steckmest goes on to say that CEO's "who do not recognize the social and political role of the corporation or are reluctant to play their role in public affairs . . . forfeit their opportunity to influence or cope more effectively with the business environment. . . . The result . . . is increased isolation of the CEO from public contact, decreased sensitivity to changing public attitudes, and misinterpretation or over-reaction to new issues—too late to change the course of the now-mature issue, but with ample time to inflict page one damage on the corporation's reputation, largely by presenting a corporate image of insensitivity or inflexibility concerning the issue."[42] These words apply not only to the chief executive officer, but to all managers whose job is affected in one way or another by public policy. According to Murray Weidenbaum, former chairman of the Council of Economic Advisors, public policy, because of its

[41] *Ibid.*, 75.
[42] *Ibid.*, p. 74.

impact on business and management, is no longer a spectator sport for business.[43]

SELECTED REFERENCES

ACKERMAN, ROBERT W. *The Social Challenge to Business.* Cambridge, Mass.: Harvard University Press, 1975.

————, AND RAYMOND BAUER. *Corporate Social Responsiveness: The Modern Dilemma.* Reston, Va.: Reston, 1976.

BOWEN, HOWARD R. *Social Responsibilities of Businessman.* New York: Harper & Row, Pub., 1953.

BUCHHOLZ, ROGENE A. *Business Environment/Public Policy: A Study of Teaching and Research in Schools of Business and Management.* St. Louis: Center for the Study of American Business, Washington University, 1979.

————, *Business Environment/Public Policy: Corporate Executive Viewpoints and Educational Implications.* St. Louis: Center for the Study of American Business, Washington University, 1980.

CARROLL, ARCHIE B., ED. *Managing Corporate Social Responsibility.* Boston: Little, Brown, 1977.

CAVANAGH, GERALD F. *American Business Values in Transition.* Englewood Cliffs, N.J.: Prentice-Hall, 1976.

CHAMBERLAIN, NEIL W. *Remaking American Values: Challenge to a Business Society.* New York: Basic Books, 1977.

————, *The Limits of Corporate Responsibility.* New York: Basic Books, 1973.

DAVIS, KEITH, WILLIAM C. FREDERICK, AND ROBERT L. BLOMSTROM. *Business and Society: Concepts and Policy Issues,* 4th ed. New York: McGraw-Hill, 1980.

EELLS, RICHARD AND CLARENCE WALTON. *Conceptual Foundations of Business.* Homewood, Ill.: Richard D. Irwin, 1961.

FRIEDMAN, MILTON. *Capitalism and Freedom.* Chicago: University of Chicago Press, 1962.

HEALD, MORRELL. *The Social Responsibilities of Business: Company and Community, 1900–1960.* Cleveland, Ohio: Case-Western Reserve, 1970.

KLEIN, THOMAS A. *Social Costs and Benefits of Business.* Englewood Cliffs, N.J.: Prentice-Hall, 1977.

MADDEN, CARL H. *Clash of Culture: Management in an Age of Changing Values.* Washington, D.C.: National Planning Association, 1972.

---

[43] Murray Weidenbaum, "Public Policy: No Longer a Spectator Sport for Business," *Journal of Business Strategy,* vol. 1, no. 1 (Summer 1980).

McGUIRE, JOSEPH W. *Business and Society.* New York: McGraw-Hill, 1963.

PRESTON, LEE E. AND JAMES E. POST. *Private Management and Public Policy.* Englewood Cliffs, N.J.: Prentice-Hall, 1975.

Research and Policy Committee of the Committee for Economic Development. *Social Responsibilities of Business Corporations.* New York: Committee for Economic Development, 1971.

SAWYER, GEORGE C. *Business and Society: Managing Corporate Social Impact.* Boston: Houghton Mifflin, 1979.

STEINER, GEORGE A. AND JOHN F. STEINER. *Business, Government, and Society,* 3rd ed. New York: Random House, 1980.

STURDIVANT, FREDERICK W. *Business and Society: A Managerial Approach.* Homewood, Ill.: Richard D. Irwin, 1977.

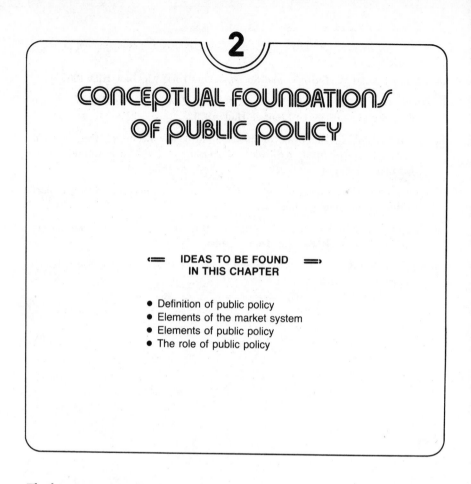

2

CONCEPTUAL FOUNDATION/
OF PUBLIC POLICY

⇐ IDEAS TO BE FOUND ⇒
IN THIS CHAPTER

- Definition of public policy
- Elements of the market system
- Elements of public policy
- The role of public policy

The business institution has been reshaped and the managerial role has been affected by many public policy measures designed to accomplish both economic and non-economic goals of society. Particularly over the last two decades, public policy has become an important determinant of corporate behavior as market outcomes have been increasingly altered through the public policy process.

Business functions in two major social processes through which decisions are made about the allocation of corporate resources. These are the market system and the public policy process. Both processes are necessary to encompass the broad range of decisions that a society needs to make about the corporation. The market mechanism and public policy are both sources of guidelines and criteria for managerial behavior.

Business has not had to concern itself throughout most of its history with the public policy process. It could assume with some confidence that the basic value system of American society was economic and thus whatever public policies resulted were generally supportive of business interests. Throughout most of American history public policy has been designed to promote business rather than interfere with its functioning.

People believed in the market mechanism and were willing to abide by most of its outcomes. Some people in society became extremely wealthy and others remained desperately poor; equality of wealth and income was not a goal of the market system or of society as a whole, for that matter. Air and water were considered to be free goods available to business management for the disposal of waste material.

With the social changes American society has recently experienced, business can no longer assume that public policy will be supportive of its interests. In fact, most of the social responsibilities of business that are now public policy measures interfere with normal business operations and result in nonproductive investments from a strictly economic point of view. Public policy measures directed toward pollution control or safety and health, interfere with the ability of business to fulfill its basic economic mission.

Thus it is important for management to have a conceptual understanding of public policy and how the public policy process differs from the market system as a resource allocator. Management also needs to understand the role that public policy plays in a market oriented society. This chapter will attempt to provide some of these important conceptual foundations which will provide a theoretical underpinning for the chapters that follow, particularly those that deal with more practical considerations.

DEFINITION OF PUBLIC POLICY

There are many concepts related to public policy that need at least a working definition to provide a framework from which to discuss more practical and action-oriented concerns. A definition of the term *public policy* itself is in order. One way to define the term is simply to say that public policy is policy made by a public body, such as government, that is representative of the interests of the larger society. Government, as stated in the last chapter, is the legitimate institution to make public policy. Whatever policy it formulates in the form of legislation, regulation, executive orders, or court decisions is public policy. Such a definition, however, is too simple—it does not do justice to the complexity of government or society and is unnecessarily restrictive.

Anderson, Brady, and Bullock state that a useful definition of public policy will indicate that public policy is a pattern of governmental activity on some topic or matter which has a purpose or goal. Public policy is purposeful, goal-oriented behavior rather than random or chance behavior.[1] It consists of *courses* of action, according to these authors, rather than separate, discrete decisions or actions performed by government officials. Furthermore, public policy refers to what governments actually do, not to stated

[1] James E. Anderson, David W. Brady, and Charles Bullock III, *Public Policy and Politics in America* (North Scituate, Mass.: Duxbury Press, 1978), pp. 4–5.

goals of action. With these criteria in mind, the authors offer the following as their definition of public policy.

> A goal-directed or purposeful course of action followed by an actor or set of actors in an attempt to deal with a public problem. This definition focuses on what is done, as distinct from what is intended, and it distinguishes policy from decisions. Public policies are developed by *governmental institutions* and officials through the political process (or politics). They are distinct from other kinds of policies because they result from the actions of legitimate authorities in a political system.[2]

Preston and Post offer a much different definition of public policy. They refer to policy, first of all, as principles which guide action. They stress the idea of generality, by referring to principles rather than specific rules, programs, practices or the actions themselves, and also emphasize activity or behavior as opposed to passive adherence.[3]

Public policy, then, refers to the principles that guide action relating to society as a whole. These principles may be made explicit in law and other formal acts of governmental bodies, but Preston and Post are quick to point out that a narrow and legalistic interpretation of the term public policy should be avoided. Policies can be implemented without formal articulation of individual actions and decisions. These are called implicit policies by Preston and Post.[4]

There is no need to repeat here a large collection of definitions from different authors to get a working understanding of the concept. The first definition is unnecessarily restrictive. Government need not engage in a formal action for public policies to be put into effect. A good example is the moratorium on nuclear power development. Government has not formalized such a moratorium, yet the public has decided through various means outside of government that no further nuclear power plants shall be built.

The Preston and Post definition, however, confuses principles and action. Principles can guide action, but the principles themselves are not necessarily the policy. Policy does more appropriately refer to a specific course of action with respect to a problem, but not to the principles that guide the action. Monetary policy is a specific course of action taken by the Federal Reserve Board to either tighten or loosen the money supply. The principles that guide this action are derived from some kind of theory, either monetarist or otherwise, but these principles do not constitute the policy itself.

Thus public policy is a specific course of action taken collectively by

---

[2] *Ibid.*, p. 5.

[3] Lee E. Preston and James E. Post, *Private Management and Public Policy: The Principle of Public Responsibility* (Englewood Cliffs, N.J.: Prentice-Hall, 1975), p. 11.

[4] *Ibid.*

society or by a legitimate representative of society, addressing a specific problem of public concern, that reflects the interests of society or particular segments of society. This definition emphasizes a course of action rather than principles. It does not restrict such action to government, it refers to the collective nature of such action, and does not claim that each and every public policy represents the interests of society as a whole.

The specific course of action that is eventually taken with respect to a problem is decided through the *public policy process*. The term public policy process refers to the various processes by which public policy is formed. There is no single process by which policy is formed.[5] The current policy on nuclear power plants was formed through a process involving public opinion, demonstrations, the media, and a host of other actions. When public policy is formalized by government, there still is no single process. Public policy can be made through legislation passed by Congress, regulations issued in the Federal Register, executive orders issued by the President, or decisions handed down by the Supreme Court. Thus the term public policy process is not entirely accurate, but is used to reduce confusion and for convenience.

The *public policy agenda* is that collection of topics and issues with respect to which public policy may be formulated.[6] There are many problems and concerns that various people in society would like to be acted on, but only those that are important enough to receive serious attention from policymakers comprise the public policy agenda. The manner in which problems attain this kind of status will be a subject of later discussion.

With these working definitions of some essential concepts in mind, we can turn to other conceptual considerations. Preston and Post state that the scope of managerial responsibility and the goals that management is to serve are determined through both the public policy process and the market mechanism.[7] Both public policy and the market mechanism are processes through which members of society make decisions about the allocation of resources for the provision of goods and services. These processes are quite different in concept and operation. In order to have a thorough understanding of public policy, it is necessary to compare and contrast these two methods of allocating resources.

ELEMENTS OF THE MARKET SYSTEM

The market system could be discussed as a holistic concept, as is done in most literature. But, it seems that our purposes would be better served by breaking the concept of the market

[5] Anderson, Brady, and Bullock, *Public Policy*, p. 6.

[6] Preston and Post, *Private Management*, p. 11.

[7] *Ibid.*, p. 13.

down into various conceptual elements and comparing and contrasting these elements with similar elements in the public policy process. Exhibit 2.1 lists the elements of both processes that will be discussed.

EXHIBIT 2.1
Conceptual Elements of the Market System and the Public Policy Process

Market System	Public Policy Process
Exchange Process	Political Process
Private Goods and Services	Public Goods and Services
Economic Value System	Diverse Value System
Self-Interest	Public Interest
The Invisible Hand	The Visible Hand
Economic Roles	Political Roles
(Producers-Consumers-Investors-Employees)	(Politicians-Citizens-Public Interest Groups)
Consumer Sovereignty	Citizen Sovereignty
Profits as Reward	Power as Reward
Business as the Major Institution	Government as the Major Institution
Operating Principles: efficiency, productivity, growth	Operating Principles: justice, equity, fairness

Source: Rogene A. Buchholz, *Business Environment and Public Policy: Implications for Management*, © 1982, p. 15. Reprinted by permission of Prentice-Hall, Inc., Englewood Cliffs, N.J.

The Exchange Process   At the heart of a market system is an exchange process where goods and services are traded between the parties to a particular transaction. In a strictly barter type of situation where money is not used, goods and services are exchanged directly for other goods and services. Where money is present, it serves as an intermediate store of value. Goods and services are exchanged for money and then the same money can be used to purchase other goods and services immediately or some time in the future. Money has little or no value in and of itself, but it is valued for what it represents and what it can purchase. The use of money greatly facilitates exchange over a barter type of economy.

Thus, in the market system, all kinds of exchanges between people and institutions are continually taking place. People exchange their labor for wages and salaries, and in turn exchange this money for goods in a retail establishment. Investors exchange money for new stock or bond issues in a

Conceptual Foundations of Public Policy

corporation which exchanges this money for raw materials or new plants and equipment. Farmers exchange their produce for money which may be used to buy new farm machinery or seed for the next planting.

Decisions as to whether or not to exchange one thing for another are made by individuals and institutions acting in their own self-interest, based on the particular value they attach to the entities being exchanged. People decide whether the item they want is of sufficient value to warrant the sacrifice of something they already have that is of value to them. Exchanges will not normally take place unless there is an increase of value to both parties of the exchange.

In the market, then, resources are allocated according to the preferences of individuals for one kind of merchandise over another, one job over another, or the stock of one corporation over another. Thus the values assigned to particular goods and services and the resulting decisions concerning allocation of resources for the production and distribution of these goods and services are made through an exchange process.

Private Goods and Services   The goods and services that are exchanged in the market system are private in the sense that they can be purchased and used by individual persons or institutions. They become the private property of the persons who attain them and do not have to be shared with anyone. The goods and services exchanged in the market are thus *divisible* into individual units and can be totally consumed and enjoyed by the people or institutions who obtain the property rights to them.

Thus one can buy a house, car, or a piece of furniture, and these items become private property to enjoy and use entirely in one's own self-interest. People can also contract for or purchase services and have a legal right to expect that the services will be provided. The legal system supports this concept of property rights and enables people to enforce these rights if necessary to protect their property from unwanted encroachment by others. This social arrangement provides a degree of security for people regarding their own property and forces them, in turn, to respect the property rights of others. Thus property rights can be assigned to the goods and services traded in the market because of their divisibility into individual units that can be privately enjoyed and consumed.

Common Economic Value System The values of all these entities that are exchanged in the market system are able to be expressed in common units that form an underlying economic value system. The worth of an individual's labor, the worth of a particular product or service, the worth of a share of stock can all be expressed in economic terms. This is not to suggest that the fundamental value of every-

33

thing is economic in nature. One person might value a particular piece of residential property because of the view it commands of the surrounding countryside, thus making the aesthetic value of the property of primary concern. Another person might desire a particular art object because of its religious or historical value. But, in order for exchange to take place where money is involved, these other values eventually have to be translated into economic values.

This economic value system thus serves as a common denominator in that the worth of everything can be expressed in a common unit of exchange, such as dollars and cents. This facilitates the exchange process and makes it possible for individuals to assess trade-offs more easily than if such a common denominator were not available. People can make an informal benefit-cost analysis when making a decision in the marketplace by comparing the benefits a good or service will provide them with the costs involved in acquiring the product or service. People enter a store, for example, with money they have earned. They assess the price of the goods available by comparing the benefits these goods will provide to the real costs (the effort involved in earning the money) of attaining them. Since both sides of this benefit-cost equation are expressed in the same units, this assessment can be made rather easily.

This common value system allows a society to allocate its resources according to the collective preferences of its members. All the diverse values that people hold in relation to private goods and services are aggregated through the market system into a collective demand schedule. If a particular product is not valued very highly by great numbers of people, aggregate demand for that product will not be very high. Its price will have to be low in order for it to be sold, if it can be sold at all, and not many resources will be used for its production. If a particular job is valued very highly by society and the people who can perform the job are scarce relative to demand, the wage or salary paid will have to be high to attract people to perform the job. Resources are thus allocated according to the values of society as expressed through the exchange process. Resources will go where the price, wage and salary, or return on investment are highest, all other things being equal.

Self-Interest

People are free, in a market economy, to use their property, choose their occupation, and strive for economic gain in any way they choose—subject, of course, to limitations that may be necessary to protect the right of all people to do the same thing. Society may also place limitations on the use of property and choice of occupation because of moral standards. Some occupations are illegal, as are certain uses of property.

The pursuit of self-interest is assumed to be a universal principle of human behavior, with a powerful advantage, as far as motivation is concerned, over other forms of human behavior. The pursuit of one's own interest is believed to elicit far more energy and creativity from human beings than would the pursuit of someone else's interests, especially under coercive conditions. Not only is it often difficult to determine what the interests of other people are, it is also difficult to find a way to sustain a high level of motivation if much of the effort one expends goes for the benefit of other people.

The definition of self-interest in a market economy is not provided by government for all its citizens but is determined by each individual participating in the exchange process. If the self-interest of an individual were defined by someone else, the concept would have no meaning. Thus self-interest is an individual concept. Yet, within a market system, the definition of self-interest is not completely arbitrary, depending on the whims of each individual. The existence of a common underlying economic value system makes the definition of self-interest take on a certain economic rationality.

If one is engaged in some aspect of the productive process, economic rationality dictates that self-interest consists of maximizing one's return on his or her investment. Entrepreneurs are expected to maximize profits, investors to maximize their returns in the stock market, and sellers of labor are expected to obtain the most advantageous terms for themselves. Consumers are expected to maximize the satisfaction to themselves through their purchases of goods and services on the marketplace. If one were to seek the lowest return on investment or the least satisfaction from goods and services, this would be viewed as irrational behavior under normal circumstances.

The Invisible Hand

Resources are allocated in a market system by an invisible hand, a mythological concept, but one that is a crucial element of a market system. There is no supreme authority in government such as a planning commission that makes decisions for the society as a whole about what goods and services are produced and in what quantities, and allocates resources accordingly. These decisions are made by the individuals who participate in the marketplace and express their preferences as based on their self-interest. These preferences are aggregated by the market, and elicit proper responses from the productive mechanism of society to supply the goods and services desired.

The invisible hand consists of the forces of supply and demand that result from the aggregation of individual decisions by producers and consumers in the marketplace. Resources are allocated to their most productive use as defined by these individuals collectively. According to Adam Smith, society as a whole benefits more from this kind of a resource allocation process than if someone were to consciously try to determine the best interests of society. Pursuit of one's own selfish ends, without outside interference, is believed to result in the greatest good for the greatest number of people.

> As every individual, therefore, endeavours as much as he can both to employ his capital in the support of domestic industry, and so to direct that industry that its produce may be of the greatest value; every individual necessarily labours to render the annual revenue of the society as great as he can. He generally, indeed, neither intends to promote the public interest, nor knows how much he is promoting it. By preferring the support of domestic to that of foreign industry, he intends only his own security; and by directing that industry in such a manner as its produce may be of the greatest value, he intends only his own gain, and he is in this, as in many other cases, led by an invisible hand to promote an end which was no part of his intention. Nor is it always the worse for the society that it was no part of it. By pursuing his own interest he frequently promotes that of the society more effectually than when he really intends to promote it.[8]

Economic Roles

The marketplace requires certain roles to be performed in order for it to function. All of these roles have an economic character to them. People can be producers who turn raw materials into goods that sell on the market, consumers who buy these goods and services for their use, investors who provide capital for the producers, or employees who work for producers and receive wages or salaries in exchange for their contributions to the production process. All of these roles are vital to the functioning of a market system. They are called economic roles because people are pursuing their economic self-interest in performing them. There are other important roles to be performed in society, of course, but economic roles are dominant in a society organized around free market principles.

Consumer Sovereignty

The most important economic role in a market system is performed by the consumer. At least in theory, consumers, through their choices in the marketplace, guide the productive apparatus of society and collectively decide what goods and services get produced and in what quantities. When there is enough demand for a product, resources will be allocated for its production. If there is not enough demand, the product will not be produced and resources will go elsewhere.

Consumer sovereignty is not to be confused with consumer choice. In any society, consumers always have a choice to purchase or not to purchase the products available in the marketplace. Consumer choice exists in a totally planned economy. Consumer sovereignty implies that the range of

---

[8] Adam Smith, *The Wealth of Nations* (New York: Modern Library, 1937), p. 423.

products with which consumers are confronted is also a function of their own decisions, not the decisions of a central planning authority. Thus consumers are ultimately sovereign over the entire system.

There are those who would argue that consumer sovereignty in today's marketplace is a fiction—that consumers are manipulated by advertising, packaging, promotional devices, and other sales techniques to buy a particular product. Sometimes this manipulation is said to be so subtle that the consumer is unaware of the factors influencing his or her decision. Thus the demand function itself has come under control of corporations and consumer sovereignty is a myth. Producers are sovereign over the system, and consumers are made to respond to the producers decisions about what to produce.[9]

While there may be some truth to these views, they do not constitute the whole truth. It is hard to believe that consumers are totally manipulated by these techniques. They still have to make choices among competing products, and the producers selling these products are all trying to manipulate the consumer. In the final analysis, the individual consumer is still responsible for his or her decision. Undoubtedly many factors besides the particular sales techniques employed by a company influence the purchase decision. In the absence of a central authority making production decisions for the entire society, it is safe to assume that some degree of consumer sovereignty exists. As long as there are competing products or acceptable substitutes, some products may not sell well enough to justify continued production. They disappear from the marketplace, not because producers desire to remove them, but because consumers have decided not to buy them in sufficient quantities.

Profits as Reward

The reason products disappear when they do not sell is because there is no profit to be made. Profits are the lifeblood of a business organization, and without profits a business organization normally cannot survive. Profits are a reward to the business organization or entrepreneur for the risks that have been taken in producing a good or service for the market. If the management of a business organization guesses wrong and produces something people do not want and cannot be persuaded to buy, they will find that the market is a stern taskmaster. No rewards will be received for this effort, and the product will be removed from the market.

Profits are also a reward for combining resources efficiently to be able to meet or beat the competition in producing a product for which there is a demand. Some entrepreneurs may be able to pay lower wages, employ a more efficient technology, or have some other competitive advantage. A

---

9 See, for example, *John Kenneth Galbraith, The New Industrial State* (Boston: Houghton Mifflin, 1967).

lower price can be charged and high-cost producers are driven from the market. This effort is rewarded with increased profits as society benefits from having its resources used more efficiently.

Business as the Major Institution The major institutional actor in the market system is the business organization that is driven by the profit motive to produce goods and services to meet consumer demand. This is not to suggest that business is the only institution that is producing something useful for society. Hospitals provide medical services and governments produce a wide range of goods and services for citizens. But these other institutions are not driven by the profit motive as is business and cannot offer the full range of goods and services that business can when functioning in a market economy. The business organization is the primary productive institution in a market economy, and most of the decisions about the allocation of society's resources for the production of private goods and services are made within the walls of the business institution.[10]

Operating Principles The primary operating principles that are used to measure performance in a market system are concepts such as efficiency, productivity, and growth. There are quantitative measures for these concepts, and while they may be imprecise in many respects, these measures at least provide some idea as to how well the market system is functioning. If economic growth is declining or negative, the economy is judged to be functioning poorly, and policy measures are taken to try to correct this deficiency. These principles are thus crucial to the operation of a market system. Good performance along these dimensions of efficiency, productivity and growth helps a great deal to make market outcomes acceptable to society.

ELEMENTS OF PUBLIC POLICY The public policy process can be broken down into comparable elements to facilitate discussion and comprehension of the concept. Such a procedure will enable a comparison with the market system to be made element by element, rather than trying to compare the complex concepts in their entirety.

[10] At first glance, it might seem that such an active role for business conflicts with the principle of consumer sovereignty described earlier. If productive institutions are guided by consumers as they make choices in the marketplace, management decisions could be seen as merely responses to the choices made by consumers. But business organizations are not merely passive entities in the market system, and real decisions are made in these organizations about whether or not to meet consumer demand, what technology to employ, etc., that take consumer preferences into account along with many other factors. Thus the principle of consumer sovereignty does not mean business is simply a passive responder.

Political Process   Instead of an exchange process, values are assigned to particular entities in the public policy process and decisions are made about allocation of resources through a political process. The political process is a complex amalgam of power and influence that involves many actors pursuing different interests who try to persuade and influence others in order to achieve their objectives. Politics has often been called the art of the possible, meaning a balancing of interests is necessary to resolve conflicts in order to arrive at a common course of action. People usually have to be willing to give up something in order to reach agreement among all the members of a group. The usual outcome of the political process reflects the principle that no one gets everything of what he wants and yet everyone has to get something in order to satisfy himself or herself that the objective is worth pursuing. Thus compromise and negotiation are necessary skills to participate effectively in the political process.

The function of a political process is to organize collective effort to achieve some goal or objective that individuals or private groups find difficult, if not impossible, to achieve by themselves. People participate in the exchange process because they believe they can achieve their individual objectives better by making some kind of trade, but the parties to the exchange do not have to share objectives or agree on a course of action. Some people in a community, however, may want to build a road, which no one person in the community can or would want to build alone. To get the road built, enough people in the community have to agree they want a road and are willing to contribute the necessary resources. But even after this decision is made, these people are going to have different ideas as to what kind of road should be built or where it should be located. These differences have to be resolved through the political process in order for the road to be constructed.

The outcome of the political process is not usually under the control of a single individual or group as is the outcome of an exchange process. The outcome of the political process depends on how much power and influence one has, how skillful one is at compromising and negotiating, and the variety and strength of other interests involved. Decisions can be made by vote (where the majority rules) by building a consensus, or by exercising raw power and coercing other members of a group to agree with your course of action. Outcomes are highly uncertain, in most instances, and contain many surprises.

The outcome of the exchange process is much more certain, as people usually know that their decisions are directly connected to the outcome. If people choose to part with a sum of money, they only do so because they know they will receive a product or service they want in return. Producers sell their products for a specific sum of money, not for some promise to pay an unspecified amount. The value of goods and services, as well as money, changes over time. But at the moment of exchange, people usually have a pretty good idea of what they are getting.

In the political process, especially if it involves a representative democracy, people are not always certain what they are getting. They may vote for a candidate who supports the issues they favor and who seems to share similar values. But elected public officials may not carry out their campaign promises, and even if they do, their vote may count for nothing in the final outcome if few others voted the same way on the issues.

People pursue their own interests through the political process based on their belief concerning objectives being sought collectively. These values cannot be expressed directly or precisely, particularly in a representative democracy. Individual preferences are rarely matched because of the need for compromise, and the outcome is highly uncertain because of the complex interactions that take place between all the parties to a transaction. Yet resources for the attainment of public policy objectives are allocated through the political process that combines individual preferences into common objectives and courses of action.

Public Goods and Services

Public policy decisions have to be made through a political process because of the nature of the goods and services that are provided. These goods and services can appropriately be referred to as public goods and services (see box) as distinguished from the private goods and services described in the market system.

Public goods and services are *indivisible* in the sense that the quantity produced cannot be divided into individual units to be purchased by people according to their individual preferences. One cannot, for example, buy a piece of clean air to carry around and breathe wherever one goes. Nor can one buy a share of national defense over which one would have control. This indivisibility gives these goods their public character because if people are to have public goods and services at all, they must enjoy roughly the same amount.[11] No one owns these goods and services individually—they are collectively owned and private property rights do not apply. There is nothing to be exchanged and decisions about these goods and services cannot be made through the exchange process.

One might argue, however, that even though public goods and services have these characteristics, they could still be provided through the market system rather than the public policy process. Suppose, for example, the market offered a consumer the following choice: two automobiles in a dealer's showroom are identical in all respects, even as to gas mileage. The only difference is that one car has pollution control equipment to reduce

---

[11] John Rawls, *A Theory of Justice* (Cambridge, Mass.: Harvard University Press, 1971), p. 266.

The concept of public goods and services needs further explanation. The literature about this subject usually refers to national defense as the best example of a public good—something tangible provided by government for all its citizens that cannot be provided by the citizens for themselves.

Pollution is generally considered to be an example of an externality, defined as either a beneficial or detrimental (pollution is detrimental) effect on a third party (homeowner who lives close to a polluting factory) who is not involved in the transaction between the principals (customer and producer) who caused the pollution because of their activities in the marketplace. Yet the results of pollution control (clean air and water) can also be called a public good as they are entities with beneficial physical characteristics for human health that are widely shared in different amounts by people in society.

Something like equal opportunity might be called a social value in that it is a particular goal of our society that is important for many of its members because of their individual values or ethical sensibilities. Yet if these values are widely shared or an important part of a society's heritage, policies designed to promote equal opportunity also produce a public good in that it is good for society to implement its basic values.

Thus the concept of public goods and services as used here is an all-inclusive concept that refers to all these various outcomes of the public policy process. This broader use also includes the maintenance of competition when this is a basic value of a society and maintenance of economic stability that makes it possible for people to find employment and maintain or improve their material standard of living.

Source: Rogene A. Buchholz, *Business Environment and Public Policy: Implications for Management*, © 1982, p. 21. Reprinted by permission of Prentice-Hall, Inc., Englewood Cliffs, N.J.

emissions of pollutants from the exhaust while the other car has no such equipment. The car with the pollution control equipment sells for $500 more than the other.

If people value clean air, it could be argued that they would choose the more expensive car to reduce air pollution. However, such a decision would be totally irrational from a strictly self-interest point of view. The impact that one car out of all the millions on the road will have on air pollution is infinitesimal—it cannot even be measured. Thus there is no relationship in this kind of a decision between costs and benefits. One would, in effect, get nothing for one's money unless many other people made the same decision. Such actions, however, assume a common value for clean air that doesn't exist. Thus the market does not offer consumers this kind of choice. Automobile manufacturers know that pollution control equipment won't sell in the absence of federally-mandated standards.

There is another side to the coin, however. If enough people in a given area did buy the more expensive car so that the air was significantly cleaner, there would be a powerful incentive for others to be free riders. Again, the impact of any one car would not alter the character of the air over a region. One would be tempted to buy the polluting car for a cheaper price and be a free rider by enjoying the same amount of clean air as everyone else and not paying a cent for its provision.

Because of these characteristics of human behavior and the nature of public goods and services, the market system will not work to provide these goods and services for a society that wants them. When goods are indivisible among large numbers of people, the individual consumer's actions as expressed in the market will not lead to the provision of these goods.[12] Society must register its desire for public goods and services through the political process because the bilateral exchanges facilitated by the market are insufficiently inclusive.[13] Only through the political process can compromises be reached that will resolve the value conflicts that are inevitable in relation to public goods and services.

Diverse Value System

Value conflicts are more pronounced in the public policy process because of the existence of a diverse value system. There is no underlying value system into which other values can be translated. No common denominator exists by which to assess trade-offs and make decisions about resource allocation to attain some common economic objective, such as improving one's material standard of living or increasing the nation's gross national product.

What is the overall objective, for example, of clean air and water, equal opportunity, occupational safety and health, and similar public goods and services? One could say that all these goods and services are meant to improve the quality of life for all members of society. If this is the objective, how can benefits be assessed in relation to costs, and trade-offs analyzed?

The costs of pollution control equipment, for example, can be determined in economic terms. This equipment should be beneficial to health by reducing the amount of harmful pollutants people have to breathe and improving the aesthetic dimension by making the air smell better. Safety may also be enhanced through an improvement of visibility for aircraft. The difficulty lies in translating all these diverse benefits into economic terms so that a direct comparison with costs can be made.

[12] Gerald Sirkin, *The Visible Hand: The Fundamentals of Economic Planning* (New York: McGraw-Hill, 1968), p. 45.

[13] James Buchanan, *The Demand and Supply of Public Goods* (Chicago: Rand McNally, 1968), p. 8.

What is the price tag for the lives saved by avoiding future diseases that may be caused by pollution? What is the economic value of having three more years added on to one's life span because of living in a cleaner environment? What is the value of reducing the probability that children will be born with abnormalities because of reduction of toxic substances in the environment? What is the value of preserving one's hearing by reducing the noise emitted by machinery in the workplace? What is the appropriate value of being able to see the mountains from one's house outside of Denver?

The difficulty of expressing all these intangibles in economic terms so that people's preferences are matched should be apparent. But in spite of these difficulties, some economists advocate certain methods to place an economic value on human life. There are three such methods that have been proposed and used in some benefit-cost studies to value human life.

An early approach to placing a value on an individual's life was called the foregone earnings method. This is an idea based upon the discounted cash flow technique. It calculates the present value of estimated future earnings that are foregone due to premature death. In addition, estimated medical costs and other associated expenses are often included.

A newer method has arisen that is termed "willingness to pay." The value of life is estimated from questions people are asked about how much they would be willing to pay to reduce the probability of their death by a certain small amount. Results of these studies yield values anywhere between $50,000 and $8 million per life saved.

A third method is based on the analysis of wage premiums for dangerous jobs or hazardous occupations. For example, if a group of workers is paid a wage increment of $3 million for jobs that have two deaths per year above the expected frequency, they have valued each life at $1.5 million. Studies of this type have yielded values between $300,000 and $3.5 million.[14]

The diversity of economic valuation that results from these techniques is not surprising. People are going to place vastly different values on their lives. Some people may believe they are worth any economic expenditure no matter how great. Others may feel their lives are relatively worthless. People's valuation of their lives will also change with age and other circumstances. Such diversity renders the use of analytical techniques such as those described above highly questionable.

When people are making individual choices about private goods and services, a diverse value system presents no problems. Making choices about public goods and services is another matter. There seems to be no way

[14] John D. Aram, *Managing Business and Public Policy* (Boston: Pitman, 1983), pp. 229–30.

to force a translation of the diversity into a common value system that is acceptable, realistic, and appropriate. Should more money be spent on reducing the emissions from coke ovens than on improving highway safety? How much money should be spent on cleaning up existing dumping sites for hazardous wastes? For these kinds of public policy questions, the political process seems to be a reasonable way to aggregate the diversity of people's values to make a decision when there is no common value system to use for more rational calculations.

The Public Interest

The universal motivating principle in the public policy process is the public interest rather than self-interest. This principle is invoked by those who make decisions about public policy. Elected public officials often claim to be acting in the interests of the nation as a whole or of their state or congressional district. Public interest groups also claim to be devoted to the general or national welfare. These claims make a certain degree of sense. When politicians have to make a decision about the provision of some public good or service, they cannot claim to be acting in the self-interest of everyone in their constituency. When goods and services are indivisible across large numbers of people, it is impossible for individual preferences to be matched. Nor can public policy makers claim to be acting in their own self-interest; such a claim is not politically acceptable. Some more general principle such as the public interest has to be invoked to justify the action.

The definition of the public interest, however, is problematical. The term can have at least four meanings.[15] The public interest can refer to the aggregation, weighing, and balancing of a number of special interests. In this view the public interest results through the free and open competition of interested parties who have to compromise their differences to arrive at a common course of action. The public interest is the sum total of all the private interests in the community that are balanced for the common good. This definition allows for a diversity of interests.

The public interest can also refer to a common or universal interest which all or at least most of the members of a society share. A decision is in the public interest if it serves the ends of the whole public rather than those of some sector of the public, if it incorporates all of the interests and concepts of value which are generally accepted in our society. Such a definition assumes a great deal of commonality as to basic wants and needs of the people who comprise a society.

There is also an idealist perspective as to the meaning of the public interest. Such a definition judges alternative courses of action in relation to some absolute standard of value, that in many cases exists independently of

---

[15] See Douglas G. Hartle, *Public Policy Decision Making and Regulation* (Montreal, Canada: The Institute for Research on Public Policy, 1979), pp. 213–218.

the preferences of individual citizens. The public interest is more than the sum of private interests; it is something distinct and apart from basic needs and wants of human beings. Such a definition has a transcendent character and refers to such abstractions as "intelligent goodwill" or "elevated aspirations" or "the ultimate reality" which human beings should strive to attain. The difficulty with this definition is finding someone with a God-like character who can define these abstractions in an acceptable manner.

Another definition of the public interest focuses on the process by which decisions are made rather than the specification of some ideal outcome. This definition involves the acceptance of some process, such as majority rule, to resolve differences among people. If the rules of the game have been strictly followed, which in a democratic setting means that interested parties have had ample opportunity to express their views, then the outcome of the process has to be in the public interest by definition.

These definitions all have their problems, making an acceptable definition as difficult to arrive at as a specific public policy itself. Most public policies undoubtedly reflect all of these definitions in some manner. One additional caveat must be mentioned. Those in a position of power and influence can never really escape their own self-interest and legitimately claim to be acting solely in the public interest or general good of society, however it is defined. Politicians want to get reelected and will vote for those goods and services they believe have an appeal to the majority of their constituency. Public interest groups want to extend their power and influence in society, and might be more appropriately called special interest groups. Thus the definition of the public interest can never be entirely divorced from the self-interest of those who are doing the defining.

The Visible Hand

Whatever definition of the public interest is invoked, resources are allocated in the public policy process by a visible hand. That visible hand is the group of decision makers in the public policy process who have been most active and influential in arriving at a common course of action. They are the ones who consciously allocate resources for the production of public goods and services they believe the public wants—those goods and services they believe serve the public interest. If they make the wrong decisions and do not adequately serve the public interest, however it may be defined, they can be held accountable and removed from their position of power and influence.

Something of a supply and demand process occurs here in that if enough citizens demand something, at least in a democratic society, the system will eventually respond. But the decisions about resource allocation are visible in that certain people in the public policy process—elected public officials, government bureaucrats, and public interest groups can be held accountable for these decisions if they are not in the public interest and thus not acceptable throughout the entire society. The market system does not fix responsibility so precisely, as decisions about resource allocation are made by thousands of people participating in the marketplace. The concept of the invisible hand is thus appropriate for a market system but not for the public policy process.

Political Roles

People play different roles in the public policy process than they do in the market system. These roles, of course, have a political character. Elected public officials are directly involved in the public policy process, but they are few in number relative to the total population. The same can be said of other government workers such as those who serve on congressional staffs or regulatory agencies and have a real influence on public policy outcomes.

The average person simply plays the role of citizen by voting for a representative of his or her choice, contributing money to a campaign, and writing to elected public officials on particular issues. At the extreme, this role could involve driving one's tractor to Washington, D.C. and clogging the city streets in protest of certain governmental actions. Joining large social movements such as the civil rights movement is another way for the average person to exercise political influence. Widespread support for issues such as this has an effect on the voting of elected public officials. Finally, people can join public interest groups or support them with contributions and fulfill a political role in this fashion. These are political roles because they involve some degree of compromise and negotiation to arrive at common objectives and courses of action.

Citizen Sovereignty

Citizens are supposedly sovereign over the public policy process as consumers are supposedly sovereign over the market system. The vote is the ultimate power that citizens have in a democratic system. Public officials can be voted out of office if they do not perform as the majority of citizens in their constituency would like. The citizens can then vote someone else into office whom they believe will make decisions about allocation of resources for production of public goods and services that are more consistent with the citizens' preferences. In the interim period between votes, citizens can express their preferences and try to influence the outcome of the public policy process either individually, through contact with public officials, or collectively, through participation in interest groups.

Power as Reward

The reward for a public official or candidate for office is the attainment of power and influence in the public policy process. If an incumbent has done a good job in office—assessed citizen preferences correctly and worked to supply the public goods and services the citizens of his or her constituency want—he or she will most likely be reelected and retain the power that has been acquired. If there is enough dissatisfaction with the incumbent, and a newcomer comes along who appears to be more responsive to citizen preferences and makes promises that people believe, that new person may be elected to office and granted the power that goes with the office.

The elected public official seeking power can be compared with the entrepreneur seeking profits. While power is not a quantifiable concept as is profit, it is no less a powerful motivator for those who want to be in positions of influence. Power accrues to people who make correct decisions, who are skillful at compromise and negotiation, and who can persuade people that they can be trusted with power and will use it in the public interest so that the society as a whole benefits. Power is the lifeblood of politicians. Without it they will wither and die and eventually fade away into oblivion.

Government as the Major Institution   The major institutional force operative in the public policy process is government, primarily the federal government and to a lesser extent state and local government. Other institutions are also active in the public policy process. Business, for example, has always been and will continue to be an institutional force in the public policy process. Public interest groups are another institutional force.

But government is the principal institution involved in formulating public policy that shapes the behavior of business organizations. Government promotes business through tariff protection, subsidies, tax credits, and tax breaks. In some situations, government becomes a guarantor of business survival. It regulates business in four aspects: competitive behavior, industry regulation, social regulation, and labor-management relations. Government is a buyer of goods and services from private business. In this capacity it can promote such public policy goals as equal opportunity through the terms of the contract it makes with private business. It manages the economy through the use of fiscal and monetary policies. In all of these activities government is engaged in the public policy process and shapes business behavior. Most of the decisions about the allocation of resources for the production of public goods and services are made by government, which has a legitimate right to formulate public policy for the society as a whole.

Operating Principles   The operating principles of the public policy process are concepts like justice, equity, and fairness. These concepts are often invoked to justify the decisions made in the public policy process about resource allocation. While efficiency is certainly a consideration in many public policy measures, it will in many cases be sacrificed in the interests of justice, equity, and fairness. There are no quantitative measures for these concepts but nonetheless, society has some idea as to how well the public policy process is performing along these lines. If certain courses of action are seen as grossly unfair to enough people in society, pressures will mount to change the policies. These principles are important to the operation of the public policy process and make the outcome acceptable to society. If justice, for example, has been served by a policy, an outcome will be accepted even though it may entail great sacrifice on the part of the citizens affected.

THE ROLE OF PUBLIC POLICY

The Preston-Post view of public policy and the market system could imply that both of these processes have an equal legitimacy in society. They state that both the public policy process and market system are sources of guidelines for managerial behavior and do not specify that one or another of these processes is more important or prior in some sense to the other. Yet in American society, there is a clear sense of priorities as to the manner in which resources should be allocated.

Since government is the major institution involved in the public policy process, our attitudes toward public policy are all tied up with government. Our ideology holds that government is a necessary evil to provide for national defense and other necessary items that can't be provided in any other manner. Many believe that the best government is the government that governs least, and that government is inefficient and cannot be trusted to allocate society's resources to their best uses.

We thus have no positive theory of government because we believe our society is basically a market-oriented society. The market can be trusted to allocate resources efficiently, and government interference should be kept to a minimum. Government exists to help the private sector do its job better; government does not have the same kind of legitimacy as does the private sector for many resource allocation decisions.

Given this kind of ideology, then, what role does public policy play in society? Perhaps this role can be best understood by describing a framework of social change called the mythic/epic cycle of social change and applying this to a market-oriented society. This theory or model grows out of the post-Enlightenment critical study of the history of religions.[16] As the name suggests, this theory consists of two major cycles. The mythic cycle addresses itself to the problem of maintaining a shared sense of meaning and continuity

---

[16] See Owen Barfield, *Poetic Diction: A Study in Meaning* (New York: McGraw-Hill, 1964); Joseph Campbell, *The Hero with a Thousand Faces*, 2nd ed. (Princeton, N.J.: Princeton University Press, 1971); Edward F. Edinger, *Ego and Archetype* (Baltimore, Md.: Penguin, 1974); Mircea Eliade, *Patterns in Comparative Religion* (New York: Sheed Andrews & McMeel, Inc., 1958); and Claude Levi-Strauss, *Structural Anthropology*, translated by Claire Jacobson and Brooke Grundfest Schoepf (New York: Basic Books, 1963).

in a society. The epic cycle deals with radical change from essentially one society to another.

According to this theory, societies maintain a shared sense of meaning and a particular vision of reality through myth. Myth is that collection of shared stories which mediate ultimate reality to a given society, and is, therefore, directed toward psyche, internal reality, personal transformation, and process. Societies usually do everything they can to keep myths alive to preserve themselves and maintain continuity for as long as possible. Societies undergo radical change, however, through the process of an epic struggle of a cultural hero. Epic focuses on history, human relationships, and events. Together these cycles provide a model for a society in equilibrium and a society undergoing radical change.[17]

Applied to a capitalistic system (Figure 2.1), the primal mythical reality is Adam Smith's notion of the invisible hand, a mythical view of reality regarding how a society provides itself with material goods and services. The invisible hand is a secularized version of God, who promises abundance to his people. If the invisible hand is left alone to do its work (laissez faire) and competition prevails, everyone's cup will run over with wealth and riches. People can pursue their own self-interest and society as a whole will benefit. Thus stories of free enterprise and entrepreneurship are all part of this primal reality.

Figure 2.1
Mythic/Epic Cycle Applied to Capitalism and Socialism

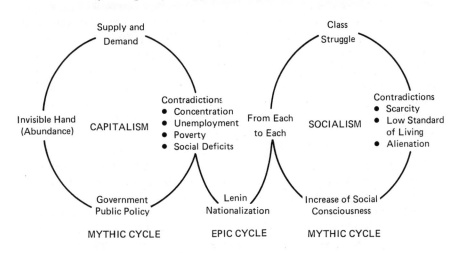

Source: Rogene A. Buchholz, *Business Environment and Public Policy: Implications for Management*, © 1982, p. 78. Reprinted by permission of Prentice-Hall, Inc., Englewood Cliffs, N.J.

[17] Ken Kochbeck, "The Mythic/Epic Cycle and the Creation of Social Meaning," (unpublished paper, St. Louis: Washington University, 1979), p. 3.

This primal reality is eventually differentiated into a more scientific concept that provides a structural view of the way the system works. This view was provided by the mechanistic concept of supply and demand, that these forces are in effect the invisible hand and allocate resources to the appropriate places and provide full employment for all the members of society willing and able to work.

Eventually, however, contradictions appear that challenge the primal view of reality. The competitive free-enterprise system, left to its own devices, tends towards oligopoly or even monopoly. Thus imperfections of competition appear. Unemployment also appears, particularly during recessions or depressions, which cannot be blamed on the people themselves. Many are not able to share in the abundance a capitalistic society produces and live out the Horatio Alger story. Instead they remain hopelessly rooted in poverty. Social deficits appear in the form of pollution or toxic wastes not disposed of properly.

These contradictions require some sort of mediation if the primal vision of reality on which society rests is to be maintained. In American society, the government becomes the primary mediator to deal with these contradictions through public policy measures, to enable the system to continue functioning. The mythic cycle is profoundly conservative, and as long as adequate mediating terms can be found the society will remain stable. Change will have occurred, of course, but it will not be perceived as such because the change has been incorporated into the original mythic structure.

If these contradictions cannot be successfully mediated or reconciled, however, the epic cycle starts and the old order begins to break apart. The people who are affected by the contradictions express their alienation and oppression in what has been called a lament—a legal petition to the powers governing the universe to intervene. Eventually, a hero appears who delivers the people from their alienation and despair and becomes the leader of the new social order. That order then proceeds to maintain itself through the mythic cycle.[18]

Something like this must have happened in Czarist Russia during the Bolshevik revolution. The contradictions of the capitalistic system could not be reconciled. Eventually a hero appeared (Lenin) who promised to deliver the oppressed people from their despair by abolishing the institutions of a capitalistic society (private property) and founding a new order based on a vision of reality appropriated from Marxist theory.

The primal vision of reality in this order is the myth "to each according to his need, from each according to his ability." The differentiating principle to describe how the system works is the notion of a class struggle. Contradictions that appear include scarcity and a lower standard of living when compared with many nations of the world, but these contradictions are suc-

[18] *Ibid..* p. 4.

cessfully mediated by increasing the social consciousness of the people through purges or propaganda.

Ordinarily, then, societies operate in the mythic mode. Only when the underlying vision of reality on which the social order rests breaks down because of unreconciled contradictions does true epic appear. The epic cycle always deals with radical social change. Usually the outcome of an epic cycle is the establishment of a new social order. Should this not happen, people can face generations of oppression and anarchy. One destroys old myths and gods only at the risk that no new ones may appear to give life meaning and order.

Clearly the time frame for this model is unpredictable. The process of mythic stability can go on for generations, even thousands of years, without serious disruption. Even when the alienation stage is reached, the epic cycle may not take place for generations, or the hero figure essential to triggering rapid and radical social change may appear overnight and the revolution be accomplished in a matter of hours. The model gives no basis for estimating the time parameters for any stage or movement.[19]

Thus public policy plays the role of mediator in our society, resolving contradictions that appear from time to time. If these contradictions can be resolved to the satisfaction of enough members in the society, radical change will be prevented and society will remain essentially stable as far as its basic institutions and mode of operation is concerned. The self-understanding of that society will be preserved and most people will still believe in the same myths and ideologies.

SELECTED REFERENCES

BUCHANAN, JAMES. *The Demand and Supply of Public Goods.* Chicago: Rand McNally, 1968.

GALBRAITH, JOHN KENNETH. *Economics and the Public Purpose.* Boston: Houghton Mifflin, 1967.

————. *The New Industrial State.* Boston: Houghton Mifflin, 1967.

HARTLE, DOUGLAS G. *Public Policy Decision Making and Regulation.* Montreal: The Institute for Research on Public Policy, 1979.

OLSON, MANCUR. *The Logic of Collective Action.* Cambridge, Mass.: Harvard University Press, 1977.

PRESTON, LEE E., AND JAMES E. POST. *Private Management and Public Policy.* Englewood Cliffs, N.J.: Prentice-Hall, 1975.

RAWLS, JOHN. *A Theory of Justice.* Cambridge Mass.: Harvard University Press, 1971.

[19] *Ibid.*, p. 7.

SIRKIN, GERALD. *The Visible Hand: The Fundamentals of Economic Planning.* New York: McGraw-Hill, 1968.

SMITH, ADAM. *The Wealth of Nations.* New York: Modern Library, 1937.

3

HI/TORICAL DEVELOPMENT/ IN PUBLIC POLICY

⟸ **IDEAS TO BE FOUND** ⟹
IN THIS CHAPTER

- The rise of modern industrial society
- The Great Depression
- The postindustrial society

History provides some clear examples of the role public policy plays in society. There are clearly identifiable periods in American history when major contradictions appeared in the system that were resolved through public policy measures. During those periods of time, the market was not trusted because people either believed it could not respond effectively to the problems society was experiencing or because they were not willing to accept the outcomes that would result if the market were left alone to work things out. Thus public policy arises out of deficiencies in the market system, either real or perceived, that appear from time to time in our history. The market cannot always resolve contradictions that appear which threaten a society's basic self-understanding.

Dealing with these periods of major contradictions in our society will aid in understanding the role public policy plays, the issues that give rise to public policy measures, and the way public policy affects the economy and business. The public policies to be discussed in this chapter are still the major areas of public policy with which business has to be concerned. These public policies are by no means historical artifacts but are ongoing policies that continue to shape business behavior.

THE RISE OF MODERN INDUSTRIAL SOCIETY

The American economy grew rapidly during the period between the founding of the nation and the beginning of the Civil War. Between 1790 and 1840, the population rose from 3.9 million to 17.1 million, and the total volume of goods produced and distributed increased enormously.[1] Inventions such as the cotton gin helped to establish whole new industries, like the textile industry. Iron making dominated the metal-working industries. Other important industrial products during the period included leather, lumber, spirits and malt liquors, animal and vegetable oil, copper and brass, carriages of all kinds, and gunpowder.[2]

In spite of this growth, however, the size and nature of business enterprises in all these industries changed little. According to Alfred Chandler, the business enterprises producing and distributing these goods continued to be traditional single-unit enterprises managed by the owners and employing fewer than fifty workers.[3] The economy was comprised of many small businesses in competition with each other. There was little institutional innovation to create larger organizations.

The major constraint on the size of business organizations was the availability of energy to business. Again according to Chandler, as long as production depended on traditional sources of energy such as people, animals, and wind power, there was little incentive for businesses to create large organizations. Such sources of energy could not generate a large enough volume of output in production and number of transactions in distribution to require the creation of large business organizations. The low speed of production and slow movement of goods meant that the maximum daily activity at each point of production and distribution could be easily handled by small personally owned and managed enterprises.[4]

The major development during this period as far as industrial growth was concerned was the building of an infrastructure—the web of transportation, communication, and basic industries essential to advanced forms of industry and trade. Between 1783 and 1801, more than three hundred business corporations were chartered by the states to build roads, bridges, canals, and water systems. The corporate form of organization was used primarily for these "public utility" purposes.

Roads such as the Philadelphia-Lancaster turnpike were built. Rivers such as the Hudson, Delaware, and Susquehanna became important for transporting goods. Canals such as the Erie, which linked Albany and Buf-

---

[1] Robert R. Russel, *A History of the American Economic System* (Englewood Cliffs, N.J.: Prentice-Hall, Inc., 1964), p. 113.

[2] Alex Groner, *The American Heritage History of American Business and Industry* (New York: American Heritage Publishing Co., 1972), pp. 68–70.

[3] Alfred Chandler, *The Visible Hand: The Managerial Revolution in American Business* (Cambridge, Mass.: Belknap Press, 1977), p. 14.

[4] *Ibid.*, p. 17.

falo, were built. By 1840 more than four hundred railroad companies were operating almost three thousand miles of track, more than the total mileage in all of Europe. Finally, the communications industry flourished with the invention of the telegraph and use of other forms of communication, such as newspapers and books.[5] The development of this infrastructure was crucial for further economic growth and was supported by public policy through land grants to railroads, the use of the corporate form of organization, and similar measures.

After the Civil War, the United States experienced an unprecedented period of economic growth. Per capita wealth and income increased dramatically. There was scarcely a millionaire in the country in 1790; in 1850 there were twenty-five millionaires in New York City alone, eighteen in Boston, and another nine in Philadelphia. People in most parts of the country were generally experiencing rising standards of living with respect to food, housing, clothing, health care, and education.[6]

One definition of an industrialized country is a country in which 50 percent or more of the occupied males are engaged in nonagricultural pursuits. The United States achieved this distinction in about 1880.[7]

There were a number of reasons for this rapid growth. First, the existence of an effective transportation system meant that finished goods and raw materials could be moved around the country fairly easily. Factories could be located where labor was available and built large enough to take advantage of economies of scale. Second, changes in agriculture made it possible for a smaller and smaller proportion of the population to feed the rest of the country. This released millions of workers to take jobs in the newly-developing industries and other occupations.

A third reason was the development of a cheap source of energy to support economic growth. The opening of the anthracite coal fields in eastern Pennsylvania removed the technological constraint that Chandler claims kept business enterprises small for many years. Cheap coal provided heat for large-scale production in foundries, became the source of steam power for railroad locomotives, and became an efficient fuel for generating steam power to drive machines in factories. Coal allowed new technologies to be developed that speeded up production of goods and services and led to the rise of the modern business enterprise.[8]

The fourth factor in this growth was the emergence of a group of entrepreneurs who were able to build large-scale business enterprises to take advantage of these potentials. There were people like Commodore

[5] Groner, *American Heritage History*, pp. 83–106.

[6] Russel, *American Economic System*, p. 277.

[7] See Russel, *American Economic System*, pp. 338–39; Groner, *American Heritage History*, p. 157.

[8] Chandler, *The Visible Hand*, pp. 75–78.

Vanderbilt, Jay Gould, Daniel Drew, and Jim Fisk in railroads; Andrew Carnegie in steel; Charles Pillsbury in flour milling; John D Rockefeller in oil; and John Pierpont Morgan in banking and the steel industry. Although historians either condemn these people as robber barons or praise them as captains of industry, it seems clear that they and others like them understood the potentials of the changes taking place around them, took up the challenge, and created huge industrial enterprises that formed the foundations of our modern business system. They were an important ingredient in America's becoming an industrial society. The productive use of the capital they were able to accumulate created unprecedented economic growth for the country.[9]

Thus the modern business enterprise was born in response to a number of changes taking place in American society. The corporate form of organization increasingly began to be used to make these enterprises even larger, as it allowed more capital to be accumulated and spread the risk across large numbers of stockholders. These large enterprises were able to use mass production techniques, which permitted a relatively small working force to produce an ever-increasing output. Machinery was placed and operated in such a way that several stages of production were integrated and synchronized technologically and organizationally within a single industrial establishment.[10]

With the growth of these large individual enterprises, however, came other organizational innovations in the late nineteenth century that were eventually seen to have anticompetitive effects on the economy and society. As competition between businesses became more severe, some of these businesses tried different industrial arrangements to reduce or at least control this competition. Some of these innovations are briefly discussed below:

Gentlemen's Agreement: An informal unwritten contract among competitors in an industry to set uniform prices for their products or to divide territories so as not to compete in the same geographic markets.

Pool: A more formal arrangement by all competitors in a given industry regarding standardized prices and operations. Decisions in a pool were governed by votes, which were allocated to pool members on the basis of market share.

Trust: An actual change of ownership for a given company. Stockholders of many competing firms turned their shares (and voting rights) over to "trustees" who became directors of one large supercorporation. This large corporation then issued trust certificates back to the original stockholders.

---

[9] Groner, *American Heritage History*, pp. 155–82, 193–224.
[10] Chandler, *The Visible Hand*, pp. 240–41.

Holding Company: An arrangement, supported by state laws, which allowed companies to hold stock in other companies. Several competitors would each buy stock in a firm whose only apparent function was to set policy for the owning companies.

The use of these devices led to a high degree of concentration in some industries. Table 3.1 shows the percentage of output produced by the dominant firm in some key industries at the turn of the century. The years between 1897 and 1904 saw a great surge of business combinations and concentration in certain industries. There were 318 industrial combinations in this period that included 5,300 plants with a combined capitalization of more than $7 billion. More than one thousand different railroad lines were consolidated into six major systems that controlled almost $10 billion in capital. The trust device was particularly useful for combinations, and the trusts that were created in petroleum, cottonseed oil, linseed oil, sugar, whiskey, and lead processing came to dominate their industries for decades.[11]

Table 3.1
Concentration in Selected Industries

International Harvester	1900	85% of harvesting machines
National Biscuit	1902	70% of biscuit output
American Can	1901	90% of industry output
Corn Products	1902	80% of industry capacity
U.S. Leather	1902	60% of leather output
Distillers Securities	1902	60% of whiskey output
International Paper	1902	60% of all newsprint
American Sugar Refining	1900	100% of refined sugar

Source: Rogene A. Buchholz, *Business Environment and Public Policy: Implications for Management*, © 1982, p. 31. Reprinted by permission of Prentice-Hall, Inc., Englewood Cliffs, N.J.

There are some advantages to a concentrated industrial structure. The existence of a national market to be served by large enterprises gave them a cost advantage because of the potential volume they could produce. The combination of several small companies into a large enterprise increased production because of better coordination and planning resulting in increased efficiency. Firms had greater stability with assured sources of supply and controlled markets.

There were also many disadvantages to this industrial structure. Competition was reduced as small firms were driven out of business because of inefficiency. Competition itself was often ruthless and cutthroat as firms sometimes cut prices below cost to drive competitors out of business. Collu-

[11] Groner, *American Heritage History*, pp. 197–200.

sion between firms was not uncommon. The economic power of large firms gave them the power to dictate the terms of trade to smaller groups—such as farmers, independent groups, and wholesalers—and transcend market forces.

The contradiction that thus appeared during this period of history was that the competitive market system was destroying itself through concentration and predatory competitive practices. Such developments awakened the fear Americans have always had of concentrations of power, whether political or economic.

Regardless of the historical reasons behind the development of large enterprises, there is a certain logic behind the competitive process that would lead one to expect this kind of outcome. Competition, followed to its logical conclusion, means that some person or organization will eventually win out over all the others. The reason for engaging in competition is to win as big as possible. Furthermore, if the competitive system is completely unregulated, competitive behavior will sink to the lowest common denominator. If one competitor uses unfair methods of competition and these methods win a larger share of the market, that competitor has an unfair advantage over its competition. In the absence of rules preventing anti-competitive behavior, other competitors will have to adopt the same behavior in order to survive.

The sports world can be looked to as an example of the competitive process in action. Rules have been passed to outlaw unfair methods of competition such as the use of spitballs or holding by offensive linemen. These rules change as society and the competitive process change. But in baseball or football there is an end to the season, and one team emerges a winner over all the others and is crowned World Series or Super Bowl Champion.

The same is not true of the economy. The season can never end, and if one business or group of businesses begins to look like a big winner over others in the industry, the competitive process is threatened. The market system does not automatically insure that competition will continue indefinitely or that competition will be fairly conducted. In the late nineteenth century, it appeared that the outcome of a completely unregulated competitive process was control by one or a few firms in most industries. Such a result produced a fundamental contradiction into the heart of society's self-understanding and brought pressures on government to resolve this contradiction.

Eventually the government took action against these large industrial combinations with specific public policy measures. Two forms of government regulation were born during the late 1800s—regulation of a specific industry and regulation of competitive behavior. The former began in 1887 with the creation of the Interstate Commerce Commission (ICC) to regulate the railroads. The authority of this commission was later extended to other forms of transportation and other agencies were created to regulate communications, the airlines, and other industries. Regulation of competitive behavior began with the Sherman Antitrust Act of 1890, which made restraints of trade and attempts to monopolize an industry illegal. The antitrust area was extended in 1914 with the passage of the Federal Trade Commission Act to outlaw unfair methods of competition, and the Clayton Antitrust Act which focused on specific anticompetitive behavior.

Antitrust Legislation   There are three theories to explain the motivation behind antitrust legislation. The first is the standard theory found in most American history textbooks, which holds that these measures were the result of a strong populist movement led by farmers and other groups who were fearful of the power of these big business combinations. These groups apparently believed that the huge industrial combinations that were created were nothing more than the result of a few industrial leaders' greed and lust for power. The problem was that as these leaders accumulated more and more capital, they began to dictate the terms of trade to the rest of society rather than being subject to the pressures of competition. Something had to be done to break up these combinations and restore more competition in the economy. The government responded by passing the necessary legislation, supported by the executive branch under President Theodore Roosevelt, who became known as "the trust-buster." This was a case of the little guys against the big guys, with the little guys having the government on their side to restore a balance of power.[12]

The second theory was developed by a group of revisionist historians in the 1960s who rewrote certain periods of American history.[13] This theory holds that certain key business leaders themselves realized that not only their profits but their very existence might be challenged by cut-throat competition and other evils of a completely unregulated competitive system. The various anticompetitive arrangements that business leaders worked out among themselves were voluntary attempts to gain control over this situation and develop a more rational and stable system. But these voluntary attempts failed for one reason or another. Some business leaders came to believe that perhaps political means might succeed where voluntary means had failed, and they actively supported government regulation. If government could stabilize the system by establishing certain rules of competition and enforcing them uniformly, corporations would be able to function in a predictable and secure environment, permitting reasonable profits to be earned over the long run.

[12] Russel, *American Economic System*, pp. 363–70.

[13] See Gabriel Kolko, *The Triumph of Conservatism* (New York: Free Press, 1963); Paul Conkin, *The New Deal* (New York: Harper & Row, Pub., 1967); Ellis W. Hawley, *The New Deal and the Problem of Monopoloy* (Princeton, N.J.: Princeton University Press, 1966).

59

The third theory holds that competition disappeared not because of the lust for power of a few business leaders but because of the technological possibilities inherent in large-scale enterprise. Efficiency could be increased dramatically when all stages of production and distribution, from mining of raw materials to delivery of a finished product to the consumer, could be combined in a single business enterprise under the direction of a single management. Thus administrative coordination of these various stages became more efficient and more profitable than market coordination.[14]

Society also benefited from these large enterprises in that more goods were produced at lower prices than would otherwise be possible. But because of the growth of these large "integrated" enterprises, the visible hand of the management of these enterprises replaced the invisible hand of market forces. This happened when and where new technology and expanded markets permitted an unprecedented high volume and speed of materials through the process of production and distribution. These enterprises grew into powerful institutions and came to dominate major sectors of the economy, and the managers of these enterprises became the most influential group of economic decision-makers. But it was not good to allow such power to go completely unregulated. Competition as a regulator was disappearing and government had to assume the role through antitrust legislation.

The Sherman Act was the first piece of antitrust legislation. The most important parts of the Sherman Act are Sections 1 and 2 (see box). Section 1 attacks the act of combining or conspiring to restrain trade and focuses on methods of competition or firm behavior. This section seems to make illegal every formal agreement among firms that is aimed at curbing independent action in the market. Section 2 enjoins market structures where seller concentration is so high that it could be called a monopoly.

The Clayton Act attacks a series of business policies insofar as they could substantially lessen competition or tend to create a monopoly. The language of the Sherman Act was quite broad, leaving a good deal of uncertainty as to what specific practices were in restraint of trade and thus illegal. The Clayton Act was passed to correct this deficiency by being more specific and barring price discrimination (later supplemented by the Robinson-Patman Act), tying arrangements, and exclusive dealing arrangements. It also contained a section that was designed to slow down the merger movement by forbidding mergers which substantially lessen competition or tend to create a monopoly (later strengthened by the Celler-Kefauver Amendments).

The Federal Trade Commission Act of 1914 created the Federal Trade Commission, which was empowered to protect consumers against all "unfair methods of competition in or affecting commerce." It was left up to the

---

[14] Chandler, *The Visible Hand*, p. 8.

SHERMAN ACT OF 1890

Sec. 1. Every contract, combination in the form of trust or otherwise, or conspiracy in restraint of trade or commerce among the several States, or with foreign nations, is hereby declared to be illegal. Every person who shall make any such contract or engage in any such combination or conspiracy, shall be deemed guilty of a misdemeanor, and, on conviction thereof, shall be punished by fine not exceeding five thousand dollars, or by imprisonment not exceeding one year, or by both said punishments, in the discretion of the court.

Sec. 2. Every person who shall monopolize, or attempt to monopolize, or combine or conspire with any other person or persons, to monopolize any part of this trade or commerce among the several States, or with foreign nations, shall be deemed guilty of a misdemeanor, and, on conviction thereof, shall be punished by fine not exceeding five thousand dollars, or by imprisonment not exceeding one year, or by both said punishments, in the discretion of the court.

---

commission itself to decide what methods of competition were unfair. In 1938, the Wheeler-Lea Act amended this section to read "unfair or deceptive acts or practices in commerce" thus empowering the FTC to pursue trade practices deemed unlawful whether or not competition was affected.

The purpose of these antitrust laws is to limit the economic power of large corporations that can control markets by reducing competition through concentration. The role of government is to maintain something called a "workable competition" on the theory that resources are allocated more efficiently and prices are lower in a competitive system than one dominated by large corporations. Justice Black stated the case for antitrust legislation well when he called the Sherman Act:

> . . . a comprehensive charter of economic liberty aimed at preserving free and unfettered competition as the rule of trade. It rests on the premise that the unrestrained interaction of competitive forces will yield the best allocation of our economic resources, the lowest prices, the highest quality and the greatest material progress, while at the same time providing an environment conducive to the preservation of our democratic political and social institutions.[15]

The problem with antitrust laws is their application. Society vacillates when it comes to acceptance of the large corporation. This was evident

---

[15] Northern Pacific Ry. v. United States, 356 U.S. 1, 4 (1958).

immediately after the antitrust laws were passed, when the courts remained pro-business for several years. In 1895, for example, the Supreme Court ruled that American Sugar Refining was not a monopoly in restraint of trade and therefore not in violation of the Sherman Act. A year earlier, the court had issued an injunction against the union in the Pullman strike on the basis that it was a conspiracy in restraint of interstate commerce. In the Danbury Hatters case of 1908, the striking union was declared financially liable for damages resulting from a boycott. The Justice Department lost seven of the first eight cases it brought under the Sherman Act. Finally, in 1911, two trusts (Standard Oil and American Tobacco) were found guilty of violating the Sherman Act and ordered dissolved into several separate firms.[16]

The same ambiguity is evident in more recent years. In the 1970s, the "bigness is bad" philosophy seemed to prevail. Cases were filed against IBM and AT&T, bills were introduced into Congress to limit conglomerate mergers, and the antitrust agencies attacked oligopoly itself through the infamous cereal case (FTC vs. Kellogg et al.). In the early 1980s, the IBM and the cereal cases were dropped, and mergers were allowed between U.S. Steel and Marathon Oil, and DuPont and Conoco, for example, signaling a much softer line on antitrust litigation.

There are obvious benefits to large-scale production, distribution, and organization. Economies of scale, more efficient coordination, and increased research and development expenditures on the part of large organizations are not figments of the imagination. But empirical research has not been able to establish conclusively the superiority of either a competitive or concentrated system on dimensions like pricing or innovations that are of importance to society. The antitrust laws maintain an allegiance to the ideals of competition and institutionalize our fear of large concentrations of power. Their application remains flexible to allow the benefits of concentrated industries to be exploited when society deems appropriate.

Industry Regulation   This type of regulation is the oldest, beginning with the Interstate Commerce Commission of 1887, which was established to provide continuous surveillance of private railroad activity across the country. The inability of the states to regulate railroads effectively led to the passage of this act, which set the pattern for additional regulatory commissions of this type. Thus followed the Federal Power Commission, the Civil Aeronautics Board, and the Federal Communications Commission, all examples of industry regulation.

One reason for this type of regulation is the belief that certain natural monopolies exist where economies of scale in an industry are so great that

16 Groner, *American Heritage History*, pp. 214–15.

the largest firm would have the lowest costs and thus drive its competitors out of the market. Since competition cannot act as a regulator in this situation, the government must perform this function to regulate these industries in the public interest.

Another reason for industry regulation is that an agency may be needed to allocate limited space, as in the case of the airlines and broadcasters. The threat of predatory practices or destructive competition is often used to justify regulation of the transportation industry. Regulation may be needed, it is often argued, to provide service to areas that would be ignored by the market. An example is the provision of railroad and airline service to small towns and cities. Finally, some argue that regulation is needed to prevent fraud and deception in the sale of securities.

Thus utilities are regulated at the federal level by the Federal Energy Regulatory Commission (FERC), whose purpose is to regulate interstate aspects of the electric power and natural gas industries. This agency, associated with the Department of Energy (DOE), succeeded the Federal Power Commission (FPC) in 1977. Where federal regulation of utilities does not apply, state regulatory commissions have been created.

The Federal Communications Commission (FCC) regulates domestic and foreign communications by radio, television, wire, cable, and telephone. The Civil Aeronautics Board (CAB) promotes and regulates the civil air transport industry. Surface transportation, including trucks, railroads, buses, oil pipelines, inland waterway and coastal shippers, and express companies are regulated by the Interstate Commerce Commission (ICC). The Securities and Exchange Commission (SEC) regulates the securities and financial markets to protect the public against malpractice.

This type of regulation focuses on a specific industry and is concerned about its economic well-being. The major concerns of agencies such as the ICC is with rates, routes, and the obligation to serve. Decisions about these economic matters are primarily made through adjudicatory procedures where interested parties present their arguments. After a lengthy process of review the agency reaches a decision, which may be appealed in the courts.

While the original impetus for regulation may have come from consumers who believed they needed protection, the so-called capture theory suggests that these agencies eventually become a captive of the industry they are supposed to regulate. This happens because of the unique expertise possessed by members of the industry or because of job enticements for regulators who leave government employment. The public or consumer interest is often viewed as subordinate because the agency comes to focus on the needs and concerns of the industry it is regulating. Many view regulated companies as nothing more than a government supported cartel, that earns higher profits and charges higher prices than would be the case if competition prevailed.

Pressures for reform of industry regulation began to build. Finally, in 1978, Congress passed a deregulation bill aimed at air passenger service, which allowed airlines to offer new services without CAB approval and granted them a great degree of freedom to raise and lower their fares. The CAB itself is scheduled to go out of existence and may already have closed its doors by the time this book is published. Companies in the railroad industry were given the right to charge as little or as much as they pleased for hauling fresh fruits and vegetables instead of following FCC approved rates. Similar pressures mounted to deregulate some aspects of the trucking industry and abolish some of the FCC's control over commercial radio broadcasting.

THE GREAT DEPRESSION After 1900, the modern multi-unit industrial enterprise became a standard for managing the production and distribution of goods in America. By 1917, most American industries had acquired their modern structure. Companies like United States Steel, Standard Oil, General Electric, and Westinghouse were founded. For the rest of the century, large industrial structures such as these continued to cluster in much the same industrial groups, and the same enterprises continued to be the leaders in the concentrated industries in these groups.[17]

During the twenties, these modern business enterprises came of age. They continued to flourish and spread in those sectors of the economy where administrative coordination proved more profitable than market coordination. The entrepreneurs who had built these enterprises hired professional managers to administer them. The new technologies and expanded markets called for more and more administrative coordination to take advantage of the opportunities and increase the flow of goods and services. This created a need for business schools to train these professional managers and equip them with the administrative skills necessary to run a large, integrated business enterprise.[18]

Whole new industries were founded during the early years of the twentieth century. One leading entrepreneur in the early years of this period was Henry Ford. He brought together concepts of mass production, interchangeable parts, and central assembly with great effectiveness. The production process he put together enabled him to produce a cheap form of mass transportation by keeping costs low enough to price his product for the lowest or largest possible mass market (see box). In 1909, Ford built 10,660 cars. By 1919 there were 6.7 million cars on the road; by 1929, 27 million. The phenomenal growth of the auto industry stimulated road construction

[17] Chandler, *The Visible Hand*, p. 345.
[18] *Ibid.*, pp. 455–68.

In 1916, Ford announced a price cut from $440 to $360 on the basic Model T automobile. The stockholders brought suit against the company, claiming that Ford was unjustified in giving their money away in this fashion. Ford's defense was that the company was clearing $2 to $2.5 million a month, which is all any firm ought to make in his opinion. The court, however, held for the stockholders, ruling that it was not within the lawful powers of a corporation to conduct a company's affairs for the merely incidental benefit of shareholders and for the primary purpose of benefiting others.

© 1972 American Heritage Publishing Company, Inc. Reprinted by permission from *The American Heritage History of American Business and Industry* by Alex Groner.

and commercial construction, led to the formation of many new auto dealerships, and benefited the rubber and steel industries.[19]

The period from World War I to the Depression was one of unprecedented prosperity. Many people became new millionaires, the stock market soared, and production increased dramatically. There were many reasons for this burst of growth. The United States emerged from World War I economically and physically undamaged, giving it an advantage in world markets. Mass production methods became widely applied in many industries, increasing production of goods and services. Several major new products, such as automobiles, and electric power, created or stimulated many new jobs and markets. Installment buying became popular and, coupled with the widespread use of advertising and sales techniques, stimulated consumption of these new products. Finally there were enormous profits to be made in stock market speculation, and low margin requirements made it possible for many people to participate (see box).[20]

Between March 3, 1928 and Sept. 3, 1929, American Can went from 77 to 181⅞, AT&T from 179½ to 335⅝, Anaconda Copper from 54½ to 162, Electric Bond & Share from 89¾ to 203⅝, General Motors from 139¾ to 181⅞, and Westinghouse from 91⅝ to 313. The New York Stock Exchange soared from 236 million shares in 1923 to more than 1 billion in 1929. Five million share days became commonplace.

From: "America in 1929: The Prosperity Illusion," *Business Week*, September 3, 1979, p.9. Quoted with permission.

[19] Groner, *American Heritage History*, pp. 218–20, 275–78; "American in 1929: The Prosperity Illusion," *Business Week*, September 3, 1979, p. 6.

[20] "American in 1929: The Prosperity Illusion," *Business Week*, September 3, 1979, pp. 6–10.

Then came the crash. It is very difficult for those who did not live through this period of American history to grasp the full impact of the Depression. Statistics such as those in Table 3.2 tell only part of the story. Unemployment soared to almost twenty-five percent of the labor force—over twelve million out of fifty-two million workers in a nation of 122 million. Breadlines, clusters of tarpaper shacks called "Hoovervilles," and gray armies of job hunters became symbols of the period. Consumption spending slid by one-fifth and investment collapsed entirely. Waves of panic struck the banking system from late 1930 through 1933, forcing more than nine thousand banks with deposits of $7 billion to close their doors. More than nine million savings accounts were lost, and thousands of businesses went bankrupt because they could not take their money out of the bank.[21] Panic selling hit the stock market and paper fortunes were lost overnight when the crash began.

There is a great deal of debate over the cause of such a drastic change in the fortunes of the country, but the following seem to emerge as some of the major causes. First, the soaring stock market was more the result of speculation than increases in real physical wealth. Low margin requirements

Table 3.2
Key Statistics of the Depression of the 1930s

Index	1929	1921
Gross National Product (billions)[a]		
Current dollars	103.1	58.0
Farm income	12.0	5.3
Corporate profits	9.8	−3.0
Industrial production (1935-1939 = 100)[b]	110.0	57.0
Durable goods production (1934-1939 = 100)[b]	132.0	41.0
Steel production as percent capacity[c]	—	20.0
New private construction activity ($ billion)[d]	8.3	1.7
Automobile sales (millions of cars)[e]	5.4	1.3
Industrial stock prices (average dollars per share)[f]	311.0	65.0
Unemployment (millions)[g]	1.5	12.1
Percent of labor force	3.2	23.6
Farm products, wholesale price index (1957–1959 = 100)[g]	64.0	20.0

[a]U.S. Department of Commerce
[b]Federal Reserve Board
[c]American Iron and Steel Institute
[d]U.S. Bureau of the Census
[e]Automobile Manufacturers Association
[f]Dow Jones
[g]U.S. Bureau of Labor Statistics
Source: George A. Steiner, *Business and Society* (New York: Random House, 1971), p. 59.

[21] "A Debate That Rages On: Why Did It Happen?" *Business Week*, September 3, 1979, p. 12.

encouraged such speculation. People borrowed heavily to buy stocks and participate in the rise of the market. When the psychology of the market changed and investors sensed it had reached a peak, they began selling to get their profits and run. Panic quickly set in and the whole speculative structure collapsed rapidly.

Second, the prosperity of the late twenties was not shared by the agricultural sector. Farm purchasing power steadily deteriorated throughout this period, aggravated by the inelastic demand for farm products. Coupled with this was an inequality in the distribution of income. Most of the money in the twenties went to those who were already wealthy rather than to workers with lower incomes. Smaller proportions of total corporate income went toward wages and salaries. Much of the money that was received by the wealthy was reinvested in new productive facilities, causing an overextension of factory capacity. Workers simply could not buy all that the economy was producing.

Then the Smoot-Hawley tariff was passed, which further aggravated the situation. It was a very restrictive tariff structure that caused other countries to pass retaliatory tariffs of their own. This action curbed our exports to foreign countries just at the time that such markets were badly needed.

Finally, the Federal Reserve System adopted a restrictive monetary policy during the late twenties, which some scholars believe was the major cause of the Depression.[22] This action cut off credit to business and resulted in lagging business investment through the end of the period just before the crash.

The real causes of the Depression are many and complex. The long-term effects, however, are quite clear. New areas of public policy were created. Franklin Delano Roosevelt won the election of 1932 promising a New Deal for the American people. This New Deal consisted of a series of public policy measures (Exhibit 3.1) that were unprecedented in American history. The federal government assumed responsibility for stimulating business activity out of an economic depression and for correcting abuses in the economic machinery of the nation. It sought to relieve businesses, farmers, workers, homeowners, consumers, investors, and other groups from the distresses brought on by the adverse economic situation. In the famous one hundred days that followed Roosevelt's swearing in, the president asked for, and Congress speedily granted, an unprecedented list of emergency legislation that plunged the federal government deeply and unalterably into the affairs of society and the economy. During Roosevelt's first two years, ninety-three major pieces of legislation were passed that directly affected banking, business, agriculture, labor and social welfare. This flow of legislation set the stage for the role government would be playing a generation

---

[22] See Milton Friedman and Anna J. Schwartz, *A Monetary History of the United States* (Princeton, N.J.: Princeton University Press, 1963).

later and dramatically increased the importance of public policy to the society as a whole and business in particular.[23]

EXHIBIT 3.1
Public Policy Measures of the New Deal Period

Year	Measure	Explanation
1932	Emergency Banking Relief Act	Reopened banks under government supervision
1932	Civilian Conservation Corps	First federal effort to deal with unemployment (youth) through direct public works
1932	Federal Emergency Relief Act	Required Washington to fund state-run welfare programs
1932	Reconstruction Finance Corporation	First use of government credit to aid troubled private companies
1933	Agricultural Adjustment Act	First system of agricultural price and production supports
1933	Tennessee Valley Authority Act	First direct government involvement in energy production and marketing
1933	Glass-Steagall Banking Act	Created bank deposit insurance. Divorced commercial and investment banking. Prohibited interest on checking accounts
1933	National Industrial Recovery Act	First major attempt to plan and regulate the entire economy through the use of industry and trade associations and codes of competition. First act to allow collective bargaining and wage and hour regulation. Portions were declared unconstitutional.
1934	National Housing Act	Provided for federal mortgage insurance and for regulation of housing standards
1935	Wagner Act	Promoted collective bargaining and prohibited unfair labor practice by employers
1935	Social Security Act	Created a system of social insurance and a national retirement system
1938	Agricultural Adjustment Act	Extended price supports, instituted payments, and launched wide federal management of agriculture
1938	Fair Labor Standards Act	Provided for minimum wage, 40-hour week, overtime, and control of child labor

Source: Rogene A. Buchholz, *Business Environment and Public Policy: Implications for Management*, © 1982, p. 38. Reprinted by permission of Prentice-Hall, Inc., Englewood Cliffs, N.J.

[23] "Interventionist Government Came To Stay," *Business Week*, September 3, 1979, p. 39.

Whether all these public policy measures really pulled the economy out of the depression is again a matter of debate. The record, as shown in Table 3.3, is spotty. Unemployment never recovered its 1929 low, and gross national product in 1939 had barely recovered its 1929 high. Some historians believe that there were three parts to the depression that in effect lasted until World War II. These were: (1) the long, nearly uninterrupted decline for three and a half years to the low point of March 1933; (2) a gradual upturn for another three and a half years until August 1937; and (3) a final plunge and ascent leading to the war production period.[24]

Table 3.3
Employment and Production 1929-1942

Year	Unemploy-ment as a Percentage of the Labor Force[a]	Gross National Product per Capita in Dollars[b]	Year	Unemploy-ment as a Percentage of the Labor Force	Gross National Product per Capita in Dollars
1929	3.1	696	1936	12.7	650
1930	8.7	619	1937	9.7	682
1931	15.8	563	1938	13.2	647
1932	23.5	478	1939	12.3	702
1933	24.7	485	1940	10.1	760
1934	20.7	537	1941	7.6	903
1935	17.6	561	1942	4.4	1024

[a]People on work relief and people in the armed forces are counted as employed.
[b]Dollars all of the same purchasing power.
Source: Robert R. Russel, *A History of the American Economic System* (Englewood Cliffs, N.J.: Prentice-Hall, 1964), p. 564. Reprinted with permission.

President Roosevelt, in the late thirties, became disappointed with the performance of the economy. He called for an investigation of economic concentration, forming a Temporary National Economic Committee to do the investigation, declaring that free enterprise was ceasing to be free enterprise. Parallel with this development was the effort of Thurman Arnold, the Assistant Attorney General, to enforce the antitrust laws more vigorously.[25] These efforts became more or less academic with the advent of the war years, which called on the nation's productive capacity as never before, and ended concern about the depression for some time.

Contradictions appeared during this period of history. Unemployment threw millions of people out of work and there existed widespread poverty in a nation that only a few years before had believed that poverty would be eliminated and prosperity would be unending. Perhaps the most basic con-

[24] Groner, *American Heritage History*, p. 302.
[25] *Ibid.*

tradiction of all was intellectual—the challenge that the Depression posed to the classical, mechanistic view of the market. The classical view of the market was that it was self-correcting—that with the onset of unemployment, wages and prices would fall, demand would begin to increase, companies would respond by expanding output and hiring more workers, and these workers would then begin to buy more products. An upward spiral would be set in motion that would eventually pull the economy out of the depression. Government intervention was not necessary, and, in fact, would only interfere with the automatic mechanisms of the market system.[26]

The Depression was such a shock to the self-confidence of the nation and the distress it caused was so widespread that people came to fear that self-correction would not happen in time to do any good. They were not willing to sit around in their Hoovervilles starving to death waiting for the market to correct itself. The unregulated market was too unstable and too slow-moving to be trusted. People, including business leaders, wanted action, and they wanted it immediately. The Roosevelt administration promised action.

The government, through public policy, thus stepped in again to mediate these contradictions in the market system. Many believe that Roosevelt, instead of being the enemy of the free market, actually saved the system, and prevented an epic cycle from gaining the headway that could have taken the country into some form of socialism. In any event, three new areas of public policy came out of this historical period: the policy process known as economic management where government attempts to manage the economy and even out the business cycle, the area of labor-management relations where government supported the right of collective bargaining, and the beginnings of a welfare state based on a philosophy of entitlements.

Economic Management   The public policy measures that came out of the early part of the New Deal were part of a social welfare program designed to help victims of the Depression. The idea that public works programs, for example, should be designed to stimulate the economy through deficit spending had not yet taken root. The immediate problem was to relieve the widespread distress the Depression had caused. Only later did economic theories develop to support the notion of an on-going government involvement to even out the business cycle through countercyclical spending.[27]

These new theoretical developments came primarily from John Maynard Keynes and his followers in the form of what has since been called Keynesian economics. Keynes pointed out that classical theory was wrong on

[26] "The Scars Still Mark Economic Policy," *Business Week*, September 3, 1979, p. 22.
[27] *Ibid.*

two counts: in the real world prices and wages did not fall as expected, because of rigidities built into the system; and a reduction in wages of sufficient magnitude to enable business to begin hiring lowers a worker's income drastically and therefore reduces even further the total demand for goods in the economy. The fundamental problem, according to Keynes, was this deficiency in demand, especially the demand for investment goods by business, which kept the economy at low levels of output and employment. Thus if no one else could spend money, government should, and prime the pump by putting money back into the economy to stimulate demand for goods and services.[28]

Eventually, these notions took root, culminating in the Employment Act of 1946, in which government was given the responsibility of managing the economy on an ongoing basis rather than simply to stimulate it in crisis situations like a depression. As World War II drew to a close, there was a great deal of concern that a new period of inflation would ensue because people had earned and saved a good deal of money during the war. Many goods and services had not been generally available. After the war, it was believed there would be a tremendous jump in demand as people took this money and moved into the marketplace. The productive facilities would not be able to keep up with this surge in demand, resulting in too much money in the economy chasing after too few goods, a classic cause of inflation. It was feared this high inflation would eventually lead to another serious downturn in the economy.

To prevent this from happening, the government was given the responsibility of managing the money supply through fiscal and monetary policies. Government was to even out business cycles by pumping money into the economy when necessary, dampening demand by raising taxes, stimulating investment, becoming the employer of last resort, and using other measures designed to maintain a stable economic environment in which business and the society at large could prosper. The idea that the market was self-regulating in this regard was rejected. It was believed that a completely unregulated market system was excessively prone to waves of over-investment and excess capacity, and deficient spending and under-employment of resources. Such boom and bust periods as had been experienced throughout much of American history were simply unacceptable. Management of the economy by government to promote stability of employment and purchasing power became a matter of public policy. Rather than trusting the market and succumbing to the ups and downs of normal cyclical behavior, government took on the responsibility of keeping inflation and unemployment under control and creating the conditions for continuing economic prosperity.

[28] *Ibid.*

Labor-Management Relations   Another area of public policy that was affected by the Depression was labor-management relations. The ordeal of the working class in those years ignited a militance that swept the country and revolutionized the industrial relations system. This militancy forced the federal government to intervene in labor-management relations and to adopt a national labor policy designed to protect the rights of workers to unionize. Out of this intervention came a revived labor movement, the development of collective bargaining as it is known today, and the end of management's unilateral control of the workplace.[29]

Workers found that the market system, particularly during periods of recession and depression when jobs were not readily available, was unable to deal with problems they were experiencing—long hours, poor working conditions, low wages, and arbitrary hiring and firing practices. They began to form unions to counter the power of management with organized labor. Before the Depression, management held an overwhelming advantage over the unions. The courts upheld the right of employers to do just about anything to prevent unionism. Companies could fire workers for joining unions, force them to sign a pledge not to join a union as a condition of employment, require them to belong to company unions, and spy on them to stop unionization before it got started. The attempt to form unions without government help was not very successful. Before the Depression, the workers' interest in unionism was declining.[30]

The National Industrial Recovery Act rekindled this interest. The NIRA authorized businesses to form trade associations to regulate production, and a few union leaders insisted that the bill also gave employees the right to organize and bargain collectively. With the support of public policy and with job security at the forefront of workers' minds because of the Depression, labor leaders found it easier to organize segments of the labor force. When the NIRA was found unconstitutional in 1935, a more comprehensive labor relations law called the Wagner Act was passed. The Wagner Act extended to workers the right to organize and bargain collectively. It also proscribed employer actions that interfered with that right, and established the National Labor Relations Board as the enforcement mechanism. After World War II, two additional laws were passed to amend certain provisions of the Wagner Act, the Taft-Hartley Act of 1947 and the Landrum-Griffin Act of 1959. Thus were created the rules which govern labor-management relations today.[31]

---

[29] "The Ruins Gave Rise To Big Labor," *Business Week*, September 3, 1979, p. 26.

[30] *Ibid.*

[31] *Ibid.*, pp. 27–28.

The Welfare State   The Depression was also responsible
for the beginning of another series of
public policy measures that can be grouped loosely under the title of welfare. The initial public policies of the New Deal era, as stated previously,
were designed to alleviate distress. Many people were the victims of circumstances beyond their control. They were willing and able to work but there
simply were no jobs available. Society conceded that the unemployed were
not necessarily to blame for their situation and was willing to have government accept responsibility for helping such victims. People were not allowed
to starve while waiting for the market to correct itself and make jobs available again.

So began a philosophy of entitlements, in which people believe they
have rights to a good job, decent food, clothing, and shelter. The government has a responsibility to guarantee these rights. This philosophy has led
to a whole series of measures—such as social security, aid to families with
dependent children, medicare and medicaid, and food stamps—designed to
help people whose basic needs have not been met, for one reason or another, by the market system.[32]

The largest growth of these entitlement programs took place in the
1960s and 1970s as the nation mounted an effort to eliminate poverty and
assure every citizen a guaranteed minimum level of medical care, food, and
income. Aid to families with dependent children and medicaid programs, for
example, grew 515 percent and 905 percent respectively in the 1967–77
period. Overall payment to individuals of this sort grew at an average annual
rate of 15.3 percent during fiscal years 1966–79 compared with much lower
rates for earlier periods. These payments steadily increased as a percent of
GNP throughout most of this period (Figure 3.1). In 1981, 43 percent of the
federal budget went to direct payments for individuals.

The motivation for this growth of entitlement programs came from an
egalitarian movement in our society. These programs became a means of
promoting equality, instead of simply a means to relieve the distresses of
certain unfortunate groups. The egalitarian movement was primarily composed of blacks and other minorities, women, welfare workers, and leaders
of new unions of government employees.[33] The goal of this movement was to
promote an equality of result rather than opportunity, by transferring money
from the upper-income levels of society to the lower levels through a series
of cash-income assistance programs such as social security and in-kind assis-

[32] "A Watershed In American Attitudes," *Business Week*, September 3, 1979, pp. 46–50.

[33] John Cobbs, "Egalitarianism: Threat to a Free Market," *Business Week*, December 1,
1975, pp. 62–65; John Cobbs, "Egalitarianism: Mechanisms for Redistributing Income," *Business Week*, December 8, 1975, pp. 86–90; and John Cobbs, "Egalitarianism: The Corporation as
Villain," *Business Week*, December 15, 1975, pp. 86–88.

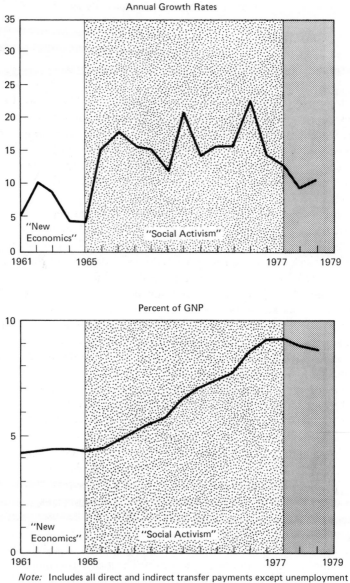

Annual Growth Rates

35

30

25

20

15

10

5

"New
Economics"

"Social Activism"

0
1961   1965   1977   1979

Percent of GNP

10

5

"New
Economics"   "Social Activism"

0
1961   1965   1977   1979

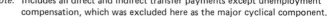

Note: Includes all direct and indirect transfer payments except unemployment
compensation, which was excluded here as the major cyclical component.

Figure 3.1
Payments for Individuals, Fiscal 1961–1979

From Michael E. Levy, "Federal Budget Policies of the 1970s: Some Lessons for the
1980s," *Stabilization Policies* (St. Louis, Mo.: Washington University Center for the
Study of American Business, 1980), p. 166. Reprinted with permission.

tance programs such as medicare and medicaid that provide basic services to needy people.

The growth of these programs and the egalitarian movement sparked a lively debate in our country. Critics were concerned about the further growth of government these programs demanded. The drive for equality of results contributes to strengthening centralized bureaucratic power because government must allocate outcomes.[34] Others raised questions about the trade-offs between equality and efficiency. In pursuing equality, society would forego any opportunity to use material resources or rewards as incentives to production. Thus any insistence on carving the pie into equal slices would shrink the size of the pie for everyone.[35] Egalitarians thus posed a threat to the business system.

> Egalitarianism is a vital counter-force to the traditional business philosophy for several reasons: (1) It has a great appeal to the masses, for it promises them their "rights" to a higher life style and greater positions of power; (2) The egalitarian thrust has necessitated (and will continue to demand) the strengthening of centralized power in order to reduce the privileges of the "haves" and the transfer of some of their largess to the "have nots"; (3) It is directly antithetical to the managerial ideology, for it tends to create a society wherein there are smaller numbers of winners and losers, and thereby reduces the capitalistic incentives, which, of course, depend upon the presence, and desirability, of inequalities; and finally, (4) Egalitarianism confuses the notion of "progress," for its emphasis is on distribution rather than on production.[36]

The growth of many of these entitlement programs was finally slowed beginning in 1981 with the Reagan administration. Programs such as food stamps, aid to families with dependent children and student loans were cut significantly. Other programs, such as social security, were not immediately cut for political reasons. These budget cuts, which will disproportionately affect lower-income groups, coupled with income tax cuts, which will disproportionately benefit upper-income groups, will go some way in reversing the egalitarian trend in our society. If these changes prove to be long lasting, 1981 could prove to be another watershed year in this area of public policy.

[34] See Dow Votaw, "The New Equality: Bureaucracy's Trojan Horse," *California Management Review*, vol. XX, no. 4 (Summer 1978), pp. 5–17.

[35] Arthur M. Okun, *Equality and Efficiency: The Big Tradeoff* (Washington, D.C.: The Brookings Institution, 1975).

[36] Joseph W. McGuire, "Today's Business Climate," *Business and Its Changing Environment*, George A. Steiner, ed. (Los Angeles: UCLA Graduate School of Management, 1978), p. 10. Quoted with permission.

THE POSTINDUSTRIAL SOCIETY

The postwar period, at least until the Arab oil embargo in 1974, was yet another period of prosperity for the United States. By later standards, inflation was very low throughout most of this period. Unemployment was also low, and there were only minor recessions until that of 1974–75. Cities and suburbs alike grew, people became wealthier, and more and more goods and services were produced until the gross national product topped the trillion-dollar mark. People were overwhelmed with new products, new services, and new inventions to make their lives easier. As more people moved into the middle class and came to own homes, buy cars, and acquire all the other amenities, society became referred to as a postindustrial society.[37]

A postindustrial society generally has three characteristics, and the United States had all three of them. The first is affluence that becomes widespread throughout much of the population. The second is a service-based economy, one in which most of the labor force is engaged in service industries, such as banking or insurance. The third characteristic is a knowledge-based society—one in which people become better and better educated and in which education is crucial to getting and keeping a good job. Unskilled jobs decline as society becomes more technologically sophisticated, demanding more highly skilled people.

If Maslow's hierarchy of needs concept is applied to a society, it seems that throughout the 1950s and early 1960s American society fulfilled its basic economic needs. It could then move up the ladder to the next level and devote attention and resources to solving some of society's social problems. This it did, first in the civil rights movement, when an attempt was made to assure equal rights to blacks and other minorities who had been treated as second-class citizens throughout our history. Soon after this movement had peaked, the feminist movement developed to press for women's rights in all areas of American life, from equal job opportunities to equal treatment in the armed services. Then came a serious concern with pollution—air and water pollution at first, then noise and visual pollution, and later toxic substances and hazardous waste disposal. Soon after that came a war on poverty, which sought to eliminate it in American society. Then came a new wave of consumerism, touched off by Ralph Nader, which dealt with product safety and quality, warranties, truth in advertising, packaging, and other aspects of the marketplace. At the end of the decade, a new concern about safety and health in the workplace surfaced. Finally, ethical concerns, stimulated by illegal campaign contributions in this country and foreign payments in other countries, came in for a great deal of attention.

Thus society experienced one social movement after another in the

[37] Daniel Bell, *The Coming of Post-Industrial Society: A Venture In Social Forecasting* (New York: Basic Books, 1973).

middle and late sixties—movements that changed the face of the country and altered fundamental values that had guided this country for years. Out of this change in values new public policy measures arose. These measures have become of increasing concern to business because many of them have interfered with the basic economic mission of business.

In the mid-1970s, American society experienced what was the worst recession since the Great Depression—an economic shock brought on primarily by the Arab oil embargo. The country survived that recession but double-digit inflation, soaring energy costs, relatively high levels of unemployment, and declining real income for many people have become the order of the day. These factors, many of which seem out of our control, confronted American society with a whole new set of challenges as it entered the 1980s, challenges that were taken up by the Reagan administration.

The initial challenge was inflation, which erodes incomes and destroys confidence in the future. Throughout the 1950s and 1960s, there were many years when inflation averaged only one percent for the entire year. During the late 1970s, the country was fortunate if inflation held to a one percent level for a month. One important reason for this high inflation was that the price of oil, which is so basic to our economy, was not under our control. Members of the Organization of Petroleum Exporting Countries (OPEC) were bent on a policy of continued increases throughout the late 1970s to maintain the value of their dollar holdings and increase the value of their oil in the ground.

The huge buildup of private sector indebtedness presented a major obstacle to the Federal Reserve System's efforts to control inflation. As long as credit was available, attempts to control the money supply had little effect on demand. People were motivated to buy now before inflation became worse. Business had also been amassing debt with a view to paying it off at some future time in inflation-cheapened dollars. Workers sought a hedge against inflation with higher wage demands that were unchecked by government guidelines. Yet at the same time, the productivity of American industry was declining. Much of the economy was indexed to inflation. Social security benefits rose automatically with increases in consumer prices. The same is true of wages that had a cost of living adjustment (COLA) as part of the contract. Add to these forces the increases in government spending, particularly for entitlement programs, and the additional cost burdens imposed on private business because of social regulation. Government spending, too, was indexed in a way, because inflation allowed the government to take in more money from taxpayers because of bracket creep. Thus inflation had built up such momentum that it was hard to wring out of the economy.

The Reagan administration declared inflation as public enemy number one and promised to get the economic situation under control. This administration instituted the largest income tax cut in history, cut federal spending—particularly with regard to entitlement programs—continued the tight monetary policy of the Carter administration, and mounted an effort to cut back on government regulation of business.

Inflation indeed was brought under control, and came down to 5–6 percent, which was still high by historic standards, but a great relief from the double-digit levels of previous years. But the cost of accomplishing this reduction was tremendous. The country entered a new recessionary period in 1981 that proved to be worse than the one experienced only a few years previously. Unemployment shot up into the double digits and bankruptcies reached record levels. Interest rates stayed in the double digits to choke off any kind of a recovery. They only began to come down in mid-1982 because the economy continued to deteriorate so badly that the demand for credit on the part of business and consumers dried up. The federal government's demand for credit, however, remained high and continued to put upward pressures on interest rates because of high federal deficits.

Thus economic conditions steadily worsened. No one seemed to have any answers to the economic problems that worked. For a time, the overall business system was operating at only 67 percent of capacity. For some industries, capacity utilization was much worse. Meanwhile, our competitive position in the world economy was eroding. Basic industries, such as steel and autos, could not compete effectively in world markets and sought protectionist measures. Plants and equipment in many of our basic industries became outmoded. Books were written about the deindustrialization of America as our basic manufacturing industries weakened and the service sector of our economy grew larger.

The contradictions that appeared in the postindustrial period were every bit as serious as in earlier periods. The social movements that appeared in the 1960s brought into question the article of faith related to economic growth—that economic growth was an unmixed blessing and the supreme objective of the country. It had been believed that economic growth was the source of all progress, social as well as economic. The engine of growth was the drive for profits by competitive private enterprise, which applied new technologies as rapidly as possible to foster economic growth. Business was thought to be solely an economic institution, and in pursuing economic objectives, business was making its maximum contribution to society.

But the civil rights movement and ecology movements, for example, pointed out that economic growth was a mixed blessing—that there were some serious social deficits in the form of discrimination and pollution that were not being treated adequately by the mindless pursuit of an ever-increasing gross national product. Discrimination was not being eliminated by the market system, as something called systemic discrimination was built into the personnel practices of our economic institutions. The market system provided no means of controlling pollution—there were no incentives to reduce pollution or dispose of toxic wastes properly to mitigate the environmental effects of new technology. These problems had to be given more direct attention in order to improve the quality of life for all citizens, a term that came to be increasingly used as a supplement or replacement of economic growth as an overall objective for the nation.

Another contradiction had to do with resource shortages. The Arab oil embargo and subsequent price increases made us aware of our dependency on foreign sources of supply. It also confronted us with the possibility of facing real limits to economic growth, a subject that had been discussed previously, but now confronted the nation as a reality rather than an academic exercise. The United States has used up a good many of its basic resources to the point where it is dependent on foreign sources for many of its raw materials. But even these foreign sources are finite. Thus the future holds a great deal of uncertainty about the cost and availability of raw materials crucial to the continued survival and operation of a sophisticated and technological society.

Questions began to be raised about the ability of a market system to allocate resources that are in short supply in an effective and acceptable manner. Does a market system which encourages exploitation of resources rather than conservation provide for future generations? Does the market system distribute pain and suffering fairly when critical resources become scarce? Is it right, for example, that those at the low end of the income scale should suffer more than others? Does not everyone have a basic right to be warm in winter and have enough gasoline for normal driving? Does the market system provide adequate incentives for the development of alternative sources of supply when the technologies are complex and expensive, and the lead times are lengthy before a private business can expect a return on investment?

Yet a third contradiction appeared in the deterioration of some of our basic industries. Industries like steel and the automobile industry needed billions of dollars to retool and invest in new technologies to become competitive in world markets. Yet the market system did not seem to be providing the capital needs of these industries or allocating enough capital resources in their direction. The incentives were lacking, and thus these industries continued to deteriorate.

Social Regulation

The social deficits that were of concern in the 1960s were the subject of government action. Again the market proved unable to respond to these problems and meet the social needs of society. A new area of public policy ensued with the passage of much legislation directed at these problems and the creation of a new form of regulation called social regulation. Congress passed all kinds of social legislation related to environmental cleanup, consumer concerns, and other social issues, outdoing the New Deal Congress of Franklin D. Roosevelt. Government also created new regulatory agencies, such as the Environmental Protection Agency (EPA), the Equal Employment Opportunity Commission (EEOC), the Consumer Product Safety Commission (CPSC), and the Occupational Safety and Health Administration (OSHA), and gave expanded powers to such existing agencies as the Food and Drug Administration (FDA). This new type of regulation affects every industry in the country rather than a particular industry, as was the old style of regulation patterned after the Interstate Commerce Commission mode. These regulatory agencies set and enforce standards which all companies are expected to meet. Every company is thus left in the same competitive position and at the same time social goods and services are supposedly provided to the society.

Thus business was forced to internalize the so-called social costs of production and respond to social problems. Business was asked to consider and mitigate the social effects of its economic decisions. The new style of social regulation concerns itself with the conditions under which goods and services are produced and the physical characteristics of products rather than rates, routes, and the obligation to serve, as did the old style of industry regulation. Social regulatory agencies are concerned with noneconomic matters and sometimes pay little or no attention to an industry's basic mission of providing goods and services to the country. They become involved with many detailed facets of the production process, interfering with the traditional prerogatives of management. OSHA, for example, sometimes specifies precise engineering controls that must be adopted. The CPSC mandates specific product characteristics it believes will protect consumers from injury.[38]

One reason for this type of regulation is related to the nature of today's workplace and marketplace. It is often argued that when goods and technology are complex and their effects largely unknown, consumers are incapable of making intelligent judgments. Workers may not know the risks they face on various jobs or may not be able to acquire the necessary information. Expert judgment is needed in these areas to protect consumers and workers from unnecessary risks that they cannot assess for themselves.[39]

Another reason for this type of regulation is the existence of situations where the actions of a firm have a harmful effect on others. The cost of external diseconomies such as air and water pollution cannot be voluntarily assumed by firms unless a government agency exists to enforce standards equally across all firms in an industry. Voluntary assumption by some firms would place them at a competitive disadvantage; regulation is needed to

---

[38] William Lilley III and James C. Miller III, "The New Social Regulation," *The Public Interest*, no. 47 (Spring 1977), p. 53.

[39] Robert E. Healy, ed., *Federal Regulatory Directory 1979–80* (Washington D.C.: Congressional Quarterly, Inc., 1979), p. 5.

make all companies meet the same standard, leaving them in the same competitive position.[40]

Agencies dealing with social regulation include OSHA whose purpose is to enforce worker safety and health regulations. The EEOC enforces the antidiscriminatory provisions of the Civil Rights Act and other related laws that have recently come under its jurisdiction. The CPSC was created to protect the public from unreasonable risks of injury associated with consumer products. Protection and enhancement of the physical environment is the responsibility of the EPA. The Bureau of Consumer Protection in the Federal Trade Commission (FTC) deals with false or deceptive advertising of consumer products. The purpose of the FDA is to protect the public against impure and unsafe food, drugs, and cosmetics, and to regulate hazards associated with medical devices and radiation. Finally, the National Highway Traffic Safety Administration (NHTSA) sets standards for motor vehicle safety and fuel economy.

National Economic Planning   This area of public planning is not yet developed, but it certainly is in the discussion stage. Two bills were introduced into Congress to set up a planning mechanism and establish national objectives.[41] The Carter administration attempted to develop a comprehensive energy plan, which consisted of a series of rewards and penalties for consumers and business organizations to adopt behaviors consistent with the goal of energy independence. Some economists advocate a national materials policy to assure the country adequate sources of supply for critical resources. The government attempted to promote the development of synthetic fuel. A massive effort was launched involving billions of dollars to provide incentives for private corporations to invest in research and development for synfuel. There has been much talk about the reindustrialization of America, which most often means the government should directly promote capital formation for modernization of plants and equipment in our basic industries.

Thus the debate has begun as to whether formal economic planning is a proper role for government in mediating the contradictions introduced by resource shortages and the deindustrialization of America. In a sense, the government does plan already, but it is ad hoc and uncoordinated, consisting of bits and pieces located in various agencies and departments that affect various sectors of the economy. The kind of planning being considered is a more comprehensive formal approach. It would specify social and economic

[40] *Ibid.*

[41] The Humphrey-Javits bill introduced into the first session of the 94th Congress (S. 1795) and the Humphrey-Hawkins bill introduced into the House (H.R. 50) and Senate (S. 50) in March 1976.

goals for the society as a whole and attempt to coordinate all the efforts of the public and private sectors toward the attainment of these goals. This is a new role the government has not as yet attempted.

One argument for national planning is simply that if government management of aggregate demand has had such success for most of the period since World War II, more such planning on an even more comprehensive basis must be better. Others argue that the difficulties we have experienced since 1974 with high inflation and unemployment make planning a necessity. We have moved into an era of resource shortages, it is said, where the market can no longer allocate resources to their best uses. The market must be supplemented by national economic planning to allocate these scarce resources in a fair and just manner so all members of society can maintain a decent quality of life.

Others point to the success corporations have had with planning and argue that government should be using some of the techniques that corporations have developed to set goals, objectives, and strategies for all its agencies. "Our government suffers from the absence of (1) an overall sense of direction, (2) well-defined national goals and objectives, (3) an integrated strategy for achieving such goals and objectives, and (4) a process for answering difficult 'What if?' questions that cut across department lines within the government."[42] The answer is a comprehensive planning system which would solve the problems of energy, national defense, environment, and other problems of this scope.

Another argument in favor of planning is that business itself would benefit from it; our present haphazard approach to problems like inflation and unemployment does not create an environment in which business can function effectively. A more coordinated and planned response to problems would create a more stable environment for business and help it to gain credibility.[43] Finally, the planning exercise, some argue, would itself be beneficial. There has been a tendency for the nation to charge off after a variety of social and economic goals, all of them desirable but not necessarily compatible with one another. Planning might introduce some realism and discipline to this process.

The arguments against planning are many and formidable. Some fear that this role would inevitably result in more government control over business and eventually produce such a concentration of economic and political power in the hands of the federal government as to threaten our pluralistic system. Such a role involves a further shift in power to government bureaucrats and gives them greater control over the daily lives of citizens.

[42] Thomas H. Naylor, "The U.S. Needs Strategic Planning," *Business Week*, December 17, 1979, p. 18.

[43] Robert Lekachman, "A Cure For Corporate Neurosis," *Saturday Review*, January 21, 1978, pp. 30–34.

Another argument against planning is that the sheer size and complexity of the socioeconomic system is simply beyond the capability of people and machines to coordinate effectively. Too many variables and too many decisions would have to be made centrally to take into account all the various interests of society. Critics of planning need only point to the efforts of the Department of Energy to allocate energy resources, and the dislocations and problems these efforts caused.

Finally, the comparison of government planning with planning by business is questioned. There is a fundamental difference, some point out, between the two processes. Business planning is based on the assumption that the ultimate decisions as to the allocation of society's resources are made by individual consumers. Thus business planning is geared to the corporate purpose of attempting to persuade consumers to buy the firm's goods or services. If the company's planning is wrong, it will suffer the consequences.

Government, on the other hand, will determine through a planning process what is in the best interests of society as a whole. If the public does not respond accordingly, the government can use its power to achieve the results it desires. This power includes promotion, procurement, regulation, ownership, and taxation. Unlike a private organization, government may not only plan, it can also command. While a business firm can set goals only for itself, government can establish goals for society as a whole and see that they are followed through some form of government control.[44]

Thus there were several periods in American history where new areas of public policy developed in response to contradictions that developed in

EXHIBIT 3.2
Major Periods of Public Policy

Historical Period	Contradictions	Public Policy
Rise of modern industrial society	Destruction of competition	Industry regulation Antitrust legislation
The Great Depression	Widespread unemployment and poverty Market not self-correcting	Economic management Collective bargaining Welfare system
Postindustrial society	Social deficits Resource shortages Deindustrialization	Social regulation National economic planning

[44] Murray L. Weidenbaum and Linda Rockwood, "Corporate Planning versus Government Planning," *The Public Interest*, no. 46 (Winter 1977), pp. 59–72.

the market system. These periods are summarized in Exhibit 3.2 in case the reader has become confused by all the detail in this chapter. Without successful mediation, these contradictions may indeed have developed sufficient pressures to result in a radical transformation of American society. Thus public policy plays a crucial role in responding to values that are not able to be incorporated into the normal workings of a market system.

SELECTED REFERENCES

ALLEN, FREDERICK LEWIS. *The Lords of Creation*. New York: Harper & Row, Pub., 1935.

BONNIFIELD, MATTHEW P. *The Dust Bowl: Men, Dirt, and Depression*. Albuquerque: University of New Mexico Press, 1979.

CHAMBERLAIN, JOHN. *The Enterprising Americans*. New York: Harper & Row, Pub., 1963.

CHANDLER, ALFRED. *The Visible Hand: The Managerial Revolution in American Business*. Cambridge, Mass.: Belknap Press, 1977.

CHANDLER, LESTER V. *America's Greatest Depression, 1929–1941*. New York: Harper & Row, Pub., 1970.

COCKRAN, THOMAS C., AND WILLIAM MILLER. *The Age of Enterprise*. New York: Harper & Row, Pub., 1942.

DEGLER, CARL N. *The New Deal*. New York: Quadrangle/The New York Times Book Co., 1970.

GALBRAITH, JOHN KENNETH. *The Great Crash—1929*, 3rd ed. Boston: Houghton Mifflin, 1972.

GRAHAM, OTIS, L. *The New Deal: The Critical Issues*. Boston: Little, Brown, 1971.

GRONER, ALEX. *The American Heritage History of American Business and Industry*. New York: American Heritage Publishing Co., 1972.

HACKER, LOUIS M. *The Triumph of American Capitalism*. New York: Simon & Schuster, 1940.

HEILBRONER, ROBERT L. *Beyond Boom and Crash*. New York: W. W. Norton & Co., Inc., 1978.

HENDRICK, BURTON. *The Age of Big Business*. New Haven: Yale University Press, 1919–1921.

JOSEPHSON, MATTHEW. *The Robber Barons*. New York: Harcourt Brace Jovanovich, 1934.

MITCHELL, BROADUS. *Depression Decade*. New York: Holt, Rinehart & Winston, 1947.

MOODY, JOHN. *The Masters of Capital*. New Haven: Yale University Press, 1921.

MORISON, SAMUEL E., AND HENRY S. COMMAGER. *Growth of The American Republic*. Oxford: Oxford University Press, 1937.

NORTON, HUGH STANTON. *The Employment Act and the Council of Economic Advisers, 1946–1976*. Columbia: University of South Carolina Press, 1977.

RUSSEL, ROBERT R. *A History of The American Economic System*. Englewood Cliffs, N.J.: Prentice-Hall, Inc., 1964.

SCHACTMAN, TOM. *The Day America Crashed*. New York: Putnam's, 1979.

4

ORIGINS OF PUBLIC POLICY

⬅️ **IDEAS TO BE FOUND** ➡️
IN THIS CHAPTER

- Values
- Ideology
- Social-political structure

How do new areas of public policy, such as those discussed in the last chapter, get started? What can explain the emergence of new issues that were previously unimportant? What elements combine to cause social change at various times in our history as a nation? How do issues find their way onto the public policy agenda so that they become of widespread concern and deserve attention by government and corporations? These kinds of questions will be discussed in this chapter as part of an attempt to understand the origins of public policy.

VALUES   Public policy begins with values.
When particular values people hold strongly are threatened or when new values are adopted, pressures are generated. If the pressures are strong and widespread, they may result in the formulation of public policy, provided no other means can be used successfully. Thus it would seem that the concept of value is a good place to start in attempting to understand the origins of public policy. In earlier chapters, the role that values play in the market system and public policy process was described, but the concept of value was never defined.

Defining and Classifying Values   There is both a subjective and an objective definition of value. The subjective definition thinks of value as a particular quality that human beings associate with certain forms of human behavior, institutions, or material goods and services. When something is valued, it is considered to be worthwhile, good, desirable, important, and esteemed or prized.[1] That something, whatever it is, is believed to contribute to one's well-being and be of benefit to him or her. Something that is valueless is considered to be worthless and is not desired for any reason. When one makes a value judgment about something, one is either attributing value to a certain action or entity and judging it to be worthwhile, good, or desirable to some degree, or deciding that the entity in question has little or no worth and is not desired.

Value conflicts exist between people and within people. One person may value clean air quite highly, while another person may not deem it very important. One person may strongly desire a vacation in Hawaii. Someone else may want to buy a new car. A single individual may want both a vacation in Hawaii and a new car, but may not be able to afford both of these good things. The same individual may value both clean air and energy independence which means burning coal that dirties the air. The market system resolves these conflicts by forcing people to translate their diversity of values into a common value system and make choices about which items are most worthwhile. The public policy process resolves value conflicts through a process of negotiation and compromise where a common course of action is agreed upon with respect to a social objective, such as clean air or energy independence.

The market system responds to this subjective definition of value by allowing people to express their desires in the marketplace for goods and services they value. The objective definition of value, on the other hand, thinks of value in more absolute terms—that certain things are good for people whether they desire them or not, or conversely, that certain things are inherently bad and people shouldn't have them in spite of their desires. There is a large market for cocaine and other narcotics, for example. There are producers and drug dealers who try to meet these needs. Yet most societies believe it is a bad thing for people to use these products and try to prevent their production, sale, and usage through the use of sanctions and penalties. To use another example, government regulators have decided auto safety is a good thing despite people's apparent disdain for safety measures, and at one point, required auto manufacturers to design cars so they couldn't be started until seat belts were fastened.

When many people in a society desire the same things or make the same kinds of value judgments, social values can be said to exist. These values show up in principles the society believes in strongly, the institutions that are most highly esteemed, the behavior a society believes is appropri-

---

[1] *Webster's New Collegiate Dictionary* (Springfield, Mass.: Merriam, 1977), p. 1292.

ate, and the objectives people pursue. Social values, then, are values held in common because it is believed that certain principles, institutions, behavior, and objectives will produce a desirable state of affairs for all members of that society.

When a relatively homogeneous value system exists in a society over a period of time, that society is stable and experiences relatively little social change. When a homogeneous value system begins to break up and large segments of society begin to express so-called nontraditional values, social change of some kind seems inevitable. Social change of this sort usually brings about changes in the major institutions of society to incorporate these new values.

Values can be measured along several dimensions to evaluate their importance and strength in influencing a society's behavior. These dimensions are shown in Exhibit 4.1 which can be used as a model to determine the values of a given society. If these dimensions can be measured accurately, one can get some idea of the dominant value system in a society and where values fall in a scale of priorities.

Extensiveness has to do with how widespread a value is throughout a society. Recent surveys show, for example, that support for cleaning up the environment is widespread throughout all segments of society. Competition is something Americans have valued throughout their entire history and are likely to do so for the foreseeable future. Freedom is something Americans value with great intensity and will go to great lengths to protect and preserve. The heroic welcomes given to astronauts, particularly the first ones, says something about how strongly Americans value adventure and exploration of new frontiers.

Values can also be classified into certain categories, such as those shown in Exhibit 4.2, which can aid in understanding how values relate to each other and simplify an analysis of value change. Values that fall into the same category relate to each other in a cluster and form a value system. Using such categories, one can make a comparative analysis in terms of which values are more dominant than others in our society.

Many would argue that American society is dominated by an economic value system. Elbing and Elbing, for example, believe that the business institution is the supreme institution in our society. What is good for business is believed to be good for the entire country. The ultimate social values for society are assumed to be the outgrowth of economic values created by business organizations. Social and ethical problems not solved through the production of goods and services traded on the marketplace are viewed as peripheral problems.[2]

Others may not agree that economic values are so dominant, at least as

[2] Alvar O. Elbing, Jr. & Carol J. Elbing, *The Value Issue of Business* (New York: McGraw-Hill, 1967), p. 57.

EXHIBIT 4.1
Value Dimensions

---

1. Extensiveness of the value in the total activity of the system. What proportion of a population and of its activities manifests the value?
2. Duration of the value. Has it been persistently important over a considerable period of time?
3. Intensity with which the value is sought or maintained, as shown by effort, crucial choices, verbal affirmation, and reactions to threats to the value—for example, promptness, certainty, and severity of sanctions.
4. Prestige of value carriers—that is, of persons, objects, or organizations considered to be bearers of the value. Culture heroes, for example, are significant indexes of values of high generality and esteem.

From Robin M. Williams, Jr., *American Society: A Sociological Interpretation*, 3rd. ed. (New York: Knopf, 1970), p. 448. Reprinted with permission.

EXHIBIT 4.2
Value Systems

Theoretic:	The pursuit of knowledge for its own sake—the desirability of attaining knowledge because of the pleasure it brings to an individual.
Economic:	The pursuit of those material goods and services that can be bought and sold on the marketplace, where value is determined through the exchange process.
Aesthetic:	The importance of beauty in all aspects of existence, particularly in nature.
Social:	The desire to associate and interact with other people either individually or as members of a group and affirm one's existence in this manner.
Political:	The desire to make decisions that affect many people in society and exercise power over them.
Religious:	The pursuit of the ideas and precepts of a particular religious system.
Ethical:	The desire to do the right thing, take the right action, make the right decision in accordance with a particular ethical system.

Adapted from Keith Davis and Robert L. Blomstrom, *Business and Society: Environment and Responsibility*, 3rd ed. (New York: McGraw-Hill, 1975), p. 175. Reproduced with permission.

far as their individual priorities are concerned. Some may believe that religious values are most important—that the ideals embodied in the Judeo-Christian tradition, for example, are most desirable to pursue. Intellectuals may hold a certain disdain for economic values and believe the marketplace caters to the vulgar tastes of the masses. For them, the pursuit of knowledge may be the most important value system in their scale of priorities.

Redefining and Changing Values   Values change in response to many influences in society. Technology is one such influence. It may be possible for some things to be done that could never have been done before or to do something more easiy or inexpensively than before, changing the benefit-cost ratio. The invention of the airplane eventually made it possible to travel long distances with relative ease and at increased speeds, making distant places accessible. Most people probably desire good physical health, and modern medical technology makes it possible for more people to enjoy good health than before. Information changes the importance of certain things in our society. When it became known that using the environment for dumping our wastes has some disastrous side effects and might even change the climate of the world, the importance of the environment increased dramatically and more resources were allocated to cleaning it up.

Shifts in population have an effect on the dominant value systems in society. If the aged come to constitute an increasing proportion of the population, the values they hold as a group will tend to exercise more influence over the society as a whole. The same will hold true if young people come to constitute an increasing proportion of the population, as was true of American society in the 1960s.

Another factor influencing values is education. As people attain more formal education, they may question their desires and the things that they were raised to believe were important. They may come to reject these traditional values appropriated from their families and adopt a new set of desires and goals to pursue. Education supposedly broadens one's horizons and acquaints one with new sets of possibilities. Education gives people access to different dimensions of life and thus may change their beliefs about what is worthwhile.

Changes in basic institutions, such as the family and religion, also affect values. These institutions, particularly the family, play a crucial role in the socialization of children and the transmission of values from generation to generation. Much evidence suggests that these institutions are changing. Increasing numbers of women are employed outside the home, leaving children in day care centers or nursery homes. The increasing divorce rate breaks up more and more families. Attendance at religious institutions has declined and the authority of these institutions is being questioned. As these institutions play a reduced role in value transmission, there is less continuity of values from one generation to the next.

Affluence also causes value changes. Society can be looked at from the standpoint of a Maslowian hierarchy of needs. As more and more people in society become affluent and thus fulfill their basic economic needs, they can move up the ladder to fulfill a higher order of needs. Things become important to them that were not within the range of possibility before. They may desire other goods and services besides economic ones and pursue other goals related to self-fulfillment or improving the quality of life for the whole society.

Identifying specific value changes in American society is a risky proposition, but a good deal of evidence suggests that certain value changes have taken place in recent years. These changes have not occurred throughout the entire society but are significant enough to have appeared in much of the literature related to American society. Some of these major changes are briefly described in the paragraphs that follow.

1. One traditional value is the importance that American society has attached to work and a corresponding disrespect for laziness. The traditional notion was that work had value in and of itself regardless of the nature of the work, because it was done for the glory of God (religious meaning) or to make a contribution to the wealth of society (secular meaning). Thus work had a transcendent meaning that made all jobs of equal value and made work a serious duty of humankind. This has changed for many people. Work has lost this transcendent meaning and is valued more for what it contributes to the individual's personal enjoyment and fulfillment. Many people want a job that is fulfilling and challenging and shun jobs that involve drudgery and boredom. If they cannot find this kind of job, they try to gain more leisure time away from the job to pursue their interests.

2. Related to importance of working hard was the traditional importance of deferring personal gratification until the future. There was value in providing for one's security in retirement, saving for a rainy day, building an estate for the children, and having such virtue rewarded in heaven rather than on earth. The credit card has destroyed this value, as it encourages instant gratification. One can enjoy a particular product or service right now and pay for it later. Homes can be purchased with long-term mortgages. The future is taken care of with social security or institutional retirement plans.

3. Americans have traditionally believed that opportunity for success should be—and is in fact—equal for all people in society. America was the land of opportunity to which people came from all over the world. This led to the conclusion that the successful are differentiated from the unsuccessful only by their moral virtue, their willingness to work hard and to save, and their innate abilities. Recent years have seen the recognition that equal opportunity has not always existed for certain segments of society, most notably minorities and women. It has been discovered and admitted that systemic discrimination against these groups is built into the hiring, transfer, and other employment practices of our major institutions.

4. Since there was so much opportunity, Americans have always believed that it was important to make it on one's own in the world—that the world did not owe one a living but that one had to earn his or her own place in society by working hard to make a success of something. The Depression years saw the beginnings of a philosophy of entitlement that has grown stronger. People have a right to an income, a job, and good health, but, despite one's best efforts, the marketplace doesn't always provide these. If the market system cannot respect these rights, the government should, by becoming the employer of last resort, providing in effect a guaranteed annual income, or providing health care for all its citizens.

5. The tendency to pursue material wealth as a solution to many problems and a national belief in the desirability of economic growth and improved material living standards has been a social goal of the highest priority. This value was questioned in the 1950s and 1960s by many people who dropped out of the system to pursue something more meaningful for themselves than material wealth. It is also under question today because inflation is eroding the standard of living for many people and making it difficult for the nation to maintain a consistent growth in real gross national product.

6. The traditional American attitude toward the natural environment was that it is basically a hostile force to be subdued and exploited as a readily-available source of economic growth. Our land and resources were believed to be infinite. Indeed, as the first pioneers saw the vast expanse of the western region of the country, this belief was a reasonable response. This is so no longer. We know our resources are finite and we have nearly exhausted some of them. We also recognize that we have to live in harmony with nature and that our environment has deteriorated from many years of exploitation and neglect.

7. Technological progress is closely related to growth—a faith in the ability of science and technology, supported by money and economic resources, to ultimately solve all our problems. New technologies were introduced rapidly into society as a way to sustain growth and improve the quality of life. The side effects of many technologies, however, have now become all too apparent, and some technologies, such as nuclear power, are being questioned as to whether the risks involved make them worthwhile. Technology is seen as the source of many of our problems.

8. Finally, there has been a predominance of economic values in our society. This predominance is reflected in the high priority and social approval granted to the economic institutions in our society and the men and women who manage them. Recently, the term "quality of life" has come into vogue as a concept used to broaden people's conception of the kind of life they desire for themselves. Within this conception, social values play an increasingly important part and economic values begin to lose their domi-

nance. From this change comes the pressure to make the corporation respond to social values—to make it into a socioeconomic institution.

These changes in values are not, of course, spread throughout the entire society. They tend to be concentrated among younger people, people with college educations, and people in the middle- and upper-income groups. This concentration may reflect differences in formal education or it may indicate that people are not willing to abandon traditional values until they have attained the material success inherent in the old value system. But it is important to note that values seem to be changing fastest among people one would expect to have the greatest influence over society's future.

It must also be noted that American society is not in the process of exchanging one set of values for another. It is changing from a nation with relatively homogeneous values to one in which a variety of values is tolerated and encouraged. This change is consistent with the movement toward a pluralistic society, as such a social structure allows a greater diversity of values to be expressed.

IDEOLOGY   The concept of ideology can be understood as a shared set of beliefs that are representative of a group or an entire society. An ideology is the framework of ideas that integrates and synthesizes all aspects of a group or society's experience—political, social, economic, and cultural—into a meaningful whole. Ideology legitimizes the institutions of a society and helps make their functions acceptable.[3] Ideologies help to organize values into a coherent system that provides an understanding of the world and how it functions.

Other functions ideologies perform have to do with providing purpose and identity to individuals in a society. We distinguish ourselves from people of other societies on the basis of ideology. People in the Soviet Union, for example, have the same bodily functions as we do; they get married, have children, and finally die. What, then, makes them different from those of us living in the United States? The basic differentiation is ideological. They are Communist and that makes them different and gives us an identity different from theirs.

Ideologies are simplifying devices to cut through the complexity and ambiguity of the real world. How does our economic system work, for example, when it is composed of a myriad of large and small businesses pursuing somewhat different objectives, and an amalgam of business and government functions with government bailing out a failing business and business making contributions to political campaigns. The complexity of this system is over-

---

[3] William F. Martin and George Cabot Lodge, "Our Society in 1985—Business May Not Like It," *Harvard Business Review*, vol. 53, no. 6 (November–December 1975), pp. 149-50.

whelming to the average person. Mention the word free enterprise, however, and everything falls into place and makes sense.

Ideology can also be viewed as a shared belief system that provides a blueprint or map of social reality which serves to guide human behavior in the midst of social and cultural confusion. This view of ideology focuses on the symbolic significance of ideology and sees ideology as a symbol system that provides information and meaning to a particularly confusing cultural situation.

> They [symbol systems] are extrinsic sources of information in terms of which human life can be patterned—extrapersonal mechanisms for the perception, understanding, judgment, and manipulation of the world. Culture patterns . . . are programs; they provide a template or blueprint for the organization of social and psychological processes, much as genetic systems provide such a template for the organization of organic processes . . . The reason such symbolic templates are necessary is that, as has been often remarked, human behavior is inherently extremely plastic. Not strictly but only very broadly controlled by genetic programs or models—intrinsic sources of information—such behavior must, if it is to have any effective form at all, be controlled to a significant extent by extrinsic ones.[4]

Cultural symbol systems, then, serve as an external guide or road map for human behavior. Ideologies are symbol systems of this sort that perform such a function. Ideological activity arises in times of strain, and ideologies are crucial to guide behavior when the normal institutional guides for behavior are lacking. Ideologies help people make sense of an otherwise incomprehensible social situation, enabling them to comprehend their rights and responsibilities and act purposefully.[5]

Thus ideologies are a system of shared beliefs expressed symbolically that are a response to cultural, social, and psychological strain, all of which influence each other. The loss of cultural orientation is particularly crucial, because the institutions of that culture can provide no guidelines with which to deal with the strains. Ideologies then arise to fill the gap, and provide guidelines for behavior during a cultural upheaval or transformation when people find themselves in very unfamiliar territory.[6]

While new ideologies may arise during periods of strain, they function all the time, even during periods of relative cultural stability. There is always

---

[4] Reprinted with permission of Macmillan Publishing Co., Inc., from Clifford Geertz, "Ideology as a Cultural System," in *Ideology and Discontent*, David E. Apter, ed., page 63. Copyright © 1964 by the Free Press of Glencoe, a division of Macmillan Publishing Co., Inc.

[5] *Ibid.*, pp. 63–64.

[6] Other writers hold similar views of ideology and its function: Anthony F. C. Wallace, "Revitalization Movements," *American Anthropologist*, Vol. 58 (April 1956); and José A. Moreno, *Barrios in Arms* (Pittsburgh: University of Pittsburgh Press, 1970), especially Chapter 7.

a certain amount of cultural confusion and thus a need to rely on symbolic meaning systems for guides to behavior. Ideologies that have served well during periods of strain, bringing meaning and purpose to incomprehensible social situations, are likely to be relied upon to pattern human behavior for some time.

American society thinks of itself as a market-oriented society, in which the most efficient allocation of resources takes place when goods and services are exchanged in a free market. The idea of a *free market* or *free enterprise* is an ideology that describes in the abstract how the economic system works and prescribes duties and opportunities for people who participate in the marketplace. The outcomes of the marketplace are acceptable to society because they are believed to be just and moral. The free enterprise system depends on a number of ideological components that together form a total system or way of viewing the world.

An important part of American ideology in the notion of *individualism*—that the individual is more important than the society or its institutions. Social institutions exist to facilitate the pursuit of individual interests rather than to subordinate the individual to the power of the institution as is true in a collectivist society. Individuals must be free to pursue their own self-interest as defined by themselves, not by an institution. The welfare of a community is no more than the sum total of the welfare of the individuals who make up that community.

Property rights are the best guarantee of individual freedom. By virtue of this concept, individuals are protected from the predatory powers of a sovereign government. They are free to use their property as they see fit and thus have some control over their own destiny.

The uses of property are controlled by *competition* in a free and open market for the rewards society has to offer. This competition will draw property into its most productive use, as individuals pursue their rational economic self-interest. Competition encourages high levels of economic performance from all citizens of a society, and weeds out those who are inefficient. Competition channels the interests of self-seeking individuals into socially useful purposes and keeps power from becoming unduly concentrated.

The notion of a *limited state* stems from a mechanistic view of the free market. If the market remains free and is not interfered with, it will work to everyone's advantage. The natural laws of supply and demand will allocate resources to maximize the well-being of each individual citizen and of the entire society. The government has a very limited economic function and is best when it governs least. Governmental functions should be limited to protecting private property, enforcing contracts, and providing for national security. Anything beyond this is undue interference with the natural workings of a free enterprise system.

This traditional ideology has received many challenges throughout our history. It has had to be adapted in many ways to changing historical conditions when contradictions developed that needed attention. The free enterprise system hasn't always worked satisfactorily and government has had to play a much larger role than the ideology advocates. But despite much battering, the ideology remains largely intact. We still think of ourselves as basically a free enterprise society, and public policy has a legitimacy only in correcting deficiencies in the system. The beliefs that comprise an ideology are deeply embedded in human consciousness. Commitments to an ideology are not abandoned easily or quickly.

Ideologies interact with values in a very complex manner. Values are pursued in some kind of an ideological context that either facilitates or hampers expression of the value. In general, the free enterprise system fosters values related to private goods and services. People's desires for these goods and services are consistent with the elements of free enterprise ideology. But public goods and services desired by the public generally have to be pursued through the political process. This means an expanded role for government in the allocation of resources and restrictions on individual freedom through collective action. This desire runs counter to free enterprise ideology which is then challenged by the need to respond to new values.

Ideologies thus impinge on public policy. They bring collective energies into focus and provide a blueprint for collective choice and institutional formation. Ideology helps to determine the way in which a society chooses to formulate public policies and how it responds to value changes. Ideologies prescribe certain courses of action that are acceptable and fit with a society's basic understanding of itself. They can become out of date if reality bypasses them. If this happens, public policy is developed for pragmatic reasons in a manner and magnitude that breaks the old ideology into a thousand pieces. The society then has to develop a new ideology consistent with where it is going.

SOCIAL-POLITICAL STRUCTURE

The way in which a society goes about identifying problems and developing policies to solve these problems is also a function of the social-political structure. The structure of the social-political process has a great deal to do with the kinds of problems that get attention and the public policies that are eventually adopted. There are two different ways of viewing American society from the standpoint of its social-political structure.

The Power-Elite Model

The composition of society in this model is shown in Exhibit 4.3. According to this model there are three major classes in society: the ruling elite, often referred to as the establishment; the middle class, sometimes referred to as the silent majority; and the lower class, those at the bottom end of the income scale with little wealth in their possession.

EXHIBIT 4.3
The Power-Elite Model of Society

I. The Ruling Elite or Establishment
    A. Small in numbers
    B. Upper-class background
II. The Middle Class
    A. Large
    B. Conflictual
    C. Limited importance
III. The Lower Class
    A. Large
    B. Indifferent
    C. Alienated

Source: Rogene A. Buchholz, *Business Environment and Public Policy: Implications for Management,* © 1982, p. 50. Reprinted by permission of Prentice-Hall, Inc., Englewood Cliffs, N.J.

The ruling elite or establishment is a class that is small in numbers relative to the total population. Members of this class share an upper-class background: they are most likely listed in the social register of the community in which they live, they most likely attended one of a fairly small number of preparatory schools, they are probably members of what used to be called men's clubs, and they have a good deal of wealth, much of which may have been inherited. Because of these characteristics, the establishment is a homogeneous class in that its members share similar values and ideologies.

The middle class is large, much larger than the establishment, and as a whole has control over a great deal of wealth. But it is composed of many different kinds of people with diverse backgrounds. It is a heterogeneous class in that its members do not share similar attitudes, values, and goals, and are often in conflict with one another over what issues are important and what policies should be adopted. It is difficult for the middle class to organize itself as a whole and exercise the power in society it theoretically possesses, and therefore its importance in making public policy for society is limited.

The lower class is again large in numbers, but its members have little or no wealth or even negative wealth. Many members of the lower class are indifferent toward or alienated from the rest of society. Most of their energies are taken up in seeking out an existence in what is perceived to be a basically hostile environment. Many members of this class, particularly the poorest ones, probably believe their lives do not count for much in society, that they are a forgotten class with few or no avenues through which to express their needs and opinions. Thus this class is also not very influential as far as making public policy is concerned.

From the perspective of this particular model of society, the establishment largely "runs" society. The members of the ruling elite are the "gatekeepers" of the issues society considers. Unless a particular problem is identified by this class as important, it does not get on the public policy agenda. Once an issue is on the agenda, the public policy response to that problem is a reflection of the values and ideologies of this governing elite. They decide the shape of public policy and control its implementation. They exercise a broad scope of decision-making power in the major institutions of society and have the power to employ and reward people in these institutions. Thus in elite theory, the people or the masses do not determine public policy through their demands and actions. The main tenants of elite theory can be summarized as follows.

1. Society is divided into the few who have power and the many who do not. Only a small number of persons allocate values for society; the masses do not decide public policy.

2. The few who govern are not typical of the masses who are governed. Elites are drawn disproportionately from the upper socioeconomic strata of society.

3. The movement of nonelites to elite positions must be slow and continuous to maintain stability and avoid revolution. Only nonelites who have accepted the basic elite consensus can be admitted to governing circles.

4. Elites share a consensus on the basic values of the social system and the preservation of the system. [In the United States the elite consensus includes private enterprise, private property, limited government, and individual liberty.]

5. Public policy does not reflect demands of the masses but rather the prevailing values of the elite. Changes in public policy will be incremental rather than revolutionary. [Incremental changes permit response to events which threaten the social system, with a minimum of alteration or dislocation of the system.]

6. Active elites are subject to relatively little direct influence from apathetic masses. Elites influence masses more than masses influence elites.[7]

There was a good deal of literature in the 1950s and 1960s suggesting that this structure was basically representative of our society. Books with such titles as *The Protestant Establishment, Who Rules America?* and *Amer-*

---

[7] Thomas Dye and Harmon Zeigler, *The Irony of Democracy*, 3rd ed., p. 6. Copyright © 1975 by Wadsworth Publishing Company, Inc. Reprinted by permission of the publisher, Brooks/Cole Publishing Company, Monterey, California.

ica, Inc. appeared, which tried to establish that a ruling elite did in fact exist that controlled society and ran it in their interests.[8]

William G. Domhoff, for example, in *Who Rules America?*, tried to show with some empirical evidence that there is an upper class in America that exercises control over major institutions. Membership in the national upper class is dependent on meeting the following criteria:

1. Being listed in any social register other than the Washington edition. The Washington Social Register is an index of the "political elite" as much as it is an index of the social upper class.

2. Attendance at any one of the private preparatory schools listed in the book. The list included Groton, Middlesex, St. Andrew's, and similar schools.

3. Membership in any one of the "very exclusive" gentlemen's clubs found in major cities.

4. Having a father who was a millionaire entrepreneur or a $100,000-a-year corporation executive or corporation lawyer, and (a) attendance at one of the 130 private schools listed in Kavaler's *The Private World of High Society*, or (b) belonging to any one of the exclusive clubs mentioned by Baltzell or Kavaler.

5. Marriage to a person defined as a member of the upper class by criteria 1 to 4 above. Cooptation by marriage is one of the ways by which the upper class infuses new brains and talent into its ranks.

6. Having a father, mother, sister, or brother who was listed in the social register, attended one of the exclusive private schools listed in criterion 2, or belonged to one of the exclusive gentlemen's clubs listed in the third criterion. This allowed for the reticence of some individual members of the upper class who might, for example, refuse to be listed in the social register.

7. Being a member of one of the old and still wealthy families chronicled by Amory in *Who Killed Society?* or *The Proper Bostonians*. Domhoff admitted that this criterion assumes that Amory is an accurate ethnographer of the American upper class.[9]

Domhoff then went on to show that this upper class was also a governing class in America. He defines governing class as a social upper class which owns a disproportionate amount of the country's wealth, receives a disproportionate amount of a country's yearly income, and contributes a disproportionate number of its members to the controlling institutions and key

---

[8] Edward Digby Baltzell, *The Protestant Establishment* (New York: Random House, 1964); William G. Domhoff, *Who Rules America?* (Englewood Cliffs, N.J.: Prentice-Hall, 1967); Morton Mintz and Jerry S. Cohen, *America, Inc.: Who Owns and Operates the United States?* (New York: Dial Press, 1971).

[9] Domhoff, *Who Rules America?*, pp. 34–37.

decision-making groups of the country.[10] He argued that the institutions in which the majority of decisions are made about American society (corporations, foundations, universities, the executive branch of the federal government, and the federal judiciary) are dominated by upper-class members, who can therefore be assumed to control the policies that flow from these institutions. Thus, according to Domhoff, the American upper class is also a governing class that by and large runs society, especially in light of the wealth owned and the income received by members of that exclusive social group.[11]

The Pluralist Model   The pluralist model differs from the power-elite model of society in that there are no reasonably well-defined classes with one class exercising by far the most influence on public policy. A pluralist society is composed of a number of groups, all of which wield varying degrees of influence in the public policy process. These organizations can quite properly be called interest groups because they form around shared interests. People organize and support such groups because they share common attitudes and values on a particular problem or issue. They believe they can advance their interests better by organizing themselves into a group rather than pursuing their interests individually. These groups become political when they make claims on other groups or institutions in society.

Such interest groups convey certain kinds of demands that are fed into the public policy process. They fill a gap in the formal political process by representing interests that are beyond the capacities of individuals acting alone or representatives chosen by the people. At times they perform a watchdog function by sounding an alarm whenever policies of more formal institutions threaten the interests of their members. They generate ideas that may become formal policies of these institutions and help to place issues on the public policy agenda.

Americans seem particularly inclined to form groups to pursue their common interests. There were 13,583 national associations in the United States in 1976, devoted to a variety of interests including religion, education, science, and business.[12] One study reported that 75 percent of all American adults belonged to at least one organization and 57 percent were active in at least one group.[13] The importance of associations in American life was recognized by Alexis de Tocqueville many years ago in his famous book on American democracy.

[10] *Ibid.*, p. 5.

[11] *Ibid.*, p. 11.

[12] *Encyclopedia of Associations*, Vol. I, National Associations of the U.S., 20th ed. (Detroit: Gale, 1976).

[13] Samuel H. Barnes, "Some Political Consequences of Involvement in Organizations," paper presented at the 1977 annual meeting of the American Political Science Association, quoted in Raymond E. Wolfinger, Martin Shapiro, and Fred I. Greenstein, *Dynamics of American Politics*, 2nd ed. (Englewood Cliffs, N.J.: Prentice-Hall, 1980), pp. 229–30.

Americans of all ages, all conditions, and all dispositions, constantly form associations. They have not only commercial and manufacturing companies, in which all take part, but associations of a thousand other kinds—religious, moral, serious, futile, extensive or restricted, enormous or diminutive. The Americans make associations to give entertainments, to found establishments for education, to build inns, to construct churches, to diffuse books, to send missionaries to the antipodes, and in this manner they found hospitals, prisons, and schools.[14]

Functions of Interest Groups. These interest groups perform a variety of functions for their members. Groups may perform a *symbolic* function simply by giving members the opportunity to express the interests or values they hold. Such activity serves to reinforce one's identity or provide legitimacy for certain ideas, a valuable function in and of itself. Closely related is an *ideological* function, whereby groups may provide an outlet for people who hold strong beliefs about a particular aspect of American life, such as free enterprise, and need a way to appeal to these strongly-held principles. A common function of interest groups is to promote the *economic* self-interest of their members, a function most often associated with business and labor groups. Groups can also be *informational*, disseminating information related to particular causes the group may be pursuing or technical information in which members may be interested, such as information about stamps, coins, or antique cars. Most groups collect, analyze, and disseminate information to their members to some extent. Finally, groups can perform *instrumental* functions for their members—concrete goals that are noneconomic in nature. These goals can include the efforts of antiwar groups to end American participation in Vietnam or the right to life groups that seek to outlaw abortions.[15]

Classifications of Interest Groups. Interest groups can be classified according to their primary functions. *Economic interest groups*, formed to promote the economic self-interest of their members, may not have been formed with political activity in mind, but eventually find such activity necessary to promote or protect their interests. Economic interest groups include business groups such as the National Association of Manufacturers or Business Roundtable, labor unions, and professional associations such as the National Education Association.

Solidarity groups draw on feelings of common identity based on a shared characteristic such as race, age, or sex. The basis of the group is a sense of kinship. Examples of this classification include ethnic groups, composed of members from a particular part of the world, and women's rights

[14] Alexis de Tocqueville, *Democracy in America* (New York: Shocken, 1961), Vol. II, p. 128.
[15] Norman J. Ornstein and Shirley Elder, *Interest Groups, Lobbying and Policy-making* (Washington, D.C.: Congressional Quarterly Press, 1978), pp. 29–34.

organizations. These groups may have economic interests at stake, but their primary function seems to be in maintaining or promoting an identity or consciousness related to a common characteristic shared by all members of the group.

A third category is the *public interest group* that claims to speak for the public. Whether such groups should be called "public" interest groups or "special" interest groups is a subject of much debate. The fact is that such groups do not necessarily appeal to the economic self-interest of their members nor do they share common characteristics such as a solidarity group. They exist to promote noneconomic interests, such as the environment or equal opportunity. Thus they are somewhat ideological in nature but also have concrete goals in mind. Some of these groups tend to advance overall value positions covering a wide range of issues (liberalism or conservatism); others are strictly single-issue groups. Examples of public interest groups are the Nader Network and Common Cause.[16]

The Nader Network includes many specialized organizations (see Figure 4.1). The Center for the Study of Responsive Law, the original Nader unit started with the money from the General Motors settlement, has conducted many studies, including exposés of the Federal Trade Commission and Interstate Commerce Commission and a study of corporate concentration called *The Closed Enterprise System*. It also serves as a clearinghouse for other consumer groups. Congress Watch is the network's lobbying organization. The Public Interest Research Group (PIRG) serves as a coordinating and resource center for the many state PIRGs which are staffed largely by student volunteers. The state PIRGs concern themselves with state and local consumer problems. The Corporate Accountability Research Groups raised questions about the composition of corporate boards, disclosure of information, and other issues pertaining to corporate management.

Common Cause is one of the most prominent public interest groups operating in Washington. It was founded by John Gardner, a former secretary of Health, Education, and Welfare, in the mid-1970s. His public prestige and visibility helped make the organization an immediate success. Even though Gardner has since stepped down as chairman, membership remains at high levels. The organization focuses most of its efforts on governmental and institutional reform, including public financing of political campaigns, open meetings and hearings in Congress and executive agencies, and reform of laws related to lobbying disclosure.[17]

Interest Group Tactics. Interest groups have a number of tactics they can use to focus attention on the issue they are concerned with and

---

[16] Wolfinger, Shapiro, and Greenstein, *Dynamics of American Politics*, pp. 233–48.

[17] Ornstein & Elder, *Interest Groups*, p. 47.

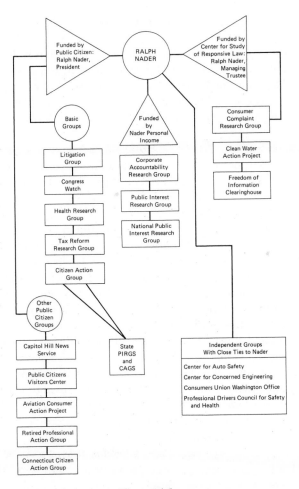

Figure 4.1
The Nader Network

win widespread support. *Boycotts* were particularly useful in the civil rights movement in the South because the black population was large and could be organized. When the blacks refused to ride the buses in Montgomery, Alabama, and boycotted white merchants in parts of the South, they had an effect because of the large numbers involved. Boycotts of lettuce in support of the California farmworkers were less successful.

The Supreme Court upheld the use of boycotts in a 1982 decision. This ruling revised a decision of a Mississippi Supreme Court that held the National Association for the Advancement of Colored People (NAACP) and ninety-one blacks liable for business losses of local merchants during the 1960s civil rights protests. The local businesses were asking for $3.5 million in damages. The Supreme Court ruled that nonviolent boycotts organized to achieve constitutional rights goals have the full protection of the First Amendment, which protects freedom of speech, and are not subject to damage suits. [18]

Interest groups can hold *public demonstrations* in support of an issue or a cause. The purpose of these demonstrations, particularly peaceful protests, is to show that a significant number of people feel very strongly about an issue and have not been able to make their voices heard through the normal political process. When such demonstrations attract thousands of people, as did some of the civil rights demonstrations and protests against the war in Vietnam, they attract widespread public attention and often induce official action through normal governmental channels. Such demonstrations can also turn violent and involve the destruction of life and property. Most public demonstrations, however, have limited political objectives and do not aim to upset the normal functioning of government and society.

The so-called "Big Business Day" was a mass demonstration organized by Ralph Nader and allies among union leaders, politicians, and economists. Demonstrations were held at 150 cities around the country charging big business with pollution, gouging of consumers, union busting, and governmental corruption, among other allegations. Nader called the demonstration the beginning of a long drive to pressure Congress to pass the Corporate Democracy Act, which would reform corporate boards of directors and require more public disclosure. [19]

The use of *terrorism* as a tactic to advance a particular interest or cause is fortunately not as widespread in the United States as it is in some parts of the world, but it is not entirely unknown. Terrorism can involve the taking of hostages, killing of government officials or people with opposite interests, hijacking of airplanes, or destroying property. Much terrorist activity is directed against "the system" and is intended to upset and interfere with the normal functioning of a society or its government.

Interest groups can also attempt to win public support through advertising in newspapers, distributing leaflets to large segments of the population, buying time on television, and using the *media* in other ways. Sometimes they become quite skillful in using the media to their advantage. The events that transpired in Selma, Alabama at the height of the civil rights movement were no accident. This particular city was chosen by civil rights groups because all the ingredients were there to make the use of nonviolent

---

[18] "High Court Ruling on Boycotts May Lead More Groups To Use Them To Make A Point," *The Wall Street Journal,* July 6, 1982, p. 13.

[19] "Nader's Antibusiness Bust," *Time,* April 28, 1980, p. 51.

demonstrations successful. The sight of dogs attacking humans and police beating people provoked moral outrage all across the country as people watched their television screens. This generated a great deal of support for the movement.

When the concern of an interest group gets picked up by the political process, the group can then *lobby* to help shape the public policies that are being developed to deal with the problem. Some of the larger groups have a large membership that provides adequate financing to be able to support full-time lobbyists in Washington, D.C. and in some state capitals.

The word "lobbying" has a rather negative connotation in many people's minds, eliciting images of behind-the-scenes arm-twisting and money changing hands under the table. Looked at in its best light, lobbying can be defined as communication with public officials to influence their decisions in a manner that is consistent with the interests of the individual or group doing the communicating. The lobbyist's purpose is a selfish one in that a lobbyist seeks to persuade others that his or her position on an issue is meritorious. Lobbying behavior is thus designed to bring about favorable outcomes from government for the group represented by the lobbyist.

The lobbyist performs a number of functions. One activity is to provide members of Congress with information. Such information, of course, tends to portray the position of the group represented favorably by the lobbyist, but it must also be accurate enough to be acceptable to members of Congress. Lobbyists also keep their constituents informed about developments in Congress or in the executive branch that may affect their interests. This information may stimulate grass roots efforts from the membership to contact their local representatives or senators. Finally, lobbyists can use publicity to support or oppose a particular bill or to put pressure on the administration or Congress.[20]

Lobbying is presently regulated by the Regulation of Lobbying Act of 1946, which defines lobbyists as those individuals whose principal purpose is to influence legislation by direct contact with members of Congress. These legally defined lobbyists must register with Congress and give quarterly reports on their spending for lobbying activities. Lobbying in the executive branch is not currently regulated by statute.

This definition allows many people who do a great deal of lobbying to avoid registering because lobbying is not necessarily their principal purpose. People who run Washington offices of corporations, for example, are not required to register because lobbying is not their primary job, even though they may lobby on various occasions. There were attempts in 1978 to change the law and make the reporting and registering requirements more stringent. However, these reform efforts failed.

[20] Wolfinger, Shapiro, and Greenstein, *Dynamics of American Politics*, pp. 252–53.

In 1978, fewer than two thousand lobbyists were registered with Congress, while the actual number was estimated at fifteen thousand, an increase from eight thousand five years previously.[21] Most large corporations probably employ lobbyists, who are located in the Washington office of the company. More than 500 corporations, including some small companies, have such offices. Many general business and industry and trade associations have their headquarters or offices in Washington for lobbying purposes.

Interest groups often form *coalitions* and work together with other groups to increase their political influence in the public policy process. Such a coalition was formed by the environmental groups in the early 1980s to counter the efforts of the Reagan administration to ease environmental constraints. These groups were able to put aside their differences and unite in a highly-knit movement or lobby, as it was called, to become a national power. As a united force, they were able to frustrate the efforts of business to make major changes in the Clean Air Act that would be more compatible with business interests.[22]

Finally, an interest group can use *litigation* to advance its interests. This has proven to be such a useful tactic for groups to use that recent years have seen a tremendous increase in litigation. Interest groups can sue the government or private parties they believe are violating the law. They can file "friend of the court" briefs, which are attempts to influence the courts through supplementary arguments. The Bakke case, regarding preferential admission of minorities to medical school, elicited more such briefs on both sides of the issue than any Supreme Court case in history.

Business groups file suit against government agencies blocking the issuance of new regulations. Environmental groups file suit against the Environmental Protection Agency pressuring it to speed up the issuance of regulations for hazardous waste disposal. Conservationists file suit against the government challenging a federal construction project, using the required environmental impact statement as the basis for their suit.

Because of the increase in litigation, the courts are deciding more and more public policy matters through interpreting laws, establishing precedent, and trying to discern the intent of Congress. As will be seen in later chapters, the courts play a crucial role in public policy-making that is likely to continue.

The Operation of a Pluralistic System. Identification of problems in a pluralistic system occurs when people who are concerned about the problem organize themselves or join an existing organization to pursue their particular interests in the problem. If the problem is of widespread concern, and the group or groups dealing with it

---

[21] "The Swarming Lobbyists," *Time*, August 7, 1978, p. 15.

[22] William Symonds, "Washington In The Grip Of The Green Giant," *Fortune*, October 4, 1982, pp. 137–41.

can attract enough financial and other kinds of support, the problem may eventually become public as people become aware of it and show varying degrees of support. Eventually government or other institutions may pick up on the problem and translate the issues being raised into formal legislation or other policy actions. These interest groups then continue to exercise influence in helping to design public policies to deal with these problems.

Thus in the pluralist model, problems are identified and policies designed in a sort of bottom-up fashion—concern about a problem can begin anywhere at the grass roots level in society and eventually grow into a major public issue that demands attention. This is in contrast to the power-elite model, a sort of top-down process in which the upper class identifies the problems, designs public policy, and forces it on the rest of society. One could see the pluralistic process at work during the social revolutions of the 1960s. Various interest groups, such as the Southern Christian Leadership Conference, Nader's groups, and the Sierra Club, were active in identifying the problems of civil rights, consumerism, and pollution respectively, and in helping to shape public policies on these problems.

Public policy, then, reflects the interests of groups, and as groups gain and lose influence, public policy is altered to reflect the changing patterns of group influence. Public policy is the result of the relative influence of the group in the policy-making process, and results from a struggle of these groups to win public and institutional support. As one theorist claims, "What may be called public policy is the equilibrium reached in this [group] struggle at any given moment, and it represents a balance which the contending factions or groups constantly strive to weigh in their favor."[23]

In theory, a pluralistic system is an open system. Anyone with a strong enough interest in a problem can pursue this interest as far as it will take him or her. Membership in a particular social or income class or of a particular race does not prevent one from participating in the public policy process. Power is diffused in a pluralistic system and dominant power centers are hard to develop in such a competitive arrangement. The existence of many interest groups also provides more opportunities for leadership, making it possible for more people with leadership ability to exercise these talents.

But interest groups themselves, particularly as they become large, tend to be dominated by their own leadership. This leadership usually formulates policy for the group as a whole, and the public stance of an interest group often represents the views of a ruling elite within the interest group itself rather than all of the rank and file membership. Interest groups in many cases also draw most of their membership from better educated, middle- or upper-class segments of society. Many minorities and particularly the poorer elements of society are not adequately represented. Their problems

---

[23] Earl Latham, *The Group Basis of Politics* (New York: Octagon Books, 1965), p. 36, as quoted in Anderson, Brady, and Bullock, *Public Policy and Politics*, p. 416.

are likely to be ignored unless championed by other people who are more likely to participate in public policy making.

Improved public policy decisions should result from such a structure since more people, particularly those who are closest to the problem, have an input in decision making. Yet a pluralistic system is a system of conflict because interest groups compete for attention and influence in the public policy process, and such competing interests do not necessarily result in the best public policy decisions. Conflict can get out of control and result in social fragmentation, making a policy decision for society difficult to reach. This is particularly true when interest groups are unwilling to compromise, in which case reaching a public policy decision for society as a whole may be impossible. Furthermore, some interests are not adequately represented.

A pluralistic system does seem to allow for more interests to be represented than does a society structured along the power-elite model. More people should have a chance to promote their particular values and interests and have a chance to govern society. This is a mixed blessing. As a society becomes more pluralistic, the interests represented will be more diverse, and the direction in which society is moving will be less clear. The lack of central direction for society, which an elite provides, can be a disadvantage as society is pulled to and fro by the competition of many different interests with varying degrees of power and influence.

Any society is undoubtedly a mixture of both these models, with elements of an establishment and interest groups helping to identify problems and develop public policies to deal with them. It could be argued that societies tend to lean toward one model or the other at various points in their history. If this is true, a great deal of evidence suggests that our society is leaning toward the pluralistic model at present. Interest groups have proliferated in the last decade, have become sophisticated in the use of various tactics, and have wielded influence in the public policy process far beyond what their actual numbers would suggest. Few, if any, books are written about an "establishment" anymore, suggesting that it either has disappeared or is not influential enough to worry about. Congress itself is fragmented, without the power-brokers of past years, and is thus more subject to grass roots lobbying. This kind of structure has implications for public policy making which has been the subject of much discussion.

Some observers have characterized our society as one of interest group pluralism, whereby the federal government is subject to the pressures of special interest groups. Because of the changes in the seniority system in Congress and the proliferation of subcommittees, Congress has become a collection of independent power centers. The interest groups can thus take their case directly to individual congressmen and establish close working ties with the subcommittee(s) in their areas of interest. The result is the infamous "iron triangle" composed of the interest groups, the congressional subcommittee, and the relevant federal agency, which becomes the focus of public policy making. This kind of process encourages government to act on individual measures without attention to their collective consequences. Policy is not made for the nation as a whole, but for narrow autonomous sectors defined by the special interests. While these groups may claim to be acting in the public interest, such claims are suspect.

> . . . the problem with the so-called public interest groups is not their venality but their belief that they alone represent the public interest. The confidence these groups have had in pursuing their numerous and sometimes far-reaching missions is not always warranted, especially when their activities—and their demands—are scrutinized in the context of the full effects of the government regulations which they so often instigate or endorse with tremendous zeal.[24]

Another problem with interest group pluralism is the removal of public policy making from public scrutiny. Decisions are made behind closed doors, effectively removed from popular control. As stated by Everett Carl Ladd, "The public cannot hope to monitor the policy outcomes that result from the individual actions of 535 Senators and Representatives operating through a maze of iron triangles."[25] The solution to this fractionalism, according to some observers, is a revitalized party system where the claims of interest groups can be adjusted to mesh with a coherent program that represents more of a national interest. The proliferation of interest groups makes necessary strengthened parties that can cope with the multiple organized pressures of interest group pluralism.

These concepts of value, ideology and social-political structure are tied together in Figure 4.2 to show how public policy originates in our society. Values, which are subject to various influences, and ideologies composed of various elements, work their way through the social-political structure whether organized along power-elite or pluralist lines or some combination thereof. All of these elements become mixed and intertwined in a very complex fashion, but the result may be that a particular issue finds its way onto the public policy agenda to become the subject of formal or informal public policy making where a common course of action is decided upon. The manner in which the formal public policy process works to decide upon this common course of action is the subject of the next chapter.

[24] Murray L. Weidenbaum, *The Future of Business Regulation* (New York: AMACOM, 1979), p. 146.

[25] Everett Carl Ladd, "How To Tame The Special-Interest Groups," *Fortune*, vol. 102, no. 8 (October 20, 1980), p. 72.

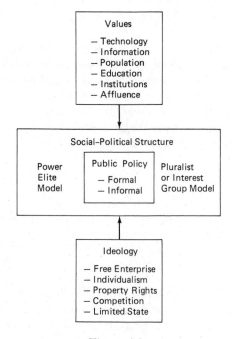

Figure 4.2
Social Model

SELECTED REFERENCES

ALLPORT, G., P. VERNON, AND G. LINDZEY. *Study of Values, Test Booklet and Manual*, 3rd ed. Boston: Houghton Mifflin, 1960.

BAIER, KURT, AND NICHOLAS RESCHER. *Values and the Future: The Impact of Technological Change on American Values*. New York: Macmillan, 1969.

BALTZELL, EDWARD DIGBY. *The Protestant Establishment*. New York: Random House, 1964.

BERRY, JEFFREY M. *Lobbying for the People: The Political Behavior of Public Interest Groups*. Princeton, N.J.: Princeton University Press, 1977.

BOULDING, KENNETH E. *The Meaning of the Twentieth Century: The Great Transition*. New York: Harper & Row, Pub., 1964.

CAVANAGH, G. F. *American Business Values in Transition*. Englewood Cliffs, N.J.: Prentice-Hall, 1976.

DAHL, ROBERT A. *Democracy in the United States: Promise and Performance*. Chicago: Rand McNally, 1972.

DOMHOFF, WILLIAM G. *Who Rules America?* Englewood Cliffs, N.J.: Prentice-Hall, 1967.

ELLUL, JACQUES. *The Technological Society*, trans. John Wilkinson. New York: Knopf, 1964.

Harvard University, Program on Technology and Society: 1964 to 1972, A Final Review. Cambridge. Mass.: Harvard University Press, 1972.

KELSO, WILLIAM A. *American Democracy Theory: Pluralism and Its Critics.* Westport, Conn.: Greenwood Press, 1978.

LODGE, GEORGE CABOT. *The New American Ideology.* New York: Knopf, 1978.

McCREADY, W. C. AND A. M. GREELEY. *The Ultimate Values of the American Population.* New York: Russell Sage Publications, 1976.

MESTHENE, EMMANNUEL G., ED. *Technology and Social Change.* Indianapolis: Bobbs-Merrill, 1967.

MEYERS, WILLIAM, AND PARK RINARD. *Making Activism Work.* New York: Gordon & Breach, 1972.

MINTZ, MORTON, AND JERRY S. COHEN. *America, Inc.: Who Owns and Operates the United States?* New York: Dial Press, 1971.

NICHOLLS, DAVID. *The Pluralist State.* New York: St. Martin's Press, 1975.

ORNSTEIN, NORMAN J., AND SHIRLEY ELDER. *Interest Groups, Lobbying and Policymaking.* Washington, D.C.: Congressional Quarterly Press, 1978.

REICH, C. *The Greening of America.* New York: Random House, 1970.

ROKEACH, M. *The Nature of Values.* New York: Free Press, 1973.

SCHUMPETER, J. A. *Capitalism, Socialism, and Democracy,* 3rd ed. New York: Harper & Row, Pub., 1950.

SUTTON, F. X. ET AL. *The American Business Creed.* Cambridge, Mass.: Harvard University Press, 1956.

TOFFLER, ALVIN. *Future Shock.* New York: Bantam, 1970.

WOLFINGER, RAYMOND E., MARTIN SHAPIRO, AND FRED I. GREENSTEIN. *Dynamics of American Politics,* 2nd ed. Englewood Cliffs, N.J.: Prentice-Hall, 1980.

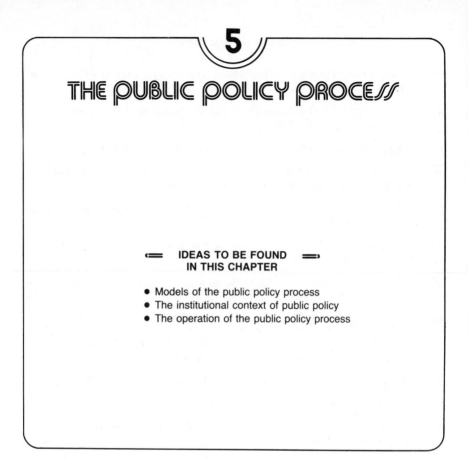

THE PUBLIC POLICY PROCESS

The public policy process, as stated in Chapter Two, refers to all the various processes by which public policy is made in our society. Formulation of public policy is not limited to formal acts of government, but can be achieved by interest groups that bring issues to public attention and attempt to influence public opinion as well as government. If interest groups are successful in raising issues and public opinion becomes strong enough, there may be no need for formal government action. Again, the moratorium on the building of nuclear power plants is a good example of this process at work. The government has taken no formal action to stop the building of nuclear power plants, yet the public at large is so concerned about safety and disposal of radioactive waste that such a moratorium exists. Utility companies know that if they go ahead with any new plants, they will be faced with a great deal of opposition, perhaps eventually even from government. Incidents like Three Mile Island, of course, have a great deal to do with shaping public opinion on this issue. The media, especially movies like *The China Syndrome*, play a major role. So the public policy process exists in society at large and may or may not involve formal government action. This process is a complex mixture of interest groups, public opinion, the media, government and other elements. Thus some kind of an overview of this larger process is necessary.

Most public policy that affects business, however, is the result of formal governmental action, particularly at the federal level. Interest group pressure and public opinion eventually translate into some kind of legislation or regulation that prescribes a specific form of business behavior. If one wants to influence government, one must understand how it works and where to intervene for maximum effect. This chapter will present both an overview of the larger public policy process, and a detailed examination of the way in which government translates public preferences into specific public policies.

MODELS OF THE PUBLIC POLICY PROCESS   There are various ways to describe the larger public policy process in order to understand its operation. Anderson, Brady, and Bullock describe six stages of the public policy process (Exhibit 5.1). The first stage, *problem formation*, involves a situation where human needs, deprivation, or dissatisfaction appear that must be addressed. If enough people believe the nature of the problem is such that government should respond, it then becomes a public rather than a private problem. Public problems involve large numbers of people and have broad-ranging effects, including consequences for people not directly involved, such as a strike by railroad workers that affects the entire society.[1]

Not all problems get the attention of government, however, and reach the *policy agenda* stage. Those that do reach this stage, get there by a variety of routes. Whether a problem gets on the public policy agenda or not depends on the power, stature, and number of people in the interest group. Political leadership is another factor in agenda setting, with the President of the United States being most important in this regard because of his position. Crisis events, such as wars and depressions, as well as protests and demonstrations, also put problems on the policy agenda.[2]

The stages of *policy formulation* and *adoption* involve the development of proposed courses of action for dealing with public problems. Policy formulation does not automatically mean adoption, of course, as many policy proposals are never formally adopted by the government. Public policies to address particular problems are formulated by the President and his immediate advisors, other members of the executive branch, career and appointed administrative officials, specially appointed committees and commissions, and legislators who introduce bills for consideration by the Congress. While

[1] James E. Anderson, David W. Brady, and Charles Bullock III, *Public Policy and Politics In America* (North Scituate, Mass.: Duxbury Press, 1978), p. 7.

[2] *Ibid.*, p. 9.

EXHIBIT 5.1
The Policy Process

Policy Terminology	1st Stage Problem Formation	2nd Stage Policy Agenda	3rd Stage Policy Formulation	4th Stage Policy Adoption	5th Stage Policy Implementation	6th Stage Policy Evaluation
Definition	Relief is sought from a situation that produces a human need, deprivation, or dissatisfaction	Those problems, among many, which receive the government's serious attention	Development of pertinent and acceptable proposed courses of action for dealing with public problems	Development of support for a specific proposal such that the policy is legitimized or authorized	Application of the policy by the government's bureaucratic machinery to the problem	Attempt by the government to determine whether or not the policy has been effective
Common Sense	Getting the government to see the problem	Getting the government to begin to act on the problem	The government's proposed solution to the problem	Getting the government to accept a particular solution to the problem	Applying the government's policy to the problem	Did the policy work?

Source: James E. Anderson, David W. Brady, and Charles Bullock III, *Public Policy and Politics In America*, p. 8. Copyright © 1978 by Wadsworth Publishing Company, Inc. Reprinted by permission of the publisher, Brooks/Cole Publishing Company, Monterey, California.

the most formal adoption strategy is one of proposal, congressional approval, and presidential signature, there are other adoption strategies that exist in government.[3]

Policy implementation, the fifth stage of the policy process, involves the actual application of an adopted policy. The administrative agencies are the primary implementors of public policy, but the courts and Congress are also involved. Congress may override the decisions of an agency such as the Federal Trade Commission, and the courts interpret statutes and administrative rules and regulations when there is a question about a specific application. The agencies, often delegated substantial authority by Congress, have a wide range of discretion in implementing policy because their mandates are often broad and ill-defined in their enabling legislation. The Federal Trade Commission Act, for example, specifies that unfair methods of competition are illegal. It is left up to the FTC and courts to decide what specific methods are unfair on a case by case basis. Thus the agencies make "administrative law" through implementing the statutes passed by Congress. The application of a public policy passed by Congress can actually change the nature of the policy itself, as implementation often affects policy content[4].

Policy evaluation, the last stage, involves an attempt to determine whether the policy has actually worked. Such an evaluation can lead to additional policy formulation to correct deficiencies. According to Anderson, Brady, and Bullock, there are two types of policy evaluation. The first is a "seat of the pants" or political evaluation that is usually based on fragmentary evidence and may be ideologically biased. The other is a systematic evaluation that seeks to objectively measure the impact of policies and determine how well objectives are actually accomplished. Such an evaluation focuses on the effects which a policy has on the problem to which it is directed.[5]

Preston and Post present other models of the public policy process that focus more on the dynamics of decision making rather than on stages of policy making. They describe three models: optimization, incrementalism, and power-bargaining. The *optimization* model is epitomized by most economists and many bureaucrats who regard the public policy process as the rational search for optimal solutions to well-defined problems. The elementary principles of such an approach are maximization (attaining the highest level of output for a given level of input) and minimization (incurring the least possible cost or inconvenience in order to achieve a given result). The optimization model is a useful analytical construct, but it is limited by its stringent analytic requirements and limited scope. It is an intellectual abstraction, according to Preston and Post, setting forth formal relationships

---

[3] *Ibid.*, pp. 9–10.
[4] *Ibid.*, pp. 10–11.
[5] *Ibid.*, pp. 11–12.

among given conditions. But it takes no account of the way in which policy goals are articulated, alternatives proposed, and preferences discovered. Thus it is at best only a partial model of the public policy process.[6]

The *incrementalist* approach holds that policy formulation proceeds by small steps and changes rather than a comprehensive analysis in search of some optimal state of affairs. Incrementalism involves fragmenting a complex problem that no one fully understands, into smaller manageable problems. Thus a piece of a larger problem is coped with by a specific policy, then the consequences of this first policy are dealt with, and so on, until the larger problem is alleviated or is no longer of concern. Rather than adopting a comprehensive revision of the welfare system, for example, and searching for an optimal solution such as a guaranteed income or other sweeping change, welfare reform from an incrementalist perspective focuses on small changes in one or more programs such as food stamps or medicaid, coping with the consequences of these changes, making other small changes, and so on ad infinitum.

Some argue that incrementalism is the only possible approach to such large problems as poverty because of political constraints. Any suggestion of comprehensive reform exposes every aspect of the existing system to endless debate because of vested interests, guaranteeing political stalemate. Thus every administration is politically constrained to pursue an incremental strategy of reform.[7] Such a strategy, however, leaves much to be desired. Incrementalism has been called the science of "muddling through," without a clear sense of direction or idea of what policy would be most preferred from the standpoint of some overriding principle or objective.

The *power bargaining* model is more of a political model, focusing on the strength and goals of various power centers within society, and on the processes of conflict bargaining and cooperation. Public policy is to be explained primarily in terms of the interaction of groups possessing some degree of social and political power. Conflict between these groups is resolved and an equilibrium reached through bargaining and compromise. The essence of power is the ability to impose penalties or distribute rewards. The outcome of the policy process depends on the penalizing and rewarding abilities of conflicting groups.[8]

Preston and Post then go on to describe what they call an *institutional-systems* model of the public policy process that integrates these three models into a comprehensive framework (Figure 5.1). The primary initiative in identifying issues for public policy consideration in this model is based in society at large and its various constituent elements. Formal policy making

[6] Lee E. Preston and James E. Post, *Private Management and Public Policy* (Englewood Cliffs, N.J.: Prentice-Hall, 1975), pp. 62–64.

[7] See Frederick Doolittle, Frank Levy, and Michael Wiseman, "The Mirage of Welfare Reform," *The Public Interest*, no. 47 (Spring 1977), p. 77.

[8] Preston and Post, *Public Policy*, pp. 67–71.

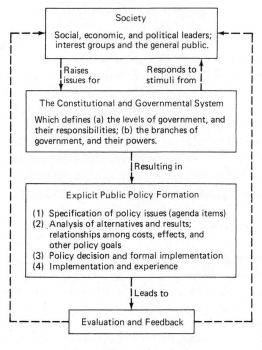

Figure 5.1
Institutional Systems Model
of the Public Policy Process

Source: Lee E. Preston and James E. Post, *Private Management and Public Policy*, © 1975, p. 72. Reprinted by permission of Prentice-Hall, Inc., Englewood Cliffs, N.J.

takes place within the constitutional and governmental system that defines the levels and branches of government, their responsibilities and power, and relationship to each other. These aspects of the system are of long duration and subject to only incremental change. The process of explicit policy formation involves the stages of problem identification, analysis, policy decision, implementation, and experience. This last stage, experience, leads to evaluation and feedback to the society at large which may require policy changes. This model accommodates the optimization model with its inclusion of analysis, acknowledges incrementalism in the relative permanence of the constitutional and governmental system, and includes power and bargaining at all stages.[9]

THE INSTITUTIONAL CONTEXT OF PUBLIC POLICY

These general models of the public policy process highlight the crucial importance of governmental institutions in formulating public policy for

[9] *Ibid.* pp. 71–73.

the society as a whole. Thus to gain a more detailed knowledge of the public policy process, these institutions must be described and examined. The constitution established three branches of government: the legislative, executive, and judicial. We will describe in more detail the institutional structure of Congress, the policy-making powers of the executive branch, and the role and structure of the courts in policy making. There is a fourth aspect of the institutional structure, however, that is often called a fourth branch of government. This fourth branch consists of the administrative agencies that actually implement most public policies, and may actually determine policy content through the implementation process.

Congress   The Constitution grants the Senate and House of Representatives all legislative power, which on the surface, seems to give Congress the sole power to approve formal public policy measures. That this is not true will be seen later, as other branches of government also have legislative power. While the Constitution may have intended a separation of power between the legislative, executive, and judicial branches of government, what the Constitution really did was to establish three institutions with shared power acting as a check and balance on each other. While the most important function of Congress is indeed legislative—enacting laws—it has many other powers and responsibilities: it plays an essential role in amending the Constitution; it appropriates money to operate the federal government and, through the numerous grant-in-aid programs, much of state and local government; it has the power to impeach and try the President, Vice-President, and all civil officers of the United States for grave criminal offenses; it creates administrative agencies and performs certain oversight functions with respect to these agencies; it confirms Presidential appointees to the courts and high executive posts in government; and it has broad investigative powers regarding matters of public policy and administration. These are just some of the responsibilities Congress has of a nonlegislative nature.

Article I of the Constitution contains the so-called "great compromise" under which members of the House are chosen for two-year terms on the basis of population, and two senators are chosen from every state for six-year terms. This arrangement was a compromise between representatives to the Constitutional Convention from heavily-populated states, who wished representation to be based on population, and from less populated states who demanded equal representation for all states. This compromise resulted in some inevitable differences in the power and organization of the two houses of Congress.[10]

Bills concerning the raising of revenue must originate in the House, for example. It is believed that tax legislation will then be made more respon-

[10] H. H. Liebhafsky, *American Government and Business* (New York: Wiley, 1971), p. 82.

sive to the electorate because representation in the House is based on population and its members are elected every two years. The Senate, on the other hand, has the power to approve or disapprove most Presidential appointments to regulatory commissions and federal judgeships as well as concur in treaties with foreign countries.[11]

Since Congress has so much work to accomplish, organization is of crucial importance. The committee system has been developed over the years to handle this work load and provide a degree of specialization with respect to public policy problems. Each house is divided into standing committees with respect to subject matter, and these committees, in turn, may have a number of sub-committees. Each committee has a fairly stable membership and a fixed jurisdiction, such as taxes, agriculture, defense, regulation, and environment. Most of the work of Congress is done through this committee structure. When a bill is introduced into Congress, it is referred to the relevant committee, which discusses it (probably by first assigning it to a subcommittee), may amend it in some fashion, and either report on it to the entire membership or fail to do so, thus killing the bill at the committee level.[12]

There are twenty-two standing legislative committees in the House and sixteen in the Senate (Exhibit 5.2). Each representative serves on one or two of these committees, each senator on two or three of them. Once assigned to a committee, a member remains there until he or she leaves office or voluntarily moves to another committee. The ratio of party representation on each committee is roughly proportional to the ratio of Democrats and Republicans in the House or Senate as a whole. Some of the committees in the House are exclusive committees. Members of an exclusive committee may not belong to any other House committee except the Budget Committee. These exclusive committees are the Appropriations, Rules, and Ways and Means Committees. These are the three most powerful committees in the House. The Rules Committee, for example, specifies the conditions under which a bill will be considered. If the Rules Committee refuses to grant a rule to a bill, the bill can go no further.[13]

Committee chairmen used to have dominant power over almost every aspect of a committee's activity. The chairman had complete control of the subcommittees, for example, in that the chairman could create or abolish them, choose their members, and determine their jurisdiction. The Subcommittee Bill of Rights adopted in 1973 by the House Democrats changed this procedure. Each committee has to have a minimum number of standing subcommittees with fixed jurisdictions. Decisions about the organization of the subcommittee are made by the full committee's Democratic caucus.

[11] *Ibid.*, p. 83.

[12] Raymond E. Wolfinger, Martin Shapiro, and Fred I. Greenstein, *Dynamics of American Politics* (Englewood Cliffs, N.J.: Prentice-Hall, 1980), p. 329.

[13] *Ibid.*, p. 330.

EXHIBIT 5.2
Standing Committees of the House

Agriculture	Interior and Insular Affairs
Appropriations	Judiciary
Armed Services	Merchant Marine and Fisheries
Banking, Finance, and Urban Affairs	Post Office and Civil Service
Budget	Public Works and Transportation
District of Columbia	Rules
Education and Labor	Science and Technology
Energy and Commerce	Small Business
Foreign Affairs	Standards of Official Conduct
Government Operations	Veterans' Affairs
House Administration	Ways and Means

Standing Committees of the Senate

Agriculture, Nutrition, and Forestry	Finance
Appropriations	Foreign Relations
Armed Services	Government Affairs
Banking, Housing, and Urban Affairs	Judiciary
Budget	Labor and Human Resources
Commerce, Science, and Transportation	Rules and Administration
Energy and Natural Resources	Small Business
Environment and Public Works	Veterans' Affairs

Source: *1981 Official Congressional Directory—97th Congress* (Washington, D.C.: U.S. Government Printing Office, 1981).

Committee chairmen suffered some loss of power from these developments, but they still have considerable influence over committee activities.[14]

The seniority system was the sole basis for selecting committee chairmen. The member of the majority party with the longest continuous service on a committee was automatically chairman of that committee. This meant, of course, that chairs went disproportionately to older members of Congress. It also meant that chairmanships went to members from safe seats who returned to Congress year after year to build up seniority. The seniority system eventually became controversial because members with safe seats mostly came from rural areas and were more conservative than the party's congressional membership as a whole. This was a particular problem for the Democratic party because most of these safe seats were in Southern states, where conservatism, particularly with regard to civil rights, was strong. Thus

[14] *Ibid.*, pp. 334–35.

liberal legislation was being frustrated because of the power of committee chairmen.[15]

Some changes were made in this seniority system by both parties in the 1970s. In 1971, the Republican Conference decided to take an automatic secret vote on the ranking minority member of each committee. In 1973 the House Democrats did the same for the more important job of picking committee chairmen. Nominations for committee chairmen came from a new body, the Democratic Steering and Policy Committee. This revolution did not completely overturn the seniority system, as the most senior member of each committee is still likely to be its chairman. But the threat of being deposed makes the chairman subject to majority sentiment in the party. Committee chairmen can no longer use their power to flout the wishes of a strong majority of the party.[16]

The legislative process itself is complex and often cumbersome . Once a bill is introduced, it is first assigned to the committee having jurisdiction over its subject matter. This committee, in turn, usually refers the bill to a subcommittee for further discussion. Hearings are usually held by the committee or subcommittee where witnesses present facts and arguments in support of or in opposition to the bill. Expert witnesses are called on to testify as are representatives of private groups that the bill will affect. These hearings are critical for any group that may be affected, and such groups should be represented at the hearings. The hearings serve three functions: (1) they help in polishing the draft of the proposed legislation, (2) they help committee members assess the strength of support and opposition to a particular measure, and (3) they provide time to mobilize additional support or opposition by bringing the bill to public attention.[17]

After the hearings, the subcommittee then drafts a final version of the bill to be presented to the full committee. This is the final point of decision as to the exact wording of the bill for all but the most controversial items. The whole discussion process of the subcommittee is then repeated at the full committee level. If the bill is noncontroversial, the full committee may pass the bill without much discussion. The bill then goes to the House or Senate for further consideration. Scheduling in the Senate is usually accomplished by the majority leader in cooperation with the bill's floor manager, who is usually chairman of the committee where the bill was initially considered. In the House, the bill must first get through the House Rules Committee and have the rules approved by the House before the substance of the bill itself is considered.[18]

Since there are many House members, controlling floor debate is more crucial than in the Senate. Floor action is thus more tightly scheduled than

[15] *Ibid.*, p. 336.
[16] *Ibid.*, pp. 337–39.
[17] *Ibid.*, p. 354.
[18] *Ibid.*, pp. 355–56.

in the Senate where unlimited debate is permitted. The House thus disposes of much legislation more quickly than the Senate, where a more leisurely approach is usually taken. Minority rights are more respected in the Senate where a small group can prevent a bill's passage by filibustering, i.e., refusing to stop talking about the bill so a vote can be taken. A filibuster can be stopped by a successful vote for cloture, which requires the approval of sixty members.[19]

Most bills are introduced into both houses of Congress, because both houses must approve the bill before it can be sent to the President. The final versions of the same bill are usually different as passed by each house, sometimes substantially different. These differences are worked out by a Conference Committee composed of senior members of each party, who served on the relevant committee in each House. A Conference Committee is appointed for every bill as necessary and must work out a compromise between the two versions. The compromise bill is then voted on by each House, and if passed, finally goes to the President, unless held back by the Congress for political reasons.

The Executive Branch   The President of the United States is the chief figure in the executive branch, if not of the entire government. The functions and powers of the President are unmatched within the government, and thus the impact the President can have on public policy is quite significant. One academic authority on the Office of the Presidency identified the following ten functions as being most important.

Chief of State (by acting as ceremonial head of government)

Chief Executive (in supervising day-to-day activities of the Executive Branch)

Commander-in-Chief (of the military forces)

Chief Diplomat (in formulating and executing foreign policy and conducting foreign affairs)

Chief Legislator (by guiding Congress in its law-making activity)

Chief of the Party (by serving as number one political boss in his party)

Voice of the People (in calling the attention of the nation to its unfinished business)

Protector of the Peace (in taking actions in times of national disaster to restore domestic order)

Manager of Prosperity (by seeking to maintain full employment, high level production, a high rate of growth, price stability, etc.)

World Leader (in serving as leader of the "Free World")[20]

---

[19] *Ibid.*, pp. 357–58.

[20] Clinton P. Rossiter, *The American Presidency*, 2nd ed. (New York: Harcourt Brace Jovanovich, 1960), as quoted in Liebhafsky, *American Government and Business*, p. 93.

All of these functions are important, but from the standpoint of public policy that affects business, some functions are much more important than others.

As chief legislator, the President can submit proposals for legislation to Congress but has no formal authority to force Congress to adopt his proposals. Thus the President must rely on techniques of persuasion, the granting or withholding of favors, and television appearances to influence public opinion to exert pressure on members of Congress. The framers of the Constitution did not anticipate that the President would become a major source of legislation. Congress was supposed to propose the laws, and the President dispose of them by signing or vetoing the bills sent him by Congress. During the administration of Franklin D. Roosevelt, the presidency itself became a major source of legislation, initiating hundreds of bills to deal with the Depression. In the first "Hundred Days" of FDR's term, Congress passed an impressive list of major laws initiated by the President and his advisors.[21]

The presidential practice of submitting legislation to Congress became institutionalized with the Truman administration. It is now customary for the State of the Union message to be accompanied by an official presidential legislative program. As manager of prosperity, a role given to the President by the Employment Act of 1946, the President submits a legislative package he believes will promote a healthy economy. The economy has become too complex and governmental policy too significant to permit the government to rely on whatever bills happen to be introduced by congressional members. Thus the President can take the lead in developing a comprehensive package of legislation to deal with economic and social problems. Congress, of course, often does not go along with the President's proposals and has its own ideas of what public policies are appropriate.[22]

The President has thus come to play a far greater role in the legislative process than the mere exercise of veto power granted him by the Constitution. The veto remains, however, an important part of public policy formulation. More than two thousand bills have been vetoed in the history of Congress and fewer than one hundred of these have been overridden. The difference between a simple majority needed to pass a bill and a two-thirds vote needed to override a veto is significant. The veto is more likely to be used by a president facing a congress controlled by the opposite party. With the veto, a president can virtually stymie an opposite party's legislative program.[23]

As the chief executive, the President has power of appointment regarding high level cabinet positions as well as heads and commissioners of government agencies. This power gives him a great deal of influence over public

---

21 Wolfinger, Shapiro, and Greenstein, *Dynamics*, p. 409.

22 *Ibid.*, p. 410.

23 *Ibid.*, p. 415.

policy, as agency heads and commissioners determine the actions taken by the agencies. During the first term of the Reagan administration, for example, people were appointed to head the Federal Trade Commission and Environmental Protection Agency who were opposed to increases in government regulation. They tried to reverse the activist role these agencies had played in previous administrations by changing policies and cutting budgets. The man appointed to head the Interior Department changed the policy of that agency from one of conservation to one of opening up more federal land to exploration and mining.

The President can also issue executive orders which are really legislative acts affecting the various departments and agencies within the executive branch. President Johnson, for example, issued an executive order requiring affirmative action plans of most government contractors, an act which went beyond the intent of Congress in passing civil rights legislation. Upon taking office, President Reagan issued an executive order requiring a benefit-cost analysis to be performed by executive branch agencies issuing new regulations, something Congress had not done in the legislation creating the Occupational Safety and Health Administration (OSHA), an executive agency affected by the order.

The executive branch of government also contains the Cabinet and its departments, which carry out a great deal of the work of government. The President may or may not rely on the Cabinet to play a significant policy-making role in the administration. The cabinet departments are quite large and some, such as Health and Human Services and Defense, administer budgets larger than most countries of the world. The impact they have in affecting public policy is significant as they implement legislation and carry out executive functions. Very often, the cabinet departments move in directions not entirely to the satisfaction of the President.

Modern presidents are more likely to rely on advisors in the Executive Office of the President, such as the Chairman of the Council of Economic Advisors or the Director of the Office of Management and Budget, and on the White House staff for major inputs to the policy-making process. The impact these individuals can have on the President and the policy-making process depends on the power they are able to accumulate. Particularly important in this regard is the White House staff, which has been able to accumulate more power over the years. People on the White House staff generally have access to the President on a day-to-day basis, something most cabinet members do not have. The White House staff performs the functions of legislative liaison, handling of press relations, writing the President's speeches, and controlling the President's schedules and relations with major interest groups and party figures. Because of these functions, the White House staff has become a key factor in formulating legislative proposals of the President and in running the executive branch in general. The existence of these positions which are largely independent of the bureaucratic departments has contributed to what some call the institutionalization of the presidency. The expansion of agencies within the Executive Office of the President and the growing power of the White House staff, "reflects not just a need for coordination and advice, but the President's desire for officials loyal to his goals, not to the interests of career bureaucrats."[24]

The Courts

The courts play an important role in the public policy process through applying the law to specific situations when a dispute arises between affected parties. Such disputes will involve disagreements about the legal rights and duties of the parties. OSHA, for example, has the responsibility to set standards to protect the health of workers. But business might complain that a particular standard is too stringent, that OSHA has not presented conclusive evidence that the new standard will actually improve health, that proper procedures were not used in setting the standard, or that OSHA did not take economic factors into account in developing the standard. Similarily, institutions may develop affirmative action programs to comply with the civil rights laws passed by Congress, but these programs may bar certain individuals, particularly white males, from obtaining jobs and promotions they would otherwise be awarded. Some of these individuals may claim they are victims of reverse discrimination. These disputed claims will be resolved through the court system which will define and enforce the rights and duties of the affected parties.

The courts, however, do not just play a passive role in discerning the intent of Congress and applying the complexity of the law to particular situations. They can and have played an active role in ways Congress may not have intended and thus have been accused of actually legislating rather than just adjudicating disputes. The intent of Congress in passing the Sherman Antitrust Act of 1890, for example, was clearly to curb the growth of trusts and other business combinations. Yet the Justice Department lost seven of the first eight cases it brought under the act because the courts were pro-business. The first applications of the Sherman Act were to unions. In 1894, the Supreme Court issued an injunction against the union in the Pullman strike on the basis that it was a conspiracy in restraint of interstate commerce. It wasn't until 1911 that two trusts (Standard Oil and American Tobacco) were found guilty of violating the Sherman Act and ordered dissolved into separate entities.

Laws cannot be written that provide a solution to every possible quarrel that can arise in a society. Most laws passed by Congress are thus written in rather broad language and contain words like "unfair" and "reasonable,"

---

[24] *Ibid.*, p. 427.

that are subject to interpretation. What, for example, is an "unreasonable" restraint of trade, or an "unfair" method of competition? Thus the courts have to give meaning to these general phrases in specific situations. In this sense the courts make public policy, with the Supreme Court being final policymaker. It is claimed that the Supreme Court spends more of its energies making legal interpretations for the guidance of lower courts that will best serve the interests of society in the future, than on satisfying the interests of the parties to a specific quarrel.[25]

Article III of the U.S. Constitution states that "the judicial power of the United States shall be vested in one Supreme Court and in such inferior courts [courts subordinate to the Supreme Court] as the Congress may from time to time ordain and establish." Over time, the federal court system has evolved into a three-level system, consisting of district courts, the courts of appeal, and the U.S. Supreme Court (Figure 5.2).

Figure 5.2
Federal Judicial System

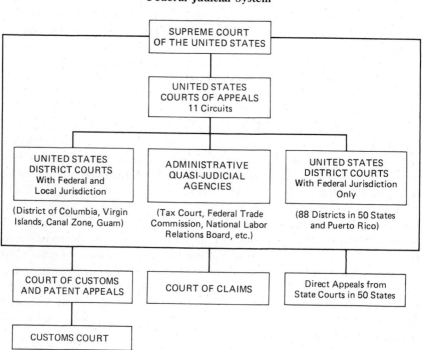

Source: Robert N. Corley, Robert L. Black, and O. Lee Reed, *The Legal Environment of Business*, 5th ed. (New York: McGraw-Hill, 1981), p.42. Reprinted with permission.

[25] *Ibid.*, pp. 480–81.

The ninety-four district courts are the basic trial courts of the system, applying the rules of law or of equity. Since they are trial courts, juries are used. The area of district court jurisdiction does not extend across state lines, as each state has at least one federal district court and some have as many as four. The work of the district courts has expanded dramatically over the past several years, as Congress has passed more laws creating federal statutory rights enforceable in federal courts. The various civil rights statutes, for example, have made it possible for many Americans, who believe they have been discriminated against, to sue somebody in a federal court. Environmental and consumer legislation has given many people access to the federal courts to pursue their policy preferences. Environmental groups have used the courts to stop or slow down projects that they claim are violating the environmental laws passed by Congress.

If either party to the litigation is not satisfied with the district court's ruling, it has the right to appeal to a court of appeal for a review of the case. There are eleven such courts of appeal, one for each of the circuits into which the United States is divided, and a twelfth for the District of Columbia (Figure 5.3). Each of these courts hears appeals from the district courts within its circuit. Decisions by a court of appeals are normally rendered by three-judge panels named by the chief judge of the circuit. In some situations, however, cases may be decided by all the judges in a given council sitting together. District court cases normally reach the Supreme Court only after having been reviewed by an appeals court. Since it is so difficult to be granted an appeal to the Supreme Court, the decision of the appeals court represents the final review for most litigants. In addition to appeals from district court decisions, the appeals court also hears appeals from the legal decisions of federal administrative agencies and regulatory commissions.[26]

There are several specialized courts in the federal system that have authority to hear cases involving specific subject matters. The Court of Customs has jurisdiction over disputes involving customs duties. Appeals from this court go to the Court of Customs and Patent Appeals, which also reviews decisions made by the U.S. Patent Office. The Claims Court deals with money claims against the United States. The Tax Court, however, is an executive agency that reviews decisions of the Internal Revenue Service. Despite its name, it is not really a court in the true sense of the word.[27]

The Supreme Court is the highest court in the land, and is primarily an appellate review court. Cases reviewed by this court are generally heard by nine judges, one of whom is appointed Chief Justice of the Supreme Court. Appeals are brought to the Supreme Court from a U.S. Court of Appeals, the Court of Customs and Patent Appeals, the Court of Claims, and the

---

[26] *Ibid.*, p. 491.

[27] Roger E. Meiners and Al H. Ringleb, *The Legal Environment of Business* (St. Paul, Minn.: West Publishing Co., 1982), p. 44.

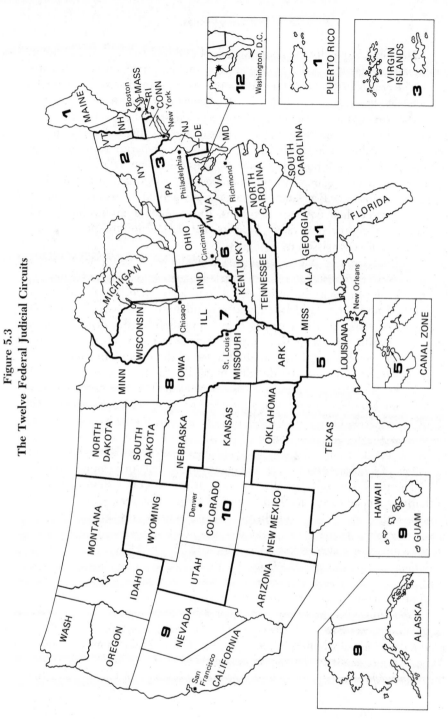

Figure 5.3
The Twelve Federal Judicial Circuits

highest courts in the states. Review is usually obtained by filing of a petition for certiorari by a lower court, which if granted, directs the lower court to send the record of the case to the Supreme Court for review. Granting of the writ, however, is at the discretion of the Supreme Court, and is not a right on the part of the parties affected. The Supreme Court cannot hear all the cases that are appealed, and thus picks those that are of substantial national importance or in which an obvious conflict exists between decisions of appeals courts. One of the important functions of the Supreme Court is to assure that there is national uniformity in interpreting federal legislation. The Supreme Court also reviews decisions of state supreme courts when a violation of the U.S. Constitution is alleged.[28]

If the Supreme Court does not grant certiorari and refuses to hear a case, the decision of the last court to deal with the case stands. Decisions made by the Supreme Court are final, in the sense that there is no further judicial review. This does not always end the matter, however, as Congress may change a statute to better reflect its intent if dissatisfied with the Supreme Court's interpretation.[29] The Supreme Court's decisions usually take the form of an order to a lower court or a government agency to carry out the mandate of the Supreme Court as reflected in the decision. Such follow-up work can take many years if complex plans are necessary to implement the court's decision.[30]

Administrative Agencies

The fourth branch of government consists of all the administrative agencies created by Congress to implement legislation in a specific area. The agencies that have the most direct impact on business are the regulatory agencies. When Congress began to pass laws to regulate business it created administrative agencies to carry out its wishes. The first such agency was the Interstate Commerce Commission (ICC) created in 1887 to deal with the railroad problem. Other regulatory agencies followed, dealing with specific industries such as communications, transportation, and financial institutions. In the 1960s and 1970s, Congress enacted hundreds of laws dealing with the environment, civil rights, consumer issues, and other social matters, and created many new agencies to implement this legislation. This new type of regulation has come to be called social regulation to distinguish it from the earlier type of regulation that dealt with a specific industry. Figure 5.4 presents an historical perspective to agency growth, showing the growth of traditional industry regulation in the New Deal era, and the surge of social regulation that is of more recent vintage.

An administrative agency has been defined as "a governmental body

28 Wolfinger, Shapiro, and Greenstein, *Dynamics*, pp. 497–98.
29 Meiners and Ringleb, *Legal Environment*, p. 44.
30 Wolfinger, Shapiro, and Greenstein, *Dynamics*, p. 499.

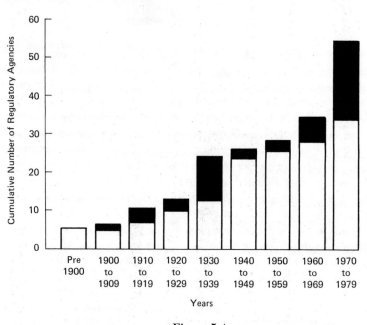

Figure 5.4
A Historical Perspective to Agency Growth

From Kenneth Chilton, *A Decade of Rapid Growth in Federal Regulation* (St. Louis, Mo.: Washington University, Center for the Study of American Business, 1979), p. 5. Reprinted with permission.

other than a court or legislature which takes action that affects the rights of private parties."[31] These agencies may be called boards, agencies, administrative departments, and so on, but in the regulatory area they are most often called commissions. The State Governmental Affairs Committee defined a regulatory commission as "one which (1) has decision-making authority, (2) establishes standards or guidelines conferring benefits and imposing restrictions on business conduct, (3) operates principally in the sphere of domestic business activity, (4) has its head and/or members appointed by the president . . . [generally subject to Senate confirmation], and (5) has its legal procedures governed by the Administrative Procedures Act."[32]

These regulatory commissions have specialized functions to implement governmental policy in specifically defined fields. Congress cannot immerse itself in all the details of each activity regulated or pass legislation that mandates specific forms of business behavior. Thus it passes laws that are broad in scope and sets general goals to be accomplished. The task of imple-

[31] John D. Blackburn, Elliot I. Klayman, and Martin H. Malin, *The Legal Environment of Business: Public Law and Regulation* (Homewood, Ill.: Richard D. Irwin, 1982), p. 65.

[32] Robert E. Healy, ed., *Federal Regulatory Directory 1979–80* (Washington D.C.: CQ, Inc., 1979), p. 3.

menting these laws is given to the regulatory agencies which are largely composed of so-called experts in areas like safety and health or the environment. Congress, for example, gives OSHA the power to set standards to improve safety and health in the workplace, but Congress does not specify what kind of standards should be established and for what substances. It is up to OSHA to determine these standards based on its expertise. In this manner, OSHA and other regulatory agencies make public policy.

Congress creates an administrative agency by passing a statute that specifies the name, composition, and powers of the agency. This statute is called the enabling legislation for the agency. The agencies are theoretically a creature of the Congress and accountable to Congress for agency activities. Congress can amend the enabling legislation to change agency behavior. Each House has oversight committees which review the work of the agencies, hold hearings, and propose amendments to the enabling legislation. Congress can also control agency activities through the appropriations process by attaching riders forbidding the agency to spend any money on particular cases. Congress can also use the legislative veto to rescind specific regulations issued by the agencies. Critics, however, argue that the legislative veto is an encroachment on executive powers, and thus its constitutionality is in question.

Agencies are also subject to specific statutes that govern their activities. The Administrative Procedures Act (APA), passed in 1946, specifies formal procedures with which agencies must comply and establishes standards and prerequisites for judicial review of agency action. Agency actions that are going to affect the environment are subject to the National Environmental Policy Act (NEPA) that requires the development of an environmental impact statement before undertaking the action. Finally, the Freedom of Information Act (FOIA) and Government in the Sunshine Act require, with certain exceptions, that agency documents be publicly available and that agency proceedings be open to the public.[33]

Judicial review of agency action is important because many of the regulations issued by agencies that are opposed by business wind up in the courts. Despite congressional oversight, the primary task of assuring that agencies comply with congressional dictates has fallen on the courts. The courts may overturn an agency's action for any of the following reasons: (1) the agency failed to comply with the procedures specified in its enabling legislation, the APA, NEPA, or FOIA; (2) the agency's action conflicts with its enabling legislation and therefore exceeds the scope of its authority; (3) the agency's decision is premised on an erroneous interpretation of the law; (4) the agency's action conflicts with the Constitution; and (5) the agency erred in the substance of its action. The last reason has to do with standards

---

[33] Blackburn, Klayman, and Malin, *Legal Environment*, pp. 67–68.

of evidence to support an agency's findings and the consideration of all relevant factors in a decision.[34]

There are two general types of regulatory agencies. Some agencies are independent in the sense that they are not located within a department of the executive branch of government. Since they are not part of the legislative or judicial branch either, a fourth branch of government seems to have emerged that combines the functions of the other three in the making, interpreting, and implementing of legislation. These independent agencies include the Civil Aeronautics Board (CAB), Consumer Products Safety Commission (CPSC), Equal Employment Opportunity Commission (EEOC), Environmental Protection Agency (EPA), Federal Trade Commission (FTC), Securities and Exchange Commission (SEC), and the ICC. In creating these agencies and making them independent, Congress sought to fashion them into an arm of the legislative branch and insulate them from presidential control. But many presidents have considered these commissions to be adjuncts of the executive branch and have argued that they should be able to coordinate and direct the independent agencies.[35]

Critics of this structure argue that the independent character of these commissions can hinder political monitoring by the executive branch and Congress that would make the agencies more responsive to social and economic change. Since Congress in particular does not always exercise its oversight function very well , the agencies can become complacent in their functions. On the other hand, these agencies can also become too zealous in their efforts, requiring new congressional action to reign them in, such as recent efforts directed toward the FTC and its rule-making authority.[36]

Another criticism is that the independent character of these agencies has weakened them by removing the benefits of more direct congressional and presidential support. In the case of industry regulation, this makes the agencies more vulnerable to pressure from the regulated industries. They become timid in defending the public interest and developing effective regulatory programs. In the case of social regulation, the independence of the agencies makes them subject to pressures from various interest groups, which may make them ignore the economic impact of their actions.[37]

Other agencies are located within the executive branch in one of the cabinet departments. These agencies include the Food and Drug Administration (FDA) as part of the Department of Health and Human Resources, the Antitrust Division of the Department of Justice, the Labor-Management Services Administration and OSHA in the Department of Labor, and the National Highway Traffic Safety Administration (NHTSA) in the Depart-

[34] *Ibid.*, 70–71.
[35] Healy, *Regulatory Directory*, p. 25.
[36] *Ibid.*
[37] *Ibid.*, p. 26.

ment of Transportation. Even here, however, there is some question whether these agencies are subject to presidential influence and guidance or whether they are free to use the regulatory authority granted them by Congress. Some believe that the President's power to appoint and dismiss cabinet officers carries with it an implicit authority to direct actions by regulatory agencies within the executive departments. Others argue that these agencies may accept White House advice, but that ultimately they are as independent as the separate regulatory commissions.[38]

Regulatory activities may be pursued in a number of ways: rate-making, licensing, granting of permits, establishing routes, establishing standards, requiring disclosure of information, and pursuing formal litigation against violators of federal standards. In general, however, the traditional industry-oriented agencies have used adjudication procedures more than rule-making procedures to carry out their functions. Rates and routes for air carriers, for example, are set in trial-like circumstances, where interested parties present their oral arguments and are cross-examined. After a lengthy process of review, the agency eventually reaches a decision, which may be appealed in the courts. The agency thus proceeds on a case-by-case basis, making law and policy much the same as a court. This procedure gives the agency considerable flexibility in developing an area of regulation over time.

The rule-making procedure is generally preferred by the newer social regulatory agencies. Rule making is the process of promulgating rules, resulting in regulations of greater certainty and consistency, and allows for broader input from the public. The APA definition of a rule is "an agency statement of general or particular applicability and future effect designed to complement, interpret, or prescribe law or policy."[39] Thus rule making is the enactment of regulations that will generally be applicable at some future time period.

Under the rule-making process, an agency must first publish a proposed regulation in the Federal Register. The Federal Register is a legal newspaper in which the executive branch of the United States Government publishes regulations, orders, and other documents of government agencies. It was created by Congress for the government to communicate with the public about the administration's actions on a daily basis.

This procedure provides an opportunity for public comment. Any interested individual or organization concerned with a pending regulation may comment on it directly in writing or orally at a hearing within a certain comment period. The Federal Register gives detailed instructions on how, when, and where a viewpoint can be expressed. After the agency receives and considers the comments, it may publish a final version of the regulation in the Federal Register or discontinue the rule-making procedure. If a final

[38] *Ibid.*, p. 31.
[39] Blackburn, Klayman, and Malin, *Legal Environment*, p. 77.

regulation is published, the agency must also include a summary and discussion of the major comments it received during the comment period. The final regulation may take effect no sooner than thirty days following its publication. After a final rule has been adopted by the agency, it is also published in the Code of Federal Regulations. The Code contains all the rules and regulations that any given agency has passed over the course of its existence.

On February 17, 1981, President Reagan issued an executive order that required agencies in the executive branch to prepare a regulatory impact analysis for each major rule being considered. The purpose of this analysis was to permit an assessment of the potential benefits and costs of each major regulatory procedure. The executive order also required that agencies choose regulatory goals and set priorities to maximize the benefits to society and choose the most cost-efficient means among legally available options for achieving the goals. This regulatory impact analysis must be submitted to the Office of Information and Regulatory Affairs (OIRA) located in the Office of Management and Budget (OMB). This analysis must pass OIRA's scrutiny before a regulation can be published. OIRA has the power to delay issuance of the regulation either in its proposed or final form.

Government agencies are very important in the public policy process. They combine the functions of the legislative branch in making administrative law, the executive branch by enforcing agency actions, and the judicial branch in ajudicating disputes. The administrative process has grown because of the need for specialized application of the laws Congress passes. Congress did not wish to increase executive power by giving these functions to the President, and thus created administrative agencies as an alternative. These agencies are subject to control by the other three branches through Congressional oversight, the presidential power of appointment and issuance of executive orders, and judicial review. They also have shown a great deal of autonomy at times in formulating public policy. Business can therefore be surprised when a law passed by Congress turns out to be quite different than anticipated after being implemented by the agencies.

THE OPERATION OF THE PUBLIC POLICY PROCESS The preceding section described the structure of government in terms of the three branches established by the Constitution and a fourth branch consisting of administrative agencies. The role these branches play in formulating public policy was outlined insofar as formal responsibilities are concerned. This kind of description, however, says nothing about the relative power of these branches in public policy making and the relative impact particular actors have in the public policy process. Such information would be extremely useful for a business executive who desires to participate in public policy formulation and use his or her time effectively.

The problem is one of finding where the power lies in government. Is Congress more powerful than the executive branch? What parts of Congress make the most impact on public policy formulation? Are the regulatory agencies the place where one should expend time and effort to affect the actual application of legislation?

The so-called traditional models of the public policy process, those which show how a bill becomes a law, for example, are of little use in this regard. They are too formal and mechanistic in their approach. Like the formal organization chart of a business, they may tell us little about how the organization really works and who has actual power to affect policy. Dan Fenn, writing in the *Harvard Business Review*, has the following to say about these traditional models.

> Like the textbook chart with the pipes and valves showing how a bill goes through Congress, they leave people and power out. They mislead us about the true nature of executive-legislative relations and make a consciously contrived system of controlled power and maximum access look centralized and monolithic.[40]

Thus we must look to nontraditional models of government to tell us how public policy is actually formulated. One such model was developed by Wallace S. Sayre and reconstructed by Walter G. Held in a Brookings publication. According to Held, "Sayre developed a model that identifies nine sets of actors or power structures in the decision-making system, sets forth their principal interests, motivations, and values, and describes the interplay among them that results in the formulation, adoption, and implementation of policies and programs by the federal government."[41]

The focal point of Sayre's analysis is the bureau leader (Figure 5.5), the level immediately below the political level in the executive branch. By bureau leader, Sayre means the head of an administrative agency. These administrative agencies include: (1) subdivisions of cabinet departments, (2) administrative agencies outside the departments such as the Veteran's Administration, (3) independent regulatory boards and commissions, (4) independent administrative boards and commissions like the Federal Home Loan Bank Board, and (5) federal corporations such as the Tennessee Valley Authority.[42]

The bureau unit has major powers for carrying out programs and proposals which makes the bureau leader pivotal in policy-making. The bureau

---

[40] Dan H. Fenn, Jr., "Finding Where The Power Lies in Government," *Harvard Business Review*, vol. 57, no. 5 (September–October 1979), p. 153.

[41] Walter G. Held, *Decisionmaking In The Federal Government: The Wallace S. Sayre Model* (Washington, D.C.: The Brookings Institution, 1979).

[42] *Ibid.*, p. 3.

Figure 5.5

The Wallace S. Sayre Model of the Federal Decisionmaking System[a]

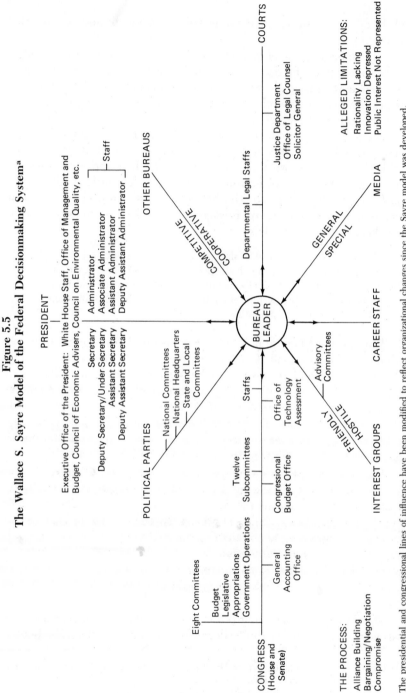

[a] The presidential and congressional lines of influence have been modified to reflect organizational changes since the Sayre model was developed.
Source: Walter Held, *Decisionmaking In The Federal Government: The Wallace S. Sayre Model* (Washington, D.C.: The Brookings Institution, 1979), p. 2.

leader can function both as an expert staff person to political superiors and general manager to subordinates within the agency. He or she is in a key position to influence the specific application of public policy measures. Bureau leaders direct large federal projects and programs or participate in determining policies and actions. Their activities draw the attention of many interest groups who wish to influence public policy.

This is not to suggest that the bureau leader is autonomous in the policy-making process. In reality, the head of an administrative agency is subject to many lines of influence, as shown in Figure 5.5. According to Held, other sets of power structures in the federal decision-making process that affect the bureau chief's decisions include the following:

The presidential line of influence, which includes executive departments and agencies and special presidential staff organizations.

The congressional line of influence, which includes the various committees, subcommittees, staffs, and special organizations established as aids to Congress.

The courts' line of influence, which is mainly exerted through legal officers in the executive branch who try to interpret what the courts are likely to do or say about actions taken or contemplated.

Other bureaus, whose activities may compete for jurisdiction, money, and other resources, or whose cooperation is required for successful performance.

The political parties, which seek to influence governmental actions to achieve their goals.

The media, both general and specialized, communicating in print or electronically.

The interest groups, whose constituents expect their agents to see that their values and desires are reflected in federal decisions.

The career staffs, who are associated with the bureau leaders, and the employees under their direction.[43]

To survive, a bureau leader must understand the nature of this system of influences and work within it to influence the outcome of the decision-making process. The leader must educate the many power centers in government about his or her activities and goals and induce them to help the bureau leader perform effectively. He or she must build alliances with other power centers in and out of government, must bargain with these power centers, and be able to reach compromises with others who have power on a given issue.[44]

[43] *Ibid.*, p. 5.
[44] *Ibid.*, p. 18.

Thus the Sayre model places primary emphasis on the heads of administrative agencies in the public policy process. It identifies the implementation stage as actually being the most crucial in policy making. The agencies actually determine the specifics of a program or proposal and carry out the wishes of Congress, the executive branch, and the courts. While Congress may pass legislation, the agencies apply it to specific situations. The President may issue an executive order affecting some agencies, but the agencies implement the order. The Courts may rule on a particular public policy issue, but the agencies may be able to circumvent much of the impact of this ruling. The bureau leader thus sits at the seat of power, according to Sayre, and others try to influence the leader's actions.

Dan Fenn uses this wheel model developed by Sayre to determine where the power lies in government. But he makes the point that one cannot answer a general question, such as who really runs the government, with this model. One can only answer the question of why a particular piece of public policy came out the way it did.[45] Thus the wheel model is not limited to bureau chiefs, but can be used to analyze decision-making processes where the bureau chief may not be the central figure.

To use the wheel model, one has to identify the key decision maker on a given issue. It may indeed be a bureau chief, but it could also be a legislator or the President himself. Once the key decision maker is identified and the power centers around him or her have been listed, one must assess the degree of interest these power centers have, evaluate their clout, and explore the possibility of forming common causes with them.[46] This wheel model, according to Fenn, can be a guide to a rational, systematic strategy for business, helping an executive select the tactics that are likely to work best in a given policy situation.[47]

Another view of where the power lies in government is presented by Clifford M. Hardin, Kenneth A. Shepsle, and Barry R. Weingast. They argue that the root of the nation's economic difficulties during the early 1980s lay in Congress itself. During the decade of the 1970s, a collection of powerful subcommittees, about 150 in each house of Congress, provided the motivation for much of the unrestrained and uncoordinated growth of the federal government. Subcommittees have grown more numerous and powerful over the past several years, and have been used more and more by Congress to conduct the main business of the nation's legislature.[48]

According to the authors, both Congress as a collective entity and the presidency have been eclipsed by the now autonomous committees and

[45] Fenn, "Power," p. 147.

[46] Ibid., p. 152.

[47] Ibid., p. 153.

[48] Clifford M. Hardin, Kenneth A. Shepsle, and Barry R. Weingast, *Public Policy Excesses: Government By Congressional Subcommittee* (St. Louis: Washington University Center for the Study of American Business, 1982), p. 1.

subcommittees of Congress. These committees and subcommittees have developed a relatively free hand in policy making within their own narrow jurisdictions. They have positioned themselves with respect to a handful of issue areas to protect relevant constituencies from changes which would adversely affect their interests.[49]

This trend towards the decentralization of Congress, transferring power from strong institutional and party leaders to committees and later to subcommittees, has been accelerated by several recent developments, according to the authors. "The Legislative Reorganization Act (1970), the Subcommittee Bill of Rights (1973), and the Committee Reform Amendments in the House (1974), served to strengthen the hand and assure the independence of the now numerous subcommittees."[50] The destruction of institutional and party power centers has resulted in the creation of new power centers, namely the committees and subcommittees of Congress.

These committees and subcommittees operate with relative independence in well-defined policy jurisdictions. They tend to be populated by those who have the highest stake in a given policy area. Thus, for example, farm-state Congressmen dominate the agricultural committees and urban legislators dominate the banking, housing, and social welfare committees.[51] Legislators tend to gravitate to the committees and subcommittees whose jurisdictions are most pertinent to their geographic constituencies.[52]

There are three reasons, according to the authors, why committees and subcommittees occupy such a key position in policy making. First, they originate legislation in specific areas of public policy. Second, they act as oversight agencies directing the activities of administrative agencies. The wise bureau chief, say the authors, ". . . had best attend to the concerns of the relevant committee and subcommittee members who can embarrass or otherwise complicate his life through the adverse publicity of oversight, and who can directly affect his bureau's authority and budget through the annual authorization and appropriations process."[53] Third, the committees and subcommittees can protect a program or agency from policy changes they deem undesirable. Reform proposals to alter bad programs can fall on deaf ears or have little effect if actually put into operation, if they are not consistent with the interests of committee and subcommittee members.[54] They are in a position to sabotage, water down, or simply ignore ameliorative changes. Policies to reform programs are often held hostage by these legislators whose constituents benefit from the current arrangements.

Thus there are several alternative ways of viewing the operation of

[49] *Ibid.*
[50] *Ibid.*, p. 6.
[51] *Ibid.*, p. 10.
[52] *Ibid.*, p. 9.
[53] *Ibid.*, p. 11.
[54] *Ibid.*, p. 12.

government in addition to the separation of powers doctrine of the constitution or the organizational chart approach. It is important to know where the power lies in government, whether it resides in the bureau chiefs, the committees and subcommittees of Congress, the presidency, or the courts, or whether it is constantly shifting with given issues. In order to be effective in the public policy process, business must be aware of where the power lies and how the system actually operates.

SELECTED REFERENCES

ALLISON, GRAHAM T. *The Essence of Decision: Explaining the Cuban Missile Crisis.* Waltham, MA: Little, Brown, 1971.

BAUER, RAY AND KENNETH GERGEN. *The Study of Policy Formation.* Riverside, N.J.: Free Press, 1971.

BAUER, RAY, ITHIEL DE SOLA POOL, AND LEWIS A. DEXTER. *American Business and Public Policy*, 2nd ed. Chicago: Aldine, 1972.

COBB, ROGER W. AND CHARLES D. ELDER. *Participation in American Politics.* Baltimore: Johns Hopkins University Press, 1975.

DYE, THOMAS R. *Understanding Public Policy*, 3rd ed. Englewood Cliffs, N.J.: Prentice-Hall, Inc., 1978.

HELD, WALTER G. *Decisionmaking In The Federal Government: The Wallace S. Sayre Model.* Washington, D.C.: The Brookings Institution, 1979.

JONES, CHARLES O. *An Introduction to the Study of Public Policy*, 2nd ed. North Scituate, MA: Duxbury Press, 1977.

LANE, FREDERICK S. *Current Issues in Public Administration.* New York: St. Martin's Press, Inc., 1978.

LINDBLOM, CHARLES E. *Politics and Markets: The World's Political-Economic Systems.* New York: Basic Books, 1977.

PRESTON, LEE AND JAMES POST. *Private Management and Public Policy.* Englewood Cliffs, N.J.: Prentice-Hall, Inc., 1975.

REDMAN, ERIC. *The Dance of Legislation.* New York: Simon & Schuster, 1974.

STARLING, GROVER. *The Politics and Economics of Public Policy.* Homewood, IL: Dorsey Press, 1979.

TRUMAN, DAVID. *The Governmental Process: Political Interests and Public Opinion*, 2nd ed. Westminster, MD: Knopf, 1951.

WADE, L. L. AND ROBERT L. CURRY, JR. *A Logic of Public Policy.* North Scituate, MA: Duxbury Press, 1970.

THE IMPACT/ OF PUBLIC POLICY
ON BU/INE// AND MANAGEMENT

**IDEAS TO BE FOUND
IN THIS CHAPTER**

- The costs of public policy
- Impacts of public policy
  on corporate structure
- Impacts of public policy
  on top management
- The paperwork impact

The public policy process described in the last chapter has produced in the last two decades a great deal of legislation and regulation which has impacted business organizations and their management. Changes have taken place in every area of public policy—antitrust legislation, economic management, labor-management relations, entitlement programs, and particularly, social regulation—that have changed the manner in which business can be operated and have altered the management task to include a public policy dimension.

No other area of public policy has made as significant an impact on business and management in recent years as the area of social regulation. Before the Reagan administration, this area of regulation constituted a real growth industry in terms of regulations issued, budgetary increases, staff increases, and in new regulatory agencies created. The growth of this new kind of regulation has been referred to as a second managerial revolution.[1] The first managerial revolution is based on the idea that ownership and

---

[1] Murray L. Weidenbaum, *Business, Government and the Public* (Englewood Cliffs, N.J.: Prentice-Hall, 1977), p. 285.

control have been separated in the modern corporation—that decision-making power has shifted from the formal owners or stockholders, to a class of professional managers.[2] This second managerial revolution involves a further shift of decision-making power from these professional managers to a vast cadre of government regulators who are influencing, and in many ways controlling, managerial decisions of the typical business corporation. These decisions, which are increasingly subject to government influence and control, are basic to the operation of a business organization.

> No business, large or small, can operate without obeying a myriad of government rules and restrictions. Costs and profits can be affected as much by a directive written by a government official as by a management decision in the front office or a customer's decision at the checkout counter. Fundamental entrepreneurial decisions—such as what lines of business to go into, what products and services to produce, which investments to finance, how and where to make goods and how to market them, and what prices to charge—are increasingly subject to government control.[3]

The impact of social regulation, more than any other area of public policy, has made managers aware of the need to take public policy seriously. It is important to understand the impacts public policy has made on business and management to see the importance of this dimension to management. Business organizations have had to incorporate new values and objectives into their operating strategies. The environment in which managers perform their tasks has been and is being changed through public policy measures.

THE COSTS OF PUBLIC POLICY

One of the major impacts that public policy makes on business organizations is economic. While the benefits of public policy measures may be shared by society at large, or at least by significant segments of a society which may include business itself, the costs of public policy are largely borne by business organizations. Much public policy, especially that which affects business directly, seems to be a matter of diffused benefits to society as a whole and concentrated costs as far as business organizations are concerned.

In the antitrust area, for example, the costs to a business organization can be very large if litigation is necessary to defend the business against a

---

[2] Adolph A. Berle and Gardner C. Means, *The Modern Corporation and Private Property* (New York: Macmillan, 1932).

[3] Murray L. Weidenbaum, "Government Power and Business Performance," *The United States in the 1980s*, Peter Dunignan and Alvin Robushka, eds. (Palo Alto, Calif.: Stanford University, Hoover Institution, 1980), p. 200.

government suit or a suit by a private party. Since most antitrust litigation is complex, the suits take a number of years to resolve. There are seemingly endless legal costs, costs involving information, the costs of management time, and costs of uncertainty regarding the outcome. IBM, for example, is estimated to have spent millions of dollars in defending itself against government allegations. The suit was finally dropped during the Reagan administration. Even when the government wins and the trial is over, the costs can be substantial. It will undoubtedly cost AT&T a substantial amount of money to divest itself of its operating companies and comply with all aspects of the final settlement. These are only the direct costs of antitrust; there are also indirect costs related to lost investment opportunities and unrealized efficiencies that may have resulted if a merger had been permitted.

In the area of entitlement programs there are direct costs to business because it acts as a tax collector for government. Business pays a portion of social security contributions, for example, and pays money to the government for unemployment compensation. There is an even greater indirect cost involved with the overall growth of entitlement programs that is probably impossible to measure but is nonetheless of great significance.

As entitlement programs become a means of promoting equality in American society, their impact on efficiency must be noted. Some economists see an egalitarian trend as posing a serious threat to business and the economy. The late Arthur Okun, former chairman of the Council of Economic Advisors, saw the issue as one of equality versus efficiency, with American society facing a trade-off with regard to these twin objectives.[4] The American economy uses the market to determine rewards and allocate resources. Differences in wages and profits are essential to keep the economic machine running and allocate resources efficiently. Public policy efforts to promote equality represent a deliberate interference with results generated by the marketplace. In pursuing equality, society foregoes the opportunity to use material rewards as incentives to production. Inefficiencies could result which would be harmful to the welfare of the majority. "Any insistence on carving the pie into equal slices," Okun said, "would shrink the size of the pie. That fact poses the trade-off between economic equality and economic efficiency."[5]

The impact on business from an increased emphasis on equality is primarily in the area of productivity. The business system depends on inequality to motivate people to work harder and take risks associated with entrepreneurship. The drive for profits and for high-paying jobs is essential to elicit greater productivity. If these incentives are reduced through gov-

---

[4] Arthur M. Okun, *Equality and Efficiency: The Big Tradeoff* (Washington, D.C.: The Brookings Institution, 1975).

[5] *Ibid.*, p. 47.

ernment taxation to support larger entitlement programs, productivity suffers. Material incentives have always been a much more powerful motivator than moral incentives, and a reduction in the ability to use material incentives has to affect business productivity.

If the economy is not managed effectively, business organizations as well as society are directly affected. Business had a great deal of optimism that the election of President Reagan would bring about the restoration of a healthy economy. The failure of the Reagan administration to get the federal budget under control kept interest rates high, discouraged investment in new plants and equipment, and failed to stimulate consumer buying. Many businessmen eventually became skeptical about supply-side economics, which promised increases in economic growth to offset the tax cuts, and supported tax increases to reduce the federal deficit to manageable proportions. Again, business is affected by this problem through increased costs if it does borrow money, lost investment opportunities if it doesn't, and a further loss of public confidence because of plant closures and layoffs.

The area of regulation has entailed many costs for business organizations. These costs are largely hidden from public view, as the only visible costs of regulation are the costs of running the agencies themselves. But these administrative costs are only the tip of the iceberg. The bulk of the costs of regulation are compliance costs—the costs of developing and implementing affirmative action programs, the costs of installing pollution control equipment, and the costs of installing safety devices.

The first study that attempted to measure these compliance costs on a comprehensive basis was completed at the Center for the Study of American Business (CSAB), a research center directed by Murray Weidenbaum, former chairman of the Council of Economic Advisors under the Reagan administration.[6] The CSAB study estimated these compliance costs for 1976 by using the most reliable estimates for various areas of regulation that were available at the time. These estimates were then totaled to arrive at an overall figure believed to represent total compliance costs for the year. For example, figures from the Council on Environmental Quality were used for estimating compliance costs for pollution abatement. The paperwork figure came from the Commission on Federal Paperwork study.[7]

[6] Murray L. Weidenbaum and Robert De Fina, *The Rising Cost of Government Regulation* (St. Louis: Washington University Center for the Study of American Business, 1977).

[7] No cost estimates were available for the following regulatory activities: Animal and Plant Health Inspection Service, Packers and Stockyards Administration, Department of Housing and Urban Development, Antitrust Division, Drug Enforcement Administration, Federal Railroad Administration, Bureau of Alcohol, Tobacco and Firearms, Customs Service, Consumer Product Safety Commission, National Transportation Safety Board, Mining Enforcement and Safety Administration, Department of Energy, Federal Maritime Commission, Commodity Future Trading Commission, Nuclear Regulatory Commission, Comptroller of the Currency, Federal Deposit Insurance Corporation.

The basic approach followed in the study was to cull from the available literature the more reliable estimates of the costs of specific regulatory programs, to put those estimates on a consistent and reliable basis, and to aggregate the results for 1976. Where a range of costs was available for a given regulatory program, the lower end of the range was generally used. In many cases no cost estimates were available. Thus, the numbers in this study are low and surely underestimate the actual cost of federal regulation in the United States.[8]

Table 6.1 shows the results of this procedure. For 1976, the study showed expenses of approximately $3.2 billion in administrative costs and $62.9 billion in compliance costs.[9] This study clearly shows that the costs imposed on the private sector are much greater than the costs of running the agencies themselves. The estimated compliance costs in 1976 were twenty times the administrative costs for that year. Applying this multiple of twenty to the amounts budgeted for regulatory activities in subsequent years, approximations were generated, as shown in Table 6.2 for the total dollar impact of government regulation from 1977 to 1979.

Table 6.1
Annual Cost of Federal Regulation, by Area, 1976
(Millions of Dollars)

	Administrative Cost	Compliance Cost	Total
Consumer safety and health	$1,516	$ 5,094	$ 6,610
Job safety and working conditions	483	4,015	4,498
Energy and the environment	612	7,760	8,372
Financial regulation	104	1,118	1,222
Industry specific	484	$19,919	20,403
Paperwork	—	25,000	25,000
Total	$3,199	$62,906	$66,105

The Business Roundtable subsequently completed a study of the compliance costs imposed on part of its membership by six regulatory agencies or

[8] Murray L. Weidenbaum and Robert De Fina, *The Cost of Federal Regulation of Economic Activity* (Washington, D.C.: American Enterprise Institute, 1978), p. 1.

[9] This total of $66 billion is equivalent to: 4 percent of the gross national product; $307 per person living in the United States; 18 percent of the federal budget; twice the amount that the federal government spends on health; 74 percent of the amount devoted to national defense; over one-third of all private investment in new plants and equipment. *Ibid.*, p. 3.

Table 6.2
Estimated Cost of Federal Regulation of Business
(Fiscal Years, in Billions of Dollars)

	1977	1978	1979
Administrative costs	$ 3.7	$ 4.5	$ 4.8
Compliance costs	75.4	92.2	97.9
Total	$79.1	$96.7	$102.7

programs.[10] This study, which was managed by the accounting firm of Arthur Andersen and Company, claimed to be different from other regulatory cost studies because of its specificity. It dealt only with incremental costs, defined as "the direct costs of those actions taken to comply with a regulation that would not have been taken in the absence of that regulation. These incremental costs were based upon (1) information drawn from companies' accounting, engineering, and other business records, and (2) informed judgement as to which actions would have been taken in the absence of regulation."[11]

These incremental costs were classified into operating and administrative costs, research and development costs, product-related costs, and capital costs. Not only were the costs distributed into these classifications, they were also broken down by specific regulations. The study omitted secondary costs of regulation, such as productivity losses, construction delays, inflation, and misallocation of resources.

The study, released in March 1979, covered forty-eight companies in more than twenty industries. All of these participants were considered to be large corporations. Many of them were multinational, although only their domestic operations were included. The six government agencies and programs included in the study were the Environmental Protection Agency, Equal Employment Opportunity Commission, Occupational Safety and Health Administration, Department of Energy, Employee Retirement and Income Security Act, and the Consumer Protection Bureau of the Federal Trade Commission.

The incremental cost for the forty-eight companies to comply with regulations from the six agencies and programs for 1977 was $2.6 billion. Figure 6.1 shows the breakdown of this cost by the four classifications mentioned previously. Operating and administrative costs compose the bulk (42 percent) of the total. The costs by agency (Figure 6.2) show that fully 77

[10] Arthur Andersen and Company, Cost of Government Regulation (New York: The Business Roundtable, 1979).

[11] Ibid., p. ii.

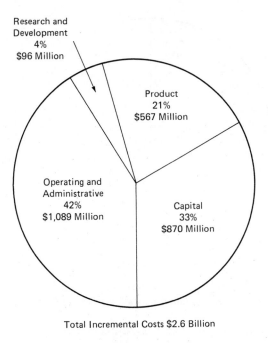

Research and
Development
4%
$96 Million

Product
21%
$567 Million

Operating and
Administrative
42%
$1,089 Million

Capital
33%
$870 Million

Total Incremental Costs $2.6 Billion

Figure 6.1
Incremental Costs Summarized in
Four Classifications

From Arthur Andersen and Company, *Cost of Government Regulation* (New York: The Business Roundtable, 1979), p. 15.
Reprinted with permission.

percent of the total incremental costs is attributable to the Environmental
Protection Agency alone.

The impact of regulation showed a wide variation among industries.
For example, the incremental cost of OSHA rules averaged $6 per year per
worker in the banking industry, but $220 per worker per year in the chemi-
cal industry. The study also identified attributes of regulation that had a high
incremental cost, which would hopefully be useful in reform efforts.

The Roundtable Study dealt with large corporations, but some believe
that government regulation has had a disproportionate adverse impact on
small business. The small firm has a limited ability to pass along regulation-
induced expenditures. As stated by Kenneth W. Chilton, Associate Director
of the Center for the Study of American Business: "Large capital expenditures to meet environmental or job safety standards above those that
would be followed voluntarily may represent merely an uneconomical application of resources for a large firm, but it may literally be a matter of the
enterprise's life or death for the small firm."[12]

[12] Kenneth W. Chilton, *The Impact of Federal Regulation on American Small Business* (St.
Louis: Washington University Center for the Study of American Business, 1978), p. 2.

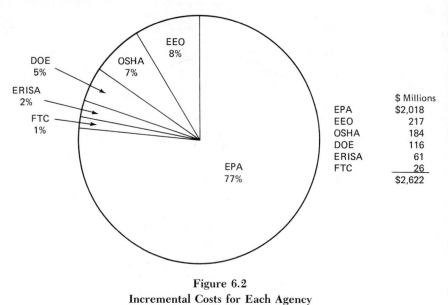

Figure 6.2
Incremental Costs for Each Agency

From Arthur Andersen and Company, *Cost of Government Regulation* (New York: The Business Roundtable, 1979), p. 19. Reprinted with permission.

The foundry industry is a case in point. Before 1968, there were approximately 4,200 foundries in the industry. Eighty-two percent of these firms employed fewer than one hundred people and 75 percent employed fewer than fifty. The total industry employed 375,000 workers. Around 1968, this industry began to lose some of its small plants due to a combination of the recession and EPA regulations. The size of the mandated EPA emission control expenditures for many of these foundries exceeded their net worth, forcing them to close down their operations. From 1968 to 1975, there were 350 verified foundry closings, and many of these were due to the impact of EPA regulations.[13]

A study by Charles River Associates examined the impact of proposed OSHA standards for air-lead exposure levels. The total compliance cost for business was estimated at $416 million (1976 dollars), with annual operating costs of $112 million. The impact on the battery industry alone, which was composed of 143 firms, was estimated to result in much larger per unit production costs for smaller plants than for larger plants. Because of this differential, about 113 single plant battery firms were forced to close, eliminating about half the productive capacity not operated by the five major battery companies.[14]

Besides these capital expenditures, the paperwork associated with gov-

[13] *Ibid.*, p. 3.
[14] "CRA Examines the Cost of Meeting OSHA Lead Standards," *Charles River Associates Research Review*, February 1978, p. 2.

ernment regulation often commands large segments of the entrepreneur's time and effort. The Commission on Federal Paperwork reported in 1977 that the five million small businesses in the country spend between $15 and $20 billion per year, or an average of over $3 thousand each on federal paperwork. The commission went on to say that "small businesses are relatively harder hit by federal information requirements than larger firms and often lack the necessary expertise to comply."[15]

Besides these effects, regulatory agencies can sometimes hurl devastating blows at a small company by releasing incorrect information about a product on which the company is dependent.[16] Some government regulations adversely affect the ability of small business to attract investment. Finally, many pension plans of small business have gone out of existence because of the increased costs of meeting pension law requirements.

Besides these direct or first-order costs of regulation, the cost to the firm of directly complying with government regulations, there are also what Murray Weidenbaum calls the indirect or second-order effects of regulation.[17] The most serious of these costs, according to Weidenbaum, are losses in productivity. Edward Denison of the Brookings Institution estimated that business productivity in 1975 was 1.4 percent lower than it would have been if business had operated under the regulatory conditions existing in 1967. Of that amount, one percent was due to pollution abatement requirements and 0.4 percent to employee safety and health programs. That productivity loss, according to Denison, amounted to a reduction of about $20 billion in the level of gross national product for that year.[18]

Besides this indirect effect on productivity, regulation can also affect employment. Older, marginal facilities may have to be closed down because they cannot meet regulatory standards and remain profitable. The minimum wage law also affects employment by pricing teenagers out of the market. Other plants that were proposed may be canceled because of the difficulty of obtaining all the regulatory permits from federal, state, and local agencies. Dow Chemical Company, for example, canceled plans in January 1977 for building a $300 million petrochemical complex in California. After two years and a $4 million expenditure, Dow had obtained only four of the sixty-five permits that were needed from federal, state, local, and regional regulatory agencies in order to build the facility.[19]

A final category of regulatory costs are the induced, or third-order

[15] Commission on Federal Paperwork, *Final Summary Report* (Washington, D.C.: U.S. Government Printing Office, 1977), p. 66.

[16] See the Marlin Toy Products Case in Murray L. Weidenbaum, *Business, Government, and the Public*, pp. 213–19.

[17] Murray L. Weidenbaum, *The Future of Business Regulation* (New York: AMACOM, 1979), pp. 16–23.

[18] *Ibid.*, p. 20.

[19] *Ibid.*, pp. 19–20.

effects. These are the actions that the firm takes to respond to the direct and indirect effects of regulation. Weidenbaum believes that these "difficult to measure impacts may, in the long run, far outweigh the more measurable costs resulting from the imposition of government influence on private sector decision making."[20]

One of these third-order effects is the impact regulation has on capital formation. This situation arises from the closing down of plants that cannot remain economically viable and meet government standards. The closing of the foundries mentioned in the previous section is an example. The other side of the coin is the difficulty in obtaining all the necessary permits and clearances necessary to construct new facilities, as the Dow Chemical case illustrates. The effect of many of these regulations is to limit new capital formation and hence economic growth.

Government regulation also has an effect on innovation in some industries. In the drug industry, for example, the volume of new drug products and new chemical entities has declined since the 1962 amendments to the Pure Food and Drug Act. These amendments required extensive premarket testing of new drugs. This drop in innovation has been accompanied by increases in the cost, duration, and risk of new product development. The results have been a sharp reduction in the rate of return on research and development investment in the drug industry and an erosion of American technological leadership in new drug development.[21]

Finally, regulation diverts management attention from its basic function of running the enterprise. Management sometimes has to devote a significant portion of its time to dealing with the impacts of regulation on the economy. The net result of these third-order effects, Weidenbaum says, "can be seen in the factories that do not get built, the jobs that do not get created, the goods and services that do not get produced, and the incomes that are not generated."[22]

The benefits of public policy do not come without cost. Business organizations have to internalize the costs of public policy objectives related to a workable competition, equality, economic stability, clean air and water, and other public goods. These costs are reflected in the cost of products, in the wages and salaries paid to employees, and in dividends paid to shareholders. Business organizations cannot simply absorb these costs, they must pass them on to the rest of society. Thus while the costs of public policy at first glance appear to be concentrated on business organizations, they are in reality also diffused throughout society.

[20] *Ibid.*, p. 23.

[21] Jerome E. Schnee, "Regulation and Innovation: U.S. Pharmaceutical Industry," *California Management Review*, Vol. XXII, No. 1 (Fall 1979), pp. 23–32.

[22] Weidenbaum, *The Future of Business Regulation*, p. 30.

IMPACTS OF PUBLIC POLICY ON CORPORATE STRUCTURE The impacts that public policy has made on the internal organization of a company are also significant. The corporation has had to adapt itself to its changing role in society as public policy measures have prescribed new responsibilities for business to fulfill. As the environment of business changes, the structure of the business organization itself has to change to incorporate new functions to carry out new responsibilities.

Public Responsibility Committees Starting at the very top of the organization, one important structural change is the development of public responsibility committees at the board level. The board of directors represents the interests of shareholders and thus must be concerned with the impact of public policy on the corporation and its prospects for success in the marketplace. This change reflects the impact that a broader constituency has been making on the corporate organization. These committees have such responsibilities as the following:

1. Identify the major constituencies—both internal and external—who normally judge the behavior and performance of the corporation; examine what they expect of the corporation's performance socially and environmentally.

2. Recommend specific issues for board and management consideration, and determine their relative priority.

3. Recommend corporate policy to respond to the priority issues.

4. Consider and recommend potential new areas of public policy and potential impacts on the corporation.

5. Examine and report to the full board on corporate attitudes toward the needs and concerns of the major constituencies of the corporation.

6. Recommend where duties and responsibilities lie throughout the company with respect to the priority public policy issues.[23]

Some of the areas with which a public responsibility committee concerns itself are affirmative action, community relations, pollution, product quality and safety, occupational safety and health, charitable contributions, and government relations. The public responsibility committee can devote more time and consideration to these issues than can the full board. The issues can then be discussed thoroughly at the board level along with the more traditional business concerns. The committee is also in a better posi-

---

[23] Reprinted by permission of the *Harvard Business Review.* Excerpt from "Public responsibility committees of the board," by Michael L. Lovdal, Raymond A. Bauer, and Nancy H. Treverton, vol. 55, no. 3 (May–June 1977), pp. 40–41. Copyright © 1977 by the President and Fellows of Harvard College; all rights reserved.

tion to monitor corporate performance in these areas than is the full board of directors. Through its actions, a public responsibility committee can indicate to all employees that top management is dedicated to public responsibility and can help spread this philosophy throughout the organization (see box).[24]

PUBLIC POLICY COMMITTEES OF THE BOARD: FORUMS FOR ELICITING ISSUES

Some companies represented in this study have established public policy or social responsibility committees—or committees with synonymous names—of the board of directors. These committees are typically composed predominantly or entirely of outside directors. One purpose they serve is to bring to management's attention, or to make sure management is following, appropriate external issues and to monitor the company's response to them. At General Motors, the public policy committee is charged with inquiring into every phase of business activity that relates to matters of public policy. Several study participants refer to these committees as "the conscience of a company," and one claims that it is the mere existence of such a committee—rather than what it does—that is important.

From James K. Brown, *This Business of Issues: Coping with the Company's Environments* (New York: The Conference Board, 1979), p. 20. Reprinted with permission.

The public responsibility committee can serve as a kind of audit committee when composed entirely of outside directors. Executives of the company concerned with affirmative action or pollution can be called before the committee to report on their activities. The committee can then report on these matters to the full board. Some companies have both a public responsibility committee at the board level to identify trends and issues and a management committee to deal with specific responses of the company.

A study completed by the Center for Research in Business and Social Policy at the University of Texas at Dallas found that in 1979, ninety companies had such committees at the board level, a 95 percent increase over the forty-six companies that reported such committees in existence in 1977.[25] The top 200 corporations of the sample on which the study was based accounted for 60 percent of the public responsibility committees while constituting only 26.9 percent of the total population. Large corporations are clearly the leaders in establishing these committees.

[24] *Ibid.*, p. 41.

[25] S. Prakash Sethi, Bernard J. Cunningham, and Patricia M. Miller, *Corporate Governance: Public Policy-Social Responsibility Committee of Corporate Board: Growth and Accomplishment* (Dallas: University of Texas Center for Research in Business and Social Policy, 1979), p. 49.

152

Twenty-seven different designations were used as names for these committees. These designations are grouped in Table 6.3 into seven different classifications. The most popular classifications were the public policy committee or social responsibility committee categories. The public policy committee classification included such titles as public interest, public policy, public issues, public affairs policy, human resources and public policy, and consumer affairs. The social responsibility committee classification included such titles as public responsibility, social responsibility, and social responsiveness.[26]

These public responsibility committees recorded the largest increase in size between 1977 and 1979 when compared with other board committees and are the largest board committees in terms of membership (Table 6.4). In 1979, the average public responsibility committee had 4.9 members with 90 percent of the companies having committee sizes between three and seven members.[27] Outside directors tended to constitute the largest proportion of the membership of these committees, with the most popular backgrounds of these outsiders being those of industrialist (32.4 percent) and academician (14.4 percent).[28]

Functional Specialists

Another structural change is the growth of functional specialists within corporate organizations. These specialized staff positions are oriented toward public policy concerns and impact the traditional functional areas of a corporation. They have been developed because of the need to comply with government regulations in such areas as the physical environment, safety and health, pensions, and affirmative action—areas where there are now people who respond to the public policy concerns expressed in regulation. They may be responsible for seeing that the company effectively responds to issues of public concern, making sure the company is in compliance with regulations, and handling the information requirements that regulations involve.

Many corporations have established a separate position for the management of environmental affairs at the directorial or vice-presidential level, with a sizable staff to deal with environmental matters. Interlake Inc., for example, a producer of steel and powdered metals in Oak Brook, Illinois, reports that its environmental staff has grown to forty people. A vice-president of the company spends about 95 percent of his time on environmental matters and states that his advice is sought on all company activities that affect the environment. *Business Week* states that this situation is not unusual. "Increasingly, corporations are upgrading the status and respon-

[26] *Ibid.*, p. 8.
[27] *Ibid.*, p. 10.
[28] *Ibid.*, p. 50.

Table 6.3
Classifications of Names Used by Corporations to Designate
Their Public Policy-Social Responsibility Committees

Type of Name	Percent of Corporations Using It
Public Policy Committee	44.5
Social Responsibility Committee	33.3
Contributions Committee—General	8.9
Contributions Committee—Education	1.1
Conflict of Interest/Ethics	6.7
Corporate Conduct/Principles	4.4
Public and Government Relations	1.1
	100.0

Source: S. Prakash Sethi, Bernard J. Cunningham, and Patricia M. Miller, *Corporate Governance: Public Policy-Social Responsibility Committee of Corporate Board: Growth and Accomplishment* (Dallas: University of Texas Center for Research in Business and Social Policy, 1979), p. 7. Reprinted with permission.

Table 6.4
Average Size of Various Board Committees

Committee	Average 1977	Size 1979
Audit Committee	4.0	4.1
Compensation Committee	4.5	4.3
Nominating Committee	4.8	4.3
Public Policy-Social Responsibility Committee	4.3	4.9

Source: S. Prakash Sethi, Bernard J. Cunningham, and Patricia M. Miller, *Corporate Governance: Public Policy-Social Responsibility Committee of Corporate Board: Growth and Accomplishment* (Dallas: University of Texas Center for Research in Business and Social Policy, 1979), p. 11. Reprinted with permission.

sibilities of their environmental managers. Their staffs and budgets are being enlarged, and many are gaining more clout with top management."[29]

Just a few years ago, most companies relegated environmental matters to the engineering department, where a small staff designed equipment to meet the few pollution control requirements which then existed. Today, because of heightened public awareness of environmental problems, widespread support of environmentalism, and increased government regulation, many companies have an organized program for handling environmental concerns.

Environmental experts have the responsibility of studying the rules

[29] "The New Corporate Environmentalists," *Business Week*, May 28, 1979, p. 154.

issued by regulatory agencies and determining what a company must do to be in compliance. This is no small task. There are more than 300 state and federal laws dealing with the environment and dozens of government agencies that administer them. In one year, more than 800 pages of federal regulations were issued on waste disposal alone.[30] The environmental staff checks company plants to see that they are in compliance with the law and meet company standards. They also point out where new projects will violate environmental laws. Such violations could result in construction delays or complete shut-down of the project. Advice from environmental experts has helped some companies save money by redesigning products or manufacturing processes to be less polluting.

The same kind of response has been made in the area of health and safety concerns. Figure 6.3 depicts a typical worker protection system in the chemical industry. The system includes worker and area monitoring for hazardous levels of dangerous substances, and chemical analysis and toxicology studies related to those substances. This information, along with medical checkups of the workers themselves, is analyzed by a computer and forms the basis of process design and safety engineering. The successful operation of such a system requires many safety and health experts. The number of industrial hygienists in the chemical industry, for example, has tripled in the last ten years. They are only part of an interdisciplinary approach to worker safety and health. The typical team consists of a variety of experts including industrial hygienists, physicians, toxicologists, and engineers.[31] Some of the functions of these experts are listed below.

Industrial Hygiene

Setting exposure limits for hazardous substances
Communicating potential health hazards
Design of engineering controls to minimize exposure
Conduct site audits and perform risk assessments
Monitor workplace exposure to hazardous chemicals
Develop staff, line, and worker training programs
Review design of equipment to reduce hazards

Occupational Medicine

Perform medical surveillance activities and biological monitoring
Conduct physical examinations of employees
Provide medical treatment to employees

[30] "Like Other New-Breed Environmental Managers, Hellman of Allied Isn't Merely A Trouble-Shooter," *The Wall Street Journal*, July 30, 1981, p. 48.
[31] "Protecting Chemical Workers," *Time*, April 28, 1980, pp. 82–83.

Give medical advice to supervisors

Conduct hazard evaluations

Provide emergency medical service

Toxicology

Conduct toxicity hazard assessments of substances

Analyze toxicity data and develop toxicology information

Conduct animal lab testing

Develop communications to employees on effects of chemicals

Provide security for hazardous materials

Take responsibility for Toxic Substances Control Act reporting and record keeping

These safety and health experts impact decision making within a corporation. In a survey of companies in the chemical industry completed in 1980, respondents were asked to rate the impact safety and health concerns were

Figure 6.3
Worker Safety Protection System

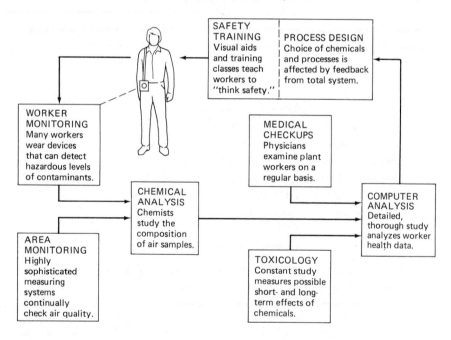

From "Protecting Chemical Workers," *Time,* April 28, 1980, p. 83. Reprinted with permission of the Chemical Manufacturers Association.

making on several categories of corporate decisions.[32] The results, shown in Table 6.5, display a clear grouping into definable categories of decisions. Decisions having to do with the building and operation of a production facility were impacted most significantly. These decisions included plant operation, building of new facilities, working conditions, and capital budgeting. The next category was a group of decisions having to do directly with the product itself, including packaging and labeling, product development, product design, pricing, product extension, and advertising. Decisions having to do with employees, wage rules, employee hiring and firing, and employee benefits were impacted the least.

Table 6.5
Impact of the Environmental, Safety, and Health Activity on Corporate Decisions
(Ranked from Greatest to the Least Impact: 1 = Great Impact; 6 = No Impact)

Plant operation	2.0
Building new facilities	2.2
Working conditions	2.4
Capital budgeting	2.5
Packing and labeling	2.5
Product development	2.6
Product design	3.6
Pricing	4.0
Product extension	4.5
Advertising	4.6
Wage rules	5.1
Employee hiring and firing	5.4
Employee benefits	5.5

Source: Rogene A. Buchholz, "The Regulatory Response In The Chemical Industry: Environment, Safety, and Health," unpublished paper.

This same kind of functional development has occurred in other areas where public policy has impacted the corporation, such as equal opportunity and consumer products. Affirmative action specialists make sure the company is in compliance with equal opportunity laws and develop affirmative action plans, particularly if the company is a government contractor. Consumer affairs offices have been developed in consumer oriented companies to handle consumer complaints and inquiries, disseminate consumer information, monitor company advertisements, provide input for product design

---

[32] Rogene A. Buchholz, "The Regulatory Response In The Chemical Industry: Environment, Safety, and Health," unpublished paper.

to improve product safety, develop warranties and guarantees, oversee product packaging and labeling, and improve quality control. There is even a professional organization called the Society of Consumer Affairs Professionals in Business that has been organized to promote professionalism among the executives who head these consumer affairs offices.

The Legal Function The growth of the legal function within corporate organizations is a result of the impact that public policy has made on the legal environment of business. Corporations are much more likely to be sued by government or private parties than in the past. Many environmental, safety and health, and consumer protection laws enacted in the past two decades carry substantial penalties for violations and provide for the right of suit by private parties. Changing notions of product and worker liability have resulted in a profusion of suits brought by citizens who assert that they have been harmed by products or environmental contamination.

Consider the case of Manville Corporation, previously known as Johns-Manville, a Denver based building materials and forest products company. The controversy was over asbestos, to which many workers were exposed while working for the company. While asbestos was once known as the miracle mineral because of its many uses, it has been increasingly recognized as a health hazard of alarming proportions. Manville, being the largest producer of the mineral in the non-Communist world, became swamped with litigation. Since 1968, the company was hit with 20 thousand lawsuits and paid out $50 million in claims. It was predicted that Manville could expect about 500 new suits a month for an eventual total of about fifty-two thousand, costing the company at least $2 billion. Accounting rules require a company to set aside funds as a reserve against anticipated claims. This $2 billion was almost as much as the $2.2 billion Manville had in total assets. To keep from being strangled, the company filed for Chapter 11 bankruptcy in 1982. This action suspended all current lawsuits and prevented new ones from being filed against the firm. The bankruptcy court thus had to deal with the present claims against the company and set guidelines for handling future claims.[33]

The Manville case, however is only one out of thousands that involves corporations in litigation. Industry sources have estimated that nearly 2.5 million workers are directly exposed to dangers in their job and that damage claims threaten to cost industry many billions of dollars. One insurance executive states that there isn't enough money in the economy to settle all the industrial claims confronting American industry today, meaning that the insurance industry could not possibly have enough funds to settle all the

[33] "Manville's Bold Maneuver," *Time*, September 6, 1982, pp. 17–18.

claims out of premiums if current trends were to persist over several years.[34]

Given this kind of environment, corporations have had to increase their in-house legal staff and in some cases, use of outside counsel. The corporate legal population grew by 18 percent in 1980, only 0.5 percent in 1981 because of the recession, but was expected to pick up again as the economy improved.[35] One reason for expanding internal staff is cost. In general, in-house attorneys cost about 35–50 percent less per hour than outsiders. In-house attorneys are more familiar with the business. Use of outside lawyers sometimes involves a great deal of education, all of which takes time and money. Using an internal legal staff saves a business the repeated problem of explaining the details of a business to an outside attorney.

Despite these advantages of in-house legal capability, many companies still find the use of outside counsel necessary. One successful trial lawyer, who defended Ford Motor Company in the Pinto case and Firestone in the 500 radial recall, claims that in-house lawyers handle mostly routine work that doesn't involve trials. Outsiders are used to solve "open-ended, unprecedented problems that require imagination—problems like how long a manufacturer can be held responsible for the performance of a product."[36]

Whether a company uses in-house lawyers or seeks outside counsel, however, it is clear that the legal environment has changed. Corporations are much more vulnerable to lawsuits than in the past because of statutory provisions and changing notions of corporate liability. Such a changing legal environment also has had impacts on the liability of top management as well as the corporation as a whole, a subject to be discussed later in this chapter.

Public Issues Management   Many corporations have developed or are developing an internal expertise in managing public issues of importance to the company. This expertise is generally referred to as "public issues management." This term does not mean that the company expects to manage a public issue with regard to society as a whole. What it does mean is that the company manages its response to a public issue the same way it manages other aspects of the business.

This expertise coordinates the company's response to public issues and, in some cases, sees that broader environmental concerns that give rise to public policy issues are incorporated into the strategic plan of the business. This expertise also assists the various functional areas in addressing

---

[34] "Companies Respond to Lawsuit Epidemic With Lawyers, Computers, and Research," *The Wall Street Journal,* June 16, 1981, p. 48.

[35] "Companies Expanding Legal Staffs as the Cost of Outside Work Soars," *The Wall Street Journal,* March 1, 1982, p. 25.

[36] "Top Trial Lawyer Gets Firm Out of Trouble With Quiet Efficiency," *The Wall Street Journal,* November 11, 1982, p. 1.

public issues and attempts to internalize an awareness of the public policy dimension throughout all levels of management. This latter task involves, among other things, providing learning experiences for management on the importance and potential impact public policy can make on the corporation.

The development of public issues management might include a structural change in the public relations function or the growth of a public affairs department. In some cases, the title of public relations has been changed to public affairs; in other cases, public relations is now considered to be a subdivision of public affairs; and in still other companies, public affairs and public relations are entirely separate departments. Some companies have also established community or urban affairs departments.

Obviously, companies have handled this change in various ways, but the major thrust of these developments is a change in the way business relates to the public. The old emphasis on public relations, which implied relations with the press and was most likely a one-way communication from business to the public, is simply not enough to deal with the new demands being forced on business by government and other groups in the public realm.

Related to this change in public relations or public affairs is the growth of Washington offices, both in numbers of people employed for this function and the influence these offices now wield in the total corporate structure. The Washington office is the "eyes, ears, and mouth" of the corporation in the nation's capital. Its primary function has changed from a concern with winning government contracts to a concern with legislative and regulatory matters that have impact on business. Its roles include gathering intelligence and tracking issues—gathering information about public issues that are at various stages of development and interpreting these issues to management. In this sense, the Washington office acts as sort of an intermediary between the federal government and corporate headquarters. Its job is also to assist in other aspects of issues management, particularly in the development of strategies to make the company's position known to the proper people in the federal government.

These changes imply that public issues are being taken much more seriously than was evident in the old public relations function. Involved in this structural change is a real concern for doing one's homework on public issues so the organization can effectively participate in the formulation of public policy.

THE IMPACTS OF PUBLIC POLICY ON TOP MANAGEMENT

Public policy has impacted the management task by adding new dimensions to management and complicating decision making. The manager of a modern corporation must consider many additional factors in decision making beyond economic considerations to run a successful business. The business organization of today serves many nontraditional constituencies that are not necessarily interested in profit or market share, and the manager must consider a broader range of noneconomic consequences before reaching a decision. There are two areas of interest in this regard that will be discussed further.

Top Management Involvement   There is no doubt that public policy concerns have penetrated into the ranks of top management. This penetration has resulted in top management's changed attitudes and behavior regarding the importance of the public policy dimension. The CEOs of many companies have been spending a great deal of time relating to constituent groups normally considered external to the company—doing things like testifying before Congress, speaking out on public issues, and talking with public interest group leaders. Many top executives now realize that the success of the business may be tied up with the ability to deal successfully with these external constituencies, particularly the government. Business cannot be run in a vacuum anymore and top management spends a considerable amount of time dealing with public policy matters.

> Top managers of corporations spend a preponderant part of their time today dealing with environmental problems. These include addressing social concerns of society, complying with new social legislation, communicating with legislators and government executives concerning new proposed laws and regulations, meeting with various self-interest groups concerning their demands and/or grievances, and administering their organizations in such a way as to respond to the new attitudes of people working in the organization. This is in sharp contrast to the top executive of a major corporation twenty years ago whose attention and decision-making was focused almost wholly on economic and technical considerations. The increased attention of top management time to social and political questions results, of course, in different allocations of time of lower-level managers than in the past. They, too, are spending more of their time on social and political issues and are being measured more and more on their performance in these areas.[37]

A Conference Board survey of 185 CEOs, published in 1976, showed that 103 of these executives were spending at least one-fourth of their time dealing with external matters and an additional seventy-two as much as half of their time (Table 6.6). Even more significant was the fact that 92 percent of these CEOs said they were spending more time on external relations than

[37] George A. Steiner, "An Overview of the Changing Business Environment and Its Impact on Business," paper presented at the AACSB Conference on Business Environment/Public Policy, Washington University, St. Louis, Summer 1979.

they were three to five years previous to the study (Table 6.7).[38] The author's own survey, completed in 1979, showed that the amount of time the CEOs spent on external matters ranged from 20–75 percent, with an average of 40 percent. The most frequently mentioned figure (mode) was 50 percent.[39] Another study completed by George Steiner in 1980, found that CEOs spent from 25–50 percent of their time on environmental matters, with a high of 80–90 percent on particular occasions. This was a major change from ten or twenty years ago when their predecessors spent very little, and in some instances, practically no time at all on external affairs.[40] Thus the importance of public policy to top management has increased dramatically in a relatively short period of time.

Table 6.6
How Much of the Chief Executive's Time
Is Spent on External Relations?

Percent of Time	Number of CEOs
0	0
1–25	103
26–50	72
51–75	6
76–100	0
Total	181*

*The total does not add up to the 185 chief executives polled. Two did not answer this question; one said the percent varies according to the occasion; one is too new in the job to estimate.

Source: Phyllis S. McGrath, *Managing Corporate External Relations: Changing Perspectives and Responses* (New York: The Conference Board, 1976), p. 49. Reprinted with permission.

The roles the CEO plays in the public policy arena, according to the Conference Board study, include (1) the personification of the company, (2) policy maker, and (3) everything to a limited degree. The chief executive officers see themselves as the principal external representatives of the company; their actions and words must at all times reflect the policies of the company. They must therefore speak before the largest and most important groups and handle the key contacts with all the various publics (top government officials, major stockholders, and so on).[41]

[38] Phyllis S. McGrath, *Managing Corporate External Relations: Changing Perspectives and Responses* (New York: The Conference Board, 1976), p . 49.

[39] Rogene A. Buchholz, *Business Environment/Public Policy: Corporate Executive Viewpoints and Educational Implications* (St. Louis: Washington University Center for the Study of American Business, 1980), p. 17.

[40] George A. Steiner, "The New Class of Chief Executive Officer," *Long Range Planning,* vol. 14, no. 4 (August 1981), p. 11.

[41] McGrath, *Managing External Relations,* p. 50.

Table 6.7
Is the Chief Executive Spending
More Time on External Relations Now
than Three to Five Years Ago?

	Number	Percent
More time	171	92
Less time	2	1
About the same	12	6

Source: Phyllis S. McGrath, *Managing Corporate External Relations: Changing Perspectives and Responses* (New York: The Conference Board, 1976), p. 49. Reprinted with permission.

As policy makers, the CEOs either initiate corporate policy on important public issues or provide the "broad thematic guidance" to policy and make the major decisions on critical public issues. The CEOs are also involved in everything else related to public policy, along with the expertise the company may have in public issues management. The CEO initiates policy, endorses external programs, sets the personal tone, and makes major public statements. The staff handles the normal day-to-day activities that can be accomplished under established policy and philosophy.[42]

The various publics to which the CEO relates, along with frequency of involvement, are shown in Table 6.8. Relations with government heads the list, which includes presenting company statements at congressional committee hearings and before regulatory agencies. Investor relations includes making presentations to major meetings of analyst societies as well as playing the leading part in the annual stockholder meeting. Membership on boards of trustees of colleges and universities and meeting with public interest group leaders are typical activities in the third category. Relations with the media is a very important role that CEOs are taking more and more seriously. Participation in associations like the Business Roundtable is a very important activity for many CEOs, given the impact such organizations can have on public policy. Finally, community involvement can include supporting charitable causes, commitment to youth projects, and involvement with other aspects of community life.[43]

The CEO is involved with many more aspects of the external environment than just the traditional ones of shareholders and customers. This amounts to a major behavioral change of the top management of a corporation. Many CEOs have become quite sophisticated in their understanding of the external environment, and through experience and hard work have managed to acquire many of the skills and attitudes necessary for handling exter-

[42] *Ibid.*
[43] *Ibid.*, pp. 51–52.

nal relations effectively. When supported by a well-organized public issues management staff that can spend time researching public issues and thinking through company responses, the CEO's effectiveness in the public policy arena can be greatly enhanced.

Table 6.8
The Role of the Chief Executive with the External Publics

Public	Number of Times Cited by 185 Chief Executives*
Government relations	124
Investor relations	74
Relations with special interest groups (consumers, customers, minorities, etc.)	52
Media relations	25
Business and professional associations membership	21
Community and civic affairs	20

*Figures are not totaled because many chief executives mentioned more than one role.
Source: Phyllis S. McGrath, *Managing Corporate External Relations: Changing Perspectives and Responses* (New York: The Conference Board, 1976), p. 51. Reprinted with permission.

Executive Liability   Another effect that public policy has had on top management is in the area of criminal liability for corporate acts of lawlessness and negligence. The traditional common law view of top management accountability shielded executives from unlawful acts of subordinates. Only when top management was directly involved in wrongdoing—actively participated in, consented to, or authorized the offending act—was there a possibility of incarceration.

But over the past several years, this special kind of limited liability has been diminished by statutory enactments regulating business activity, the definition of new statutory crimes, the imposition of new standards of personal conduct upon corporate managers, and the provision of civil and criminal penalties on both corporations and managers in case of violation.[44] Penalties for violations of antitrust laws were recently increased, for example, to a maximum of $100,000 for individuals and a three-year jail term. The Foreign Corrupt Practices Act carries with it stiff fines for making illegal foreign payments. The corporation can be fined $1 million, and officers and

[44] William A. Groening, *The Modern Corporate Manager: Responsibility and Regulation* (New York: McGraw-Hill, 1981), p. 18.

directors $10 thousand with the possibility of five years in jail. Considering the penalties associated with the newer forms of social regulation, the enforcement powers of the states, and the fact that many of the new laws allow private companies to file suit to collect damages, it can readily be seen that the potential for management involvement in litigation is substantial (Exhibit 6.1).

> Laws governing business activities have been increasing in volume and intensity as time progresses. While the first of those laws is now approaching its centennial, the rate of their enactment, the standards of responsibility, and the severity of the sanctions they impose have increased from decade to decade. The result is that today it is difficult to find any phase of business activity not subject to substantial regulation and exposure of the manager who deliberately or inadvertently fails to comply.[45]

Beginning in the late 1970s, Congress, state legislators, regulatory agencies, and the courts began to insist that top management accept personal responsibility for the actions of every individual within the organization. According to S. Prakash Sethi, this new view of liability covers health, safety, and environmental law violations involving general public welfare about which the executive may have no personal knowledge. As evidence of this trend, Sethi cites the following examples:

> The president of a Philadelphia-based supermarket chain, Acme Markets, Inc., was convicted in 1973 of violating the Federal Food and Drug Act and fined $250 after inspectors found evidence of rat infestation at a warehouse in Baltimore. The U.S. Supreme Court upheld his conviction in 1975. (United States v. John R. Park, 421 U.S. 658, 1975)

> Four managers of American Chicle and an executive of its parent company, Warner-Lambert, were charged with manslaughter and criminally negligent homicide after six workers were killed and 55 others injured in an explosion and fire at a Long Island City chewing gum plant in 1976. A New York State judge dismissed the case earlier this year, but the state intends to appeal.

> The manager of an H. J. Heinz Co. plant in Tracy, California, received a six-month suspended sentence and probation after being cited by California Food and Drug authorities for unsanitary working conditions in his plant.

> A Minneapolis municipal judge ordered Illinois-based Lloyd A. Fry Roffling Co. to select one of its executives to serve a 30-day jail term for

---

[45] *Ibid.*, p. 4.

EXHIBIT 6.1

The Risk Executives Face under Federal Law

Agency	Year Enforcement Began	Complaint May Name Individual	Maximum Individual Penalty	Maximum Corporate Penalty	Private Suit Allowed under Applicable Statute
Internal Revenue Service	1862	Yes	$5,000, three years, or both	$10,000, 50% assessment, prosecution costs	No
Antitrust Div. (Justice Dept.)	1890	Yes	$100,000, three years, or both	$1 million, injunction, divestiture	Yes
Food & Drug Administration	1907	Yes	$1,000, one year, or both for first offense; $10,000, three years, or both thereafter	$1,000 for first offense; $10,000 thereafter; seizure of condemned products	No
Federal Trade Commission	1914	Yes	Restitution, injunction	Restitution, injunction, divestiture, $10,000 per day for violation of rules, orders	No
Securities & Exchange Commission	1934	Yes	$10,000, two years, or both	$10,000, injunction	Yes

Agency	Year	Criminal prosecution	Fines / imprisonment	Civil penalties	
Equal Employment Opportunity Commission	1965	No		Injunction, back pay award, reinstatement	Yes
Office of Federal Contract Compliance	1965	No		Suspension, cancellation of contract	Yes
Environmental Protection Agency	1970	Yes	$25,000 per day, one year, or both for first offense; $50,000 per day, two years, or both thereafter	$25,000 per day, first offense; $50,000 per day thereafter; injunction	Yes
Occupational Safety & Health Administration	1970	No*	$10,000, six months, or both	$10,000	No
Consumer Product Safety Commission	1972	Yes	$50,000, one year, or both	$500,000	Yes
Office of Employee Benefits Security (Labor Dept.)	1975	Yes	$10,000, one year, or both; barring from future employment with plan; reimbursement	$100,000, reimbursement	Yes

*Except sole proprietorship
Date: BW

Reprinted from the May 10, 1976 issue of *Business Week* by special permission, © 1976 by McGraw-Hill, Inc.

the plant's violations of city air pollution standards. The sentence was rescinded because of a legal technicality.[46]

These and other examples lead Sethi to conclude that courts are rejecting the traditional view of executive liability and placing more and more blame at the top. "The new presumption is that a vigilant executive will make certain that subordinates are staying within the law. If those subordinates fail, it is proof that the executive was not properly vigilant. Thus, the executive's criminal liability accrues solely from the fact that he holds a responsible position in the corporation."[47]

At the heart of this trend to hold executives personally responsible for corporate law violations lies the problem of subjecting the corporate form of organization to effective social control. Decision making is widely diffused throughout the corporation making it difficult to fix individual responsibility for a particular violation. Many law violations are thus collective in nature, and people who contributed to the decision that resulted in a violation may have lacked the knowledge that they were violating the law or may have had no intent to do so. The trend to fix accountability to the top is an attempt to cope with this situation. Society is demanding that top executives be held responsible for the actions of their subordinates and the corporations they manage, and presumes that a vigilant executive will make certain subordinates are staying within the law. If subordinates violate the law, it is proof that the executive was not properly vigilant. The criminal liability of the executive flows solely from the fact that he or she holds a responsible position in the corporation. It is irrelevant whether the executive was directly involved in the illegal activity.[48]

The executive's favored status with respect to criminal penalties is thus changing. Tighter controls must be developed to ensure compliance with government regulations. Managers must be aware of the laws that apply to corporate behavior and must also be sure their subordinates will not unwittingly get them in trouble. This litigious potential demands more attention from top management and could result in the following effects on society and the economy.

An indiscriminate use of harsh penalties could, for instance, cause considerable damage to the social fabric by aggravating conflict between business and government. It also could adversely affect economic well-

[46] Reprinted with permission from "Who Me?: Jail As An Occupational Hazard," by S. Prakash Sethi, *The Wharton Magazine*, vol. 2, no. 4 (Summer 1978), pp. 19–20. Copyright © 1978 by the Trustees of the University of Pennsylvania.

[47] *Ibid.*, p. 22.

[48] S. Prakash Sethi, "The Expanding Scope of Executive Liability for Corporate Law Violations," in S. Prakash Sethi and Carl L. Swanson, *Private Enterprise and Public Purpose* (New York: John Wiley, 1981), pp. 267–68.

being by retarding corporate performance and economic growth. Increased personal liability may make executives more cautious about introducing new products and services into the marketplace. Indeed, there is some evidence already that increased regulatory requirements and the rapid increase in the volume of damage suits filed against corporations have led marketers to withhold new products. [49]

The federal criminal code was being rewritten a few years ago. One provision being considered of interest to management was the creation of a new kind of federal felony called "reckless endangerment." Under this concept, a company or executive who violates federal health or safety regulations so seriously that "he places another person in danger of imminent death or serious bodily injury" could be prosecuted. This provision would apply to such laws as the Federal Mine Safety and Health Act, the Food, Drug and Cosmetics Act, and the Occupational Safety and Health Act. Under a "reckless endangerment" prosecution, penalties would be much more severe than those imposed for being found in violation of the act itself. [50]

Thus the liability of top management for corporate law violations is changing because of the impact of public policy. Executives need to impose tighter controls on subordinates, provide for a reporting structure that may tell them where law violations have occurred, and even be prepared to spend a day or two in court. [51] The full implication of this trend is not yet apparent, but it certainly complicates the manager's task and exposes him or her to more public scrutiny.

THE PAPERWORK IMPACT   The cost of compliance with federal government regulations is a matter of increasing concern to business and industry. A highly visible aspect of the cost of compliance is the paperwork that regulation involves. The Federal Paperwork Commission, which was formed to study the paperwork cost for society as a whole, estimated that the paperwork costs imposed on private industry alone are approximately $25–$32 billion per year. The ten thousand largest firms are estimated to have spent $10–$12 billion on paperwork, or an average of more than $1 million each, [52] and to have filled out more than 10 billion sheets of paper a year. [53]

[49] Sethi, "Who Me?" p. 26.

[50] "A Threat To Crime-Code Reform," *Business Week*, January 28, 1980, pp. 106, 108.

[51] See "Preparing For A Day In Court," *Business Week*, March 30, 1981, pp. 144–47.

[52] U.S. Commission on Federal Paperwork, *Final Summary Report* (Washington, D.C., 1977), p. 5.

[53] Testimony of Thomas J. McIntyre, Cochairman, Commission on Federal Paperwork, before Senate Committee on Government Operations, May 3, 1976.

The amount of paperwork is, of course, directly related to the degree of government involvement in the economy. Prior to 1930, government imposed minimal paperwork burdens on business organizations. During the New Deal period and World War II, government intervention in the economy increased because of the need to finance the war effort and regulate the economy with price controls and rationing. Along with this increase in government intervention went an increase in paperwork. This increase continued with the advent of social regulation, jumping from $1.2 billion in 1950 to $30 billion in 1975.[54]

Types of Paperwork As the federal government establishes new agencies and programs, its requests for information from business and industry increase in number and in kind. These requests for information can be categorized according to the type of information they seek.

Statistical Information. Most of this information is requested by the Bureau of the Census, but the International Trade Commission, the Bureau of Labor Statistics, and the Bureau of Economic Analysis might also be involved. A typical report of this type is the Annual Survey of Manufacturers, a yearly summary of plant operations filed with the Bureau of the Census.

Financial Information. This type of information is requested primarily by the Federal Trade Commission (FTC) and the Securities and Exchange Commission (SEC). The new Line of Business Report, which was granted court approval despite a challenge by more than 200 companies, requires that specific financial data about a company's lines of business be reported. The FTC will use this information to determine whether some lines of business are anticompetitive. The SEC, among others, requires the Annual Report General Form, better known as the 10K.

Personnel and Benefits Information. Information about salaried and hourly pension plans now has to be supplied to the government because of the Employee Retirement Income Security Act. Often affirmative action plans have to be prepared and filed by companies having government contracts above a certain amount. Both types of information are requested by the Department of Labor. Annual statistics on the employment of minorities and women in various occupational categories are requested by the Equal Employment Opportunity Commission.

---

[54] National Archives and Records Service, General Services Administration, as reported in U.S. Commission on Federal Paperwork, "Study of Federal Paperwork Impact on Small and Large Businesses" (an internal draft prepared by the staff of the Commission of Federal Paperwork), July 1977, p. 10.

Environmental Information. What information is required will vary, of course, according to the industry. Most commonly, information about air pollution, water pollution, waste disposal, and drinking water usage will be required. If the company manufactures chemicals that government agencies consider to be toxic, it will be required to report on an ongoing basis detailed scientific data for all new chemicals that are developed. Agricultural chemicals are further regulated by the Federal Insecticide, Fungicide, and Rodenticide Act of 1972, which deals with the use, testing, and sale of pesticides. Numerous reports have to be filed for each product of this type the company makes. These include requests for a label, experimental-use permits, requests for new uses of an old chemical, and reports pertaining to plant shipments.

Safety and Health Information. Information about occupational injuries and illnesses is required by OSHA. While no forms have to be filed on a periodic basis with the government, records on the safety and health of the workforce must be maintained at each plant or workplace of a company.

Energy Information. Information about energy usage is required by the Department of Energy. Companies must disclose domestic natural gas reserves and domestic crude oil purchases, make energy conservation reports, and the like.

The Costs of Paperwork Complying with these requests entails costs to the company and to the economy as a whole. Not all the costs are immediately obvious and some of them, such as direct reporting costs, are astonishingly high, when compared with benefits a company can expect to receive from this reporting effort.

Direct Reporting Costs. This category includes the cost of employee time devoted to filling out reports, computer expense, the hiring of consultants, lawyers, accountants, or other professionals to prepare or review reports, and overhead costs including secretarial support, postage, rent, heat, light, supplies, and the like. Most of these costs are variable and depend on the frequency with which the report has to be completed and sent to a federal agency. They are also incremental.

Even though the information the government wants may already exist on some company report, numbers cannot simply be copied onto the federal forms. Information from many different company reports may have to be gathered to completely fill out a single federal form. Then , too, the information may have to aggregated or disaggregated. Finally, there may be some necessity for interpreting exactly what information is needed.

Start-Up Costs. Start-up costs begin with determining exactly what information is required by a federal agency. The explanation accompanying the information request may be vague and require some discussion, interpretation, or even travel to government offices.

The information requested may not be readily available on existing reports or computer files if it is different from the information the company normally requires for its own operations. A new system may have to be designed and installed to supply the information on an ongoing basis. People may have to be trained to fill out the forms and supply the right information.

Compliance with the Toxic Substances Control Act provides a recent example of a start-up cost. The act required the EPA to compile and publish an inventory of chemical substances manufactured, imported, or processed in the United States for commercial purposes. Any substance not on this list was considered a new chemical subject to premanufacture notification requirements. This inventory was compiled from inventories that manufacturers, importers, processors, or users of chemical substances were required to prepare and submit to the agency.

This inventory reporting was entirely a start-up cost to the company and could be expensive since it involved many professional people, such as chemists, in its preparation. A large chemical company estimated it spent $598,000 in 1977–78 to provide its inventory to the EPA.[55]

Avoidance Costs. Avoidance costs are expenses incurred in attempting to avoid disclosing information to the federal government. These could include the costs of lobbying efforts to support or oppose legislation introduced in Congress, attempts to change the ruling of an agency to avoid having to disclose certain types of information, legal counsel on some disclosure requirement, research into the implications and feasibility of an information request, or advertising and public relations involved in influencing public opinion. These avoidance costs are most often incurred when new areas of regulation or new reports are being considered. The legal expenses incurred in challenging the Line of Business Report and the Corporate Patterns Report mounted by over 200 corporations are good examples of avoidance costs.

Legal Exposure. As more and more information is requested by the federal government, the legal risk increases. Many of the forms filed with government agencies have to be signed by responsible corporate officals who are certifying the accuracy of the information. Honest mistakes or irresponsibility may involve the official and the corporation in litigation, the costs of which may be substantial. Such legal exposure is likely when information requirements are ambiguous or when subjective estimates are required.

---

[55] Reported in Rogene A. Buchholz, "Corporate Cost for Compliance with Government Regulation of Information," *Government Regulation of Accounting and Information*, A. Rashad Abdel-khalik, ed. (Gainesville, Fla.: University Presses of Florida, 1980).

Secondary Costs. These costs include such factors as the loss of productivity that may result from paperwork requirements, the increased construction costs resulting from inflation while the paperwork is completed on a new project, the investment disincentive that is involved in disclosing proprietary information on a new product to a government agency where it may be leaked to the company's competitors, and the negative effects on innovation that delays caused by paperwork might bring about. These costs, while extremely difficult to measure and quantify, may be the most serious of all and may be many times the total of all the other costs combined.

A Company Example The author completed a detailed study of the direct reporting costs incurred during the 1967 calendar year by a large chemical company headquartered in the United States. A summary of these costs, broken down by type of report, is shown in Table 6.9. Table 6.10 shows how much of the total cost went to satisfy the requirements of each government agency involved.

The total time required by this company to fill out federal forms came to 119,503 employee hours. If each employee works 1,880 hours per year, this total represents the equivalent of sixty-four full-time employees involved in fulfilling information requests from the federal government.

The total cost of approximately $3.5 million represented 0.07 percent of sales for that company in 1977, and 1 percent of profits—a cost of $45 per employee. If each of the top 200 companies spends $3.5 million, the cost of compliance is $700 million for these companies. This figure includes only the direct reporting costs incurred in complying with regulation by the federal government. The paperwork cost imposed by state and local governments was beyond the scope of the study.

The great majority of the direct reporting cost is in the new areas of regulation: safety and health, energy, equal opportunity, pension programs, and the environment. Table 6.11 shows that 92 percent of the total direct reporting cost was attributable to these areas. The costs of statistical and financial reporting are not a significant percentage of the total.

It is also clear that a significant amount of money is being spent to clean up the environment and control pollution problems. Fully 62.3 percent of the total paperwork cost for the company studied was attributable to information required by environmental regulations.

Table 6.9
Annual Paperwork Cost by Type of Information

Type of Report	Employee Hours	Annual Cost	Number of Reports	Cost per Report*	Percent of Total
Statistical	3,309	$ 99,270	59	$ 1,682	2.7
Financial	4,422	136,960	18	7,609	3.8
Personnel and Benefits	5,269	158,070	13	12,159	4.4
Environmental	36,800	1,104,000	15	73,600	30.9
Safety and Health	18,800	564,000	—	—	15.7
Energy	11,492	344,760	40	8,619	9.6
Agricultural Chemicals	37,600	1,128,000	—	—	31.4
Miscellaneous	1,811	54,330	7	7,761	1.5
Totals	119,503	$3,589,390	152	$111,430	100.0

*This cost is determined per individual report, no matter how often it is filed.

Source: Rogene A Buchholz, "Corporate Cost for Compliance with Government Regulation of Information," *Government Regulation of Accounting and Information*, A. Rashad Abdel-khalik, ed. (Gainesville, Fla.: University Presses of Florida, 1980), p. 34. Reprinted with permission.

Table 6.10
Annual Cost of Reports Filed with Federal Government Agencies

	Cost	Percent of Total
Department of Agriculture	$ 720	—
Department of Commerce		
Bureau of the Census	47,250	1.3
Bureau of Economic Analysis	9,960	0.3
Office of Export Administration	1,140	—
Department of the Interior		
Bureau of Mines	5,040	0.2
Geological Survey	30,960	0.9
Other	1,320	—
Department of Labor		
Bureau of Labor Statistics	12,270	0.4
Occupational Safety and		
Health Administration*	564,000	15.7
Other	132,420	3.7
Department of Energy	315,120	8.8
Department of the Treasury		
Bureau of Alcohol, Tobacco and Firearms	42,180	1.2
Federal Reserve Bank	1,410	—
Internal Revenue Service	17,100	0.5
Other	1,200	—
Cost Accounting Standards Board	750	—
Environmental Protection Agency	2,232,000	62.2
Equal Employment Opportunity Commission	25,650	0.7
Federal Trade Commission	44,050	1.2
General Services Administration	450	—
International Trade Commission	20,250	0.6
Renegotiation Board	11,700	0.3
Securities and Exchange Commission	72,450	2.0
Totals	$3,589,390	100.0

*OSHA complies with government regulations by maintaining records rather than by filing reports. The cost of maintaining these records appears here.

Source: Rogene A. Buchholz, "Corporate Cost for Compliance with Government Regulation of Information," *Government Regulation of Accounting and Information,* A. Rashad Abdel-khalik, ed. (Gainesville, Fla.: University Presses of Florida, 1980), p. 35. Reprinted with permission.

Table 6.11
Percent of Direct Reporting Cost Attributable
to New Areas of Regulation*

Safety and Health	15.7
Energy	9.6
Equal Opportunity	2.0
Pensions	2.4
Environmental	62.3
	92.0

*Statistical and financial reporting account for the remaining 8 percent.
Source: Rogene A. Buchholz, "Reducing the Cost of Paperwork," *Business Horizons*, Vol. 23, No. 1 (February 1980), p. 87. Reprinted with permission.

SELECTED REFERENCES

BROWN, JAMES K. *This Business of Issues: Coping with the Company's Environments.* New York: The Conference Board, 1979.

BUCHHOLZ, ROGENE A. *Business Environment/Public Policy: Corporate Executive Viewpoints and Educational Implications.* St. Louis, Mo.: Washington University Center for the Study of American Business, 1980.

GOLDSHMID, HARVEY J., ED. *Business Disclosure: Government's Need to Know.* New York: McGraw-Hill, 1979.

GROENING, WILLIAM A. *The Modern Corporate Manager: Responsibility and Regulation.* New York: McGraw-Hill, 1981.

MCGRATH, PHYLLIS. *Managing Corporate External Relations: Changing Perspectives and Responses.* New York: The Conference Board, 1976.

————. *Refining Corporate-Federal Relations.* New York: The Conference Board, 1979.

WEIDENBAUM, MURRAY L. *Business, Government, and the Public.* Englewood Cliffs, N.J.: Prentice-Hall, 1977.

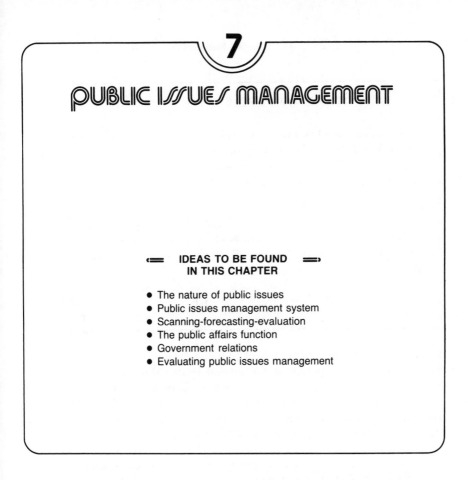

7

PUBLIC ISSUES MANAGEMENT

⟸ **IDEAS TO BE FOUND** ⟹
IN THIS CHAPTER

- The nature of public issues
- Public issues management system
- Scanning-forecasting-evaluation
- The public affairs function
- Government relations
- Evaluating public issues management

The previous chapter described in some detail the significant impacts that public policy has made on business and management. Public policies can cost substantial amounts of money, wipe out product lines overnight because of safety and health problems or involve the corporation in lengthy litigation. Thus the corporation's response to public policy should be a well thought-out and developed strategy based on research and analysis of the problems facing the company. Such a response is likely to work in the company's best interest as well as in the interests of society as a whole.

The concept of public issues management has developed to refer to an organized and intelligent effort on the part of a corporation to respond effectively to issues of public concern. A strategy is developed for the corporation's involvement in regard to a specific public issue that affects the company. The concept implies that corporations take a responsibility to become involved with public issues and develop policies on these issues in a manner comparable to the way policy is developed on traditional business concerns.

There are many elements in public issues management; not all of these elements are necessarily new in themselves. For example, public affairs,

---

DEFINITIONS OF PUBLIC ISSUES MANAGEMENT

Issues management is a program which a company uses to increase its knowledge of the public policy process and enhance the sophistication and effectiveness of its involvement in that process.

From *The Fundamentals of Issue Management* (Washington, D.C.: Public Affairs Council, 1978), p.1.

Issues management is the process by which the corporation can identify and evaluate those governmental and societal issues that may impact significantly on it. The issues can then be assigned priorities for appropriate corporate response.

From Richard A. Armstrong, "The Concept and Practice of Issues Management in the United States," Speech delivered to the National Convention, Public Relations Institute of Australia, Sydney, Australia, July 17, 1981.

---

which is an essential component of public issues management, has been a function in most corporations for several years. Many corporations, particularly the largest, have had Washington offices for the past decade that have been involved in the political process in some manner. What makes public issues management new, according to Richard A. Armstrong, President of the Public Affairs Council, is the following:

> What *is* new—is a new corporate attitude, or "mindset" which guides the Issues Management program.
>
> What *is* new—is the extent of the corporate commitment in time and people to external issues and public affairs.
>
> What *is* new—is the concept that the external relations of a company is not a function to be delegated to a staff of specialists and then quietly forgotten.
>
> What *is* new—is the awareness of the need to expand the time frame in the corporation's early warning mechanism. Most companies today try to look ahead at least three years.
>
> What *is* new—is more capable and sophisticated research personnel. A host of new titles have appeared on the scene: Director, Public Affairs Research and Planning; Public Affairs Research Analyst; Policy Analyst; Director, Public Policy Planning; Government Research Coordinator, and many more.
>
> What *is* new—is the broadened arena for action. Corporate efforts today cannot simply be focused on the legislative process, rather they must try to reach the public and those interest groups mentioned earlier.
>
> Finally, *not only new but so refreshing*—business has decided to take

the offense rather than simply defending itself. (Academics would call this being pro-active rather than reactive.) When a company can actually get involved in the policy-making process *before* the issues have become politically polarized, it can sometimes defuse them, or at least minimize their impact.[1]

The word *proactive* is a new buzzword used to describe an overall response pattern to public issues. There are four major response patterns to public issues (Exhibit 7.1) of which proactive is one of the newest, as Armstrong mentions. In the *reactive* response pattern, business is not actively concerned with public issues and opposes any change that public policy would make in corporate operations, much as business did in the late 1960s with respect to consumer legislation. As no attempt is made to anticipate public issues, business can only react, often in a not very constructive manner.

EXHIBIT 7.1
Corporate Responses to Public Issues

Reactive	Accommodative	Proactive	Interactive
Fighting Change	Adapting to Change	Influencing Change	Adjusting to and Influencing Change

The *accommodative* response means that business simply adapts to the changes involved with a public policy measure as well as possible and attempts to get on with its main line of business. The company makes no attempt to fight or influence change in any manner and again does not set up any kind of a mechanism to anticipate change. The concerns expressed in legislation and regulation are accepted as legitimate and are accommodated with the appropriate operational and organizational changes.

In the *proactive* response, business develops some kind of a mechanism to anticipate those public issues which will affect the corporation most significantly. Rather than fighting change or simply accommodating to the changes a public issue may involve, a corporation attempts to influence change by changing the environment in which issues arise and are discussed. The goal of a proactive strategy is to prevent change from becoming neces-

---

[1] Richard A. Armstrong, "The Concept and Practice of Issues Management in the United States," speech delivered to the National Convention, Public Relations Institute of Australia, Sydney, Australia, July 17, 1981.

sary, if possible, or at least to minimize the effects of a particular public issue on the corporation.

In the *interactive* response pattern, the corporation recognizes the legitimacy of public policy as a process through which public expectations are expressed and the fact that business and society are related to each other complexly. This complexity involves the use of different strategies by the corporation to adjust to changing public expectations. As stated by James Post, a professor at Boston University: "Sometimes action is taken to influence public opinion; at other times, to change corporate behavior. The two prerequisites for successfully using the interactive approach are a management commitment to anticipating external change and a willingness to adjust the corporation's normal operations to minimize the gap between performance and expectations. When consistently applied over time, an interactive approach tends to produce goals that the company and the public can accept."[2]

These latter two response patterns need to be further differentiated. The proactive and interactive corporation attempts to develop a reasonably accurate agenda of public issues with which it should be concerned, analyzes these issues for impacts, and develops a constructive response. The difference between these two response patterns is that in the proactive approach the corporation focuses its initial efforts on the external environment to try to prevent change, and only engages in internal changes if this effort fails. In the interactive approach, the corporation strikes more of a balance between its involvement in the public policy arena and changes in its own operation and organization.

The importance of public issues management to corporations is shown in Table 7.1, which reports the results of a survey of top practitioners in the field. The data show that 73.8 percent of the respondents believe public issues management is either very important or extremely important in their organization. The reasons for the importance they attach to public issues management is perhaps even more revealing (see box). Some business leaders and academics believe that the very survival of business and the business system is at stake and that business must develop better and more constructive responses to public issues than it has in the past or be faced with a further loss of credibility.

> In a world of uncertainties, where change is the one thing we can count on, businesses need the ability to anticipate and adapt successfully to change in both matters of public policy and their own market pursuits. Through a better understanding of public-policy genesis and development, organizations should be able to foresee public-policy changes and be responsive to them. Such an approach enables change—that is the

---

[2] James E. Post, "Public Affairs and Management Policy in the 1980s," *Public Affairs Review*, vol. I (1980), p. 8.

Table 7.1
Importance of Public Issues Management

Opinion	Number of Respondents	Percent
Extremely important	10	23.8
Very important	21	50.0
Somewhat important	9	21.4
Not very important	2	4.8
Not important at all	0	—
	42	100.0

Source: Rogene A Buchholz, "Education for Public Issues Management: Key Insights from a Survey of Top Practitioners," *Public Affairs Review*, Vol. III (1982), p. 68.

key concept, change—to be accommodated with minimal disruption.[3] The modern frontiers of professional management—corporate planning and external affairs—are those areas in which change is occurring most rapidly, where the least is known, where the most speculation occurs and where the opportunities for imaginative executive leadership are greatest . . . The manner in which organizations of all types, and large business corporations in particular, respond to commercial and social complexity is fundamental to their institutional legitimacy and their survival.[4]

According to David L. Shanks, Director of Corporate Public Relations and Advertising at Rexnard Corporation, proper management of public issues has many benefits, both protective and opportunistic. Public issues management (1) allows management to select issues that will have the greatest impact on the corporation, (2) allows "management of" instead of "reaction to" issues, (3) inserts relevant issues into the strategic planning process, (4) gives the company ability to act in tune with society, (5) provides opportunities for leadership roles, and (6) protects the credibility of business in the public mind.[5] Table 7.2 shows the ranking that top practitioners gave to these purposes in a recent survey. Rather than having to respond in knee-jerk fashion to issues that are already well formulated, a public issues management system provides the capability to anticipate issues and develop responses that are more likely to be consistent with the company's and society's best interests.

[3] Graham Molitor, "How to Anticipate Public-Policy Changes," *S.A.M. Advanced Management Journal*, Summer 1977, p. 4.

[4] James E. Post, "The Challenge of Managing Under Social Uncertainty," *Business Horizons*, August, 1977, pp. 51–52.

[5] James K. Brown, *This Business of Issues: Coping with the Company's Environments* (New York: The Conference Board, 1979), p. 72.

IMPORTANCE OF PUBLIC ISSUES MANAGEMENT

"In large part, the outcome of these issues determines the company's future operating environment."

"They (public issues) affect the corporation's public image, and, ultimately, the bottom line of the company."

"Ours is a high-visibility company strongly affected by public policy issues. The stakes are getting higher while the room to maneuver is getting smaller."

"In the short term, issues management has a significant bottom-line impact. In the long-run, the continued profitability and operability of the corporation depends on the public environment."

"Many public issues can have direct impacts on the company, its employees, and its stockholders, and these issues must be discussed."

"Corporate success and survival depend increasingly on sensitivity to changes in the environment in which the company does business."

"It (public issues management) allows us to deal with problems before they become crises and permits us to spot opportunities."

"Public issues have a profound impact on the manner in which a corporation conducts its business. Effective anticipation and response will determine the ultimate structure of our economic system and the role of the corporation."

"As our former chairman said, the success or failure of American business is more and more determined by governmental policy and actions."

"Management's view determines the importance, in one sense, of a function to the corporation, and such importance is relative to other management concerns."

From: Rogene A. Buchholz, "Education for Public Issues Management: Key Insights from a Survey of Top Practitioners," *Public Affairs Review*, Vol. III (1982), pp. 68-69.

THE NATURE OF PUBLIC ISSUES

The concept of public issues management implies that a public issue is distinct from an issue that arises out of a more private traditional business function. Public issues affect many people, not just one or a few, and they cannot be acted on individually. They work their way into the public policy process because of their extensive impacts and collective nature which requires society to develop a common course of action to deal with the issue. From a business point of view, a public issue can be defined as a public policy question which affects business corpora-

Table 7.2
**Important Purposes of a Public Issues Management System
(Ranked from Most Important to Least Important:
1 = Most Important, 5 = Least Important)**

Purpose	Rank Score
Allows "management of" vs. "reaction to" public issues	1.9
Allows management to select issues that will have the greatest impact on the corporation	2.5
Inserts relevant issues into the strategic planning process	2.7
Gives the company ability to act in tune with society	3.6
Protects the credibility of business in the public mind	4.3
Provides opportunities for leadership roles	4.8

Source: Rogene A. Buchholz, "Education for Public Issues Management: Key Insights from a Survey of Top Practitioners," *Public Affairs Review*, Vol. III (1982), p. 70.

tions so that business has a legitimate right to help in developing a common course of action.

Public issues can be categorized according to type, referring to the extensiveness and manner in which business is affected (Exhibit 7.2). An *operational* issue, for example, may affect one or more, but not all, units of the corporation. The issue may affect only manufacturing or marketing, or may affect only certain geographic regions. A *corporate* issue affects the corporation as a whole and can affect the way in which the entire entity functions. Issues such as corporate governance or public disclosure of information are of this nature. Finally, a *societal* issue affects the environment in which business functions. Such issues as national economic planning and regulatory reform fall in this category.

Another way to categorize public issues is according to timing. A *current* issue is presently being debated or otherwise acted on in local, state, or federal government institutions. An *emerging* issue is a public policy question with three essential characteristics: (1) its definition and contending positions are still evolving, (2) it is likely to be the subject of government action in the next three to five years, and (3) it can be acted on by affected corporations.[6] Finally, a *strategic* issue is important in the long-range planning cycle of the corporation, as such an issue concerns the future role of the corporation in society.[7]

The notion of a time frame for issues suggests that public issues have a life cycle—they go through a series of stages as they evolve. Four such stages

[6] *The Fundamentals of Issue Management* (Washington, D.C.: Public Affairs Council, 1978), p. 3.

[7] Fran Steckmest, "Some Definitions and Examples of Public Policy Issues," presented at the Public Affairs Council Workshop, Washington, D.C., May 16–17, 1978.

EXHIBIT 7.2
Example of the Three Types of Emerging Issues

I. Operational
    A. Hazardous Waste Disposal
    B. Acid Rain
    C. Water Shortages
    D. Traffic Congestion in a Plant Area
II. Corporate
    A. Federal Chartering
    B. Corporate Governance
    C. Corporate Public Disclosure
    D. Legal and Ethical Behavior
III. Societal
    A. Political/Governmental Issues
        1. Congressional Reform
        2. National Economic Planning
        3. Election Campaign Financing Reform
        4. Openness in Government
        5. Reform of the Initiative Process
        6. Regulatory Reform
    B. Personal Rights and Entitlements
        1. Personal Privacy
        2. Sexual Preference
        3. Right to a Job
        4. Comparable Worth
        5. Health Care
        6. Freedom from Risk
        7. Restitution for Losses

Adapted from F.W. Steckmest, "Some Definitions and Examples of Public Policy Issues," presented at the Public Affairs Council Workshop, Washington, D.C., May 16–17, 1978. Reprinted with permission.

have been identified.[8] The life cycle begins with *changing public expectations* that create a gap between corporate performance and what the public expects from its institutions. The seeds of a new public issue are sown when the gap becomes wide enough to affect significant numbers of people and cause extensive dissatisfaction with corporate performance.

As these new expectations enter the second stage in the life cycle, they become widely discussed in the media, become a concern for interest group discussion, and are sometimes introduced into the formal public policy process by some politicians. Thus the issue becomes a *political controversy* and is placed on the public policy agenda where it will be the subject of some kind of action.

The issue next enters the third stage, which involves the *development*

[8] James E. Post, *Corporate Behavior and Social Change* (Reston, Virginia: Reston, 1978), pp. 22–25.

of legislation dealing with the issue and its implementation. The rules of the game for business are being changed in this phase with the formal enactment of legislative and regulatory requirements. New legislation and regulations may require considerable debate and bargaining and even be the subject of court rulings. But at this stage, the issue has become institutionalized as society has changed the contract between business and society and expressed its expectations in formal legislation and regulation.

The last stage, which has been called the *government litigation* phase, is one of implementing the new rules of the game. During this period, there may be many negotiations between government and business regarding enforcement standards and timetables for meeting the new requirements. If government agencies do not believe business is successfully meeting the new rules and negotiations break down, the agencies may file suit in court to force compliance. In this stage, the adversarial relationship between business and government is most pronounced, and the opportunities for cooperation to meet public expectations severely limited.

Exhibit 7.3 shows the movement of three public issues areas through these four stages. The concept of a life cycle for public issues is important because different corporate strategies are called for at different stages. The options that are open to business for some kind of a response to the issue are different at each stage. It therefore becomes necessary for corporations to concern themselves with "goodness of fit" between the life cycle of a public issue and the response of a corporation. The development of an appropriate strategy that takes this life cycle into account is the purpose of a public issues management system.

PUBLIC ISSUES MANAGEMENT SYSTEM

The management of public issues involves a series of stages or steps that, taken together, constitute a public issues management system. Exhibit 7.4 shows the various stages of a typical public issues management system.

The first stage is one of identifying those trends and issues that are likely to affect the corporation through the public policy process. These trends and issues must be continually monitored or tracked for new developments. Forecasts must be developed to predict their probable course over the next several years. From this information, an initial screening can be made to identify those issues of greatest interest to the corporation because of their short- and long-term impacts. The purpose of this stage is to identify issues that will affect the corporation as early in their life cycle as possible.

Once issues have been identified, their potential impact on the corporation must be evaluated more thoroughly. The reason for this evaluation is to set some priorities for corporate responses. The typical corporation cannot respond to every public issue of interest—it probably does not have the resources—nor can it respond to every issue with the same level of involve-

EXHIBIT 7.3
Public Issues Life Cycle

	Phase I	Phase II	Phase III	Phase IV
	Changing Public Expectations→	Political Controversy→	Development of Legislation→	Government Litigation
Examples				
Civil Rights	1954-60	1960 (presidential campaign issue)	1964 (Civil Rights Act)	1970s (EEOC litigation backlog)
Environmental Protection	1963 (Rachel Carson *Silent Spring*)	1967 (campaign issue; political "sides" developing)	1970 (EPA established)	1970s (Tighter standards; negotiated or court-ordered settlements; nearly 300 cases in Federal courts)
Consumer Protection	1964 (Ralph Nader, *Unsafe at Any Speed*)	1968 (Presidential Consumer Affairs Advisor; proposed legislation)	1972 (Consumer Product Safety Act)	

Source: James E. Post, *Corporate Behavior and Social Change*, 1978, p. 26. Reprinted with permission of Reston Publishing Company, a Prentice-Hall Co., 11480 Sunset Hills Road, Reston, VA 22090.

ment or effort. Priorities must be set according to the potential impact of the issue on the corporation, the issue's probability of occurrence or the corporation's ability to respond. The outcome of this stage is a list of issues with priorities attached.

The next stage involves basic analysis and research on issues of highest priority. For this task, involvement of a public affairs staff devoted to public issues research is important. Involvement of functional areas—such as manufacturing when environmental issues are concerned or personnel when the issue is minority hiring—is also crucial. Outside sources can also be used at this stage, particularly consulting organizations, academia, or research centers such as the American Enterprise Institute for Public Policy Research or the Center for the Study of American Business.

At this stage, the corporation must do its homework and perform

EXHIBIT 7.4
Public Issues Management System

I. Identifying Public Issues and Trends in Public Expectations
   A. Scanning the environment for trends and issues
   B. Tracking trends and issues that are developing
   C. Developing forecasts of trends and issues
   D. Identifying those of interest to the corporation
II. Evaluating Their Impact and Setting Priorities
   A. Assessment of impact and probability of occurrence
   B. Assessment of corporate resources and ability to respond
   C. Preparation of issue priorities for further analysis
III. Research and Analysis
   A. Categorization of issues along relevant dimensions
   B. Ensuring that priority issues receive staff coverage
   C. Involving functional areas where appropriate
   D. Using outside sources of information
   E. Development and analysis of position options
IV. Strategy Development
   A. Analysis of position and strategy options
   B. Management decision on position and strategy
   C. Integration with overall business strategy
V. Implementation
   A. Dissemination of agreed-upon position and strategy
   B. Development of tactics consistent with the overall strategy
   C. Development of alliances with external organizations
   D. Linkage with internal and external communication networks
VI. Evaluation
   A. Assessment of results by staff
   B. Management evaluation
   C. Modification of implementation plans
   D. Additional research

Adapted from Donald J. Watson, "The Changing Political Environment of Business," paper presented at the Conference on Business and Its Changing Environment, UCLA, July 31, 1978; *The Fundamentals of Issue Management*, p. 2; and Ian Wilson, "Characteristics of Futures Research," material prepared for Conference on Business Environment and Public Policy, Washington University Center for the Study of American Business, July 8-13, 1979.

quality research on public issues comparable to the kind of effort devoted to technological issues in research and development laboratories. The development of a good priorities list is essential, as a corporation cannot do a thorough job of research and analysis on every public issue that is identified. Issues must be categorized as to whether they are operational, corporate or societal, current, emerging or strategic, and what stage of their life cycle they are passing through. This analysis is useful in deciding what to do about an issue, because the intent of this stage is not only to more thoroughly analyze the potential impact an issue can make on a corporation, but also to analyze the different positions and strategies that can be taken on the issue. The result is an analysis of the dimensions of an issue, including the pros and cons of different positions and strategies.

Emerging from this research and analysis phase is the development of different options that can be taken on an issue along with a recommended position that can be presented to management for consideration. The recommended position must reflect the best thinking of the corporation and be based on solid research rather than a hastily put-together reaction that will most likely not work in the corporation's best interests. Management must eventually decide to go along with the recommendation or adopt one of the other options.

Once this decision is made, strategy must be determined. Management must decide whether the position chosen calls for modification of corporate behavior to close the gap between public expectations and corporate performance, whether an attempt should be made to influence the environment by changing public expectations or legislation, or whether a mixture of both strategies should be attempted. The company can choose to lead public expectations, attempt to close the gap and meet but not exceed them, or lag behind public expectations and allow a gap between expectations and performance to continue. Figure 7.1 shows that management has a zone of discretion with respect to an issue throughout a good part of its life-cycle.

The choice of an overall strategy must then be disseminated to the appropriate people in the company who are responsible for implementation. They must develop specific tactics for changing corporate behavior, influencing public opinion, changing the thinking of public policy makers, developing a court case—whatever tactics are consistent with the strategy chosen. If other parties, such as a trade association, are involved, alliances must be built during this stage and action taken. Lobbying tactics must be developed and carried out if attempts at legislative influence are appropriate.

Linkages with internal and external communications networks must be developed as needed. For example, if grass-roots lobbying is called for, this must be communicated to the grass-roots network for it to be activated. If a change is appropriate in the way a company produces a product to reduce ecological damage, this must be communicated to the plant personnel who are in a position to make the necessary changes. External communications involves informing the public about what the company is doing to meet public expectations or engaging in a debate about the issue itself.

Finally comes the all-important stage of evaluation. Some kind of evaluation system must be developed to determine whether the public issues management effort is a success. This evaluation is extremely difficult. How much credit, for example, can any single corporate effort be given for the defeat of a bill in Congress? Or, if the bill passed when the objective was to defeat it, was this the fault of a single corporate lobbying effort? How can

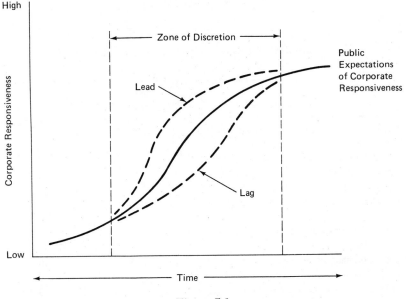

High

Corporate Responsiveness

Low

← Zone of Discretion →

Lead

Lag

Public
Expectations
of Corporate
Responsiveness

← Time →

Figure 7.1
Patterns of Corporate Responsiveness

From Robert W. Ackerman and Raymond A. Bauer, *Corporate Social Responsiveness: The Modern Dilemma*, 1976, p. 39. Reprinted with permission of Reston Publishing Co., a Prentice-Hall Co., 11480 Sunset Hills Rd., Reston, Va. 22090.

changes in public opinion be measured and attributed to a specific advocacy advertising program? What is the impact of a corporate economic education program?

These are very complex questions, and yet without some kind of evaluation by both the staff involved in public issues management and management itself, one is operating in the dark. The process of evaluation is important because the implementation tactics may have to be modified or additional research performed to develop different positions.

All through this public issues management system there are a number of key decisions that have to be made. Figure 7.2 shows these decisions in the form of a flow chart. The actual decisions and outputs of each stage are shown in the boxes. This exhibit shows the "flow" of an issue through the public issues management system.

According to a survey of public issues management practitioners completed in 1981, there have been significant improvements at almost every stage of this public issues management process over the last three years. Table 7.3 shows that 50–70 percent of the respondents believe there have been significant improvements in capability in the first five components. The relatively low percentage on the evaluation component is undoubtedly due to the difficulty of evaluating the results of the public issues management effort, a subject that will be discussed more thoroughly later in the chapter.

Table 7.3
Significant Improvements in Capability
(N = 42)

Area of Improvement	Number of Respondents	Percent
Evaluating the impact of public issues on the corporation and setting priorities.	29	69.0
Development of a strategy to respond to public issues of concern to the company.	27	64.3
Research and analysis of public issues identified as being important to the corporation.	25	59.5
Identifying public issues and trends in public expectations.	23	54.8
Implementation of strategy wih respect to public issues.	21	50.0
Evaluation of the response to a public issue.	14	33.3
Other areas	10	23.8

Source: Rogene A. Buchholz, "Education for Public Issues Management: Key Insights from a Survey of Top Practitioners," *Public Affairs Review*, Vol. III (1982), p. 69.

SCANNING–FORECASTING–EVALUATION   One of the most important elements in successful public issues management is the development of an ability to identify those public issues in the environment that will have an impact on the corporation. The earlier an issue can be identified in its life cycle, the more options business has open to it and the better chance business has to develop an effective response.

Early identification of issues can enable a corporation to be more interactive in helping to formulate public policy and change its performance, rather than being reactive (opposing every new piece of legislation or public demand), or accommodative (simply adapting itself to whatever legislation and regulation eventuates). The modern corporation must consider all factors in the environment that impinge on its operations, not just the more traditional economic and technological factors.

The need for early identification of social and political factors has become a must for many companies. Some have been confronted with a number of embarrassing situations that could have been avoided with a little forethought. Ignoring social and political trends has cost other companies a great deal of money because they have been forced to respond to public pressure or burdensome government regulation. In some cases, the very survival of the company may be at stake.

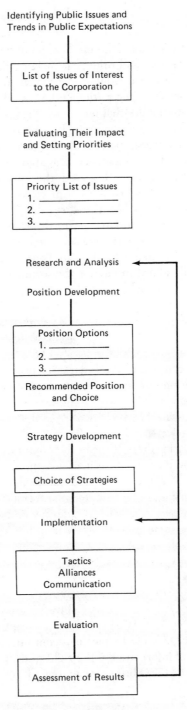

Identifying Public Issues and
Trends in Public Expectations

List of Issues of Interest
to the Corporation

Evaluating Their Impact
and Setting Priorities

Priority List of Issues
1. _____
2. _____
3. _____

Research and Analysis

Position Development

Position Options
1. _____
2. _____
3. _____

Recommended Position
and Choice

Strategy Development

Choice of Strategies

Implementation

Tactics
Alliances
Communication

Evaluation

Assessment of Results

Figure 7.2

Flow-Chart of Public Issues Management

Source: Rogene A. Buchholz, *Business Environment and Public Policy: Implications for Management.*
© 1982, p. 472. Reprinted by permission of Prentice-Hall, Inc., Englewood Cliffs, NJ.

In the late 1960s, after the publication of Ralph Nader's *Unsafe at any Speed*, General Motors and other car makers did not realize that Nader's concerns about the Corvair would set the stage for a wide-ranging consumer movement. Car buyers began demanding, and forcing manufacturers to produce, safer automobiles that met more stringent liability standards. Auto makers also failed to take action urged by environmental groups until legislation was passed mandating pollution controls in cars. By waiting until they were required to act, car manufacturers spent more to retool their plants than they would had they designed the plants with antipollution-gear capability in the first place. In another more recent example of a corporation responding to negative public pressure, the Nestle Company had to deal with a boycott of Nestle products worldwide as a result of public outrage against an infant-formula marketing scheme launched by the company. Nestle had promoted its infant formula to Third-World countries whose residents could hardly afford to pay for the formula, especially when mother's milk was readily available.[9]

Environmental Scanning　　　The first step in identifying issues is one of scanning the environment to look for developing issues that may affect the corporation. The process of scanning can be compared to a radar scan used in presenting the weather report in a television newscast. The purpose of the radar scan is to discover storms that may affect a given area sometime in the near future. The purpose of environmental scanning is to discover issues that may affect a given corporation in the near future.

There are various ways to scan the environment to discover important public issues. One method of categorizing the sources of information in the scanning process for the social and political environments is shown in Exhibit 7.5. According to this scheme, sources are categorized as internal or external, then as personal or impersonal within each of these categories. "Internal sources" refers to those within the corporation and "external sources" refers to those outside the organization. "Personal sources" means the use of people as sources, while "impersonal sources" refers to the use of reports or studies.

The chief executive officer is an obvious source of environmental information, especially if he or she is politically involved and is aware of the current political scene in Washington or at the state level. Because of time pressures, the CEO cannot be part of a continual scanning process, but can be a good source of information if the right questions are asked when time is available. When the CEO brings up an issue, it is very likely to be of concern to the company.

The board of directors is another good source of information, especially

---

[9] Adapted from "Capitalizing on Social Change," *Business Week*, October 29, 1979, p. 105.

EXHIBIT 7.5
Sources of Scanning Information

I. External
  A. Personal
   1. Consultants (Washington).
   2. Conferences (Public Affairs Council, trade associations, professional and scientific meetings, etc.).
   3. Executives and managers in other companies.
   4. Government officials (Congressmen and regulators).
   5. Representatives of public interest organizations.
  B. Impersonal
   1. Reports from trade associations.
   2. Government publications (Congressional Record, Federal Register).
   3. Newspapers and magazines.
   4. Trade and technical journals (Food and Chemical News) and books.
   5. Special consulting and reporting services.
   6. Publications of public interest organizations.
II. Internal
  A. Personal
   1. Chief executive officer.
   2. Board of directors.
   3. Washington office.
   4. Other executives and managers.
   5. Staff specialists.
  B. Impersonal
   1. Management reports and memoranda.
   2. Accounting reports.
   3. Planning reports and budgets.

Adapted from Francis J. Aguilar, *Scanning the Business Environment* (New York: Macmillan, 1967), p. 66. Copyright by The Trustees of Columbia University in the City of New York. Reprinted with permission.

when there is a public responsibility committee whose job is to be concerned about such matters. Information about the political environment, such as legislation or regulation being considered, ought to be readily available from a corporation's Washington office. Other executives and managers are also good sources of information. They can be polled directly or asked to be part of a more sophisticated process such as a Delphi exercise. Finally, staff specialists who are involved in regulatory areas can supply information about their particular area of concern.

Impersonal internal sources include management reports and memoranda that may deal with issues in the political and social environments, accounting reports that show how resources are being allocated, and planning reports and budgets that show how much money is going to be spent on an area of concern, such as pollution control. Such economic reports should be an indicator of the importance of that issue to the future of the company as assessed by those who put the budget together.

Outside consultants are very useful external personal sources of information about emerging social and political issues. These outside consultants frequently conduct research for the company to measure the effectiveness of a particular program in dealing with an issue of concern.

Conferences are a good place to pick up environmental information. Many corporate executives can be found attending conferences such as the Annual Meeting of the Academy of Management. Executives and managers of other companies may be good sources of information as are government officials in various positions. The information from these sources must be screened carefully, however, as it is more likely to be biased than information from other sources. Finally, representatives of public interest groups can be consulted on their current concerns, which they often are willing to express quite readily.

Impersonal external sources include reports from the general business and trade associations, such as the Business Roundtable, which publishes studies analyzing various aspects of the environment. Government publications are an obvious source of scanning information, particularly congressional hearings on such subjects as corporate governance or antitrust reform. The Federal Register contains regulations that affect business, both regulations being proposed and those issued in final form. Finally, the census reports contain demographic information about population trends.

Newspapers and magazines are another important source of information. Some companies and industries have a rather elaborate system for monitoring these sources. The American Council of Life Insurance, for example, has a Trend Analysis Program that depends on the efforts of over 100 volunteer monitors who work for member companies. These volunteers regularly scan one or more publications from a list of close to 100 publications, and abstract any article in their assigned area that meets the following criteria: (1) the article involves an event or an idea that is indicative of either a trend or discontinuity in the environment, and (2) it contains implications for the long-range concerns of society and the life insurance business. These abstracts are analyzed six times a year by an abstract analysis committee and may eventually find their way into a trend report for member companies.[10]

Trade and technical journals are another source of information. Some companies have a full-time employee who does nothing but monitor trade journals. Special counseling and reporting services can be useful sources of information. Finally, the publications of public interest groups must not be overlooked, especially those that are known to be influential in political circles.

There seems to be no end to sources of information for the political and social environments. Some means must be developed to organize these sources into a useful framework for analysis. Some of these sources will

[10] Brown, *The Business of Issues*, pp. 22–25.

obviously be more important than others, and it is best to have the entire picture in mind when making these judgments. The next step in the identification process is deciding what to do with all this scanning information. How can all this information be put together in a forecast that is useful for planning purposes?

Environmental Forecasting   Forecasting can be defined as the attempt to predict some future event or condition as a result of rational study and analysis of pertinent data. Forecasting is, in this sense, not an intuitive guess about the future, but is an educated guess based on actual data and analysis that provide evidence for a particular kind of development. To continue the analogy with a weather report, once the radar scan has discovered some storms in the area, a forecast will predict what will happen to these storms. Are they likely to hit an area or miss it entirely? Will they intensify or weaken before reaching a given area? Forecasting is very difficult at best, but if a few simple laws are followed (see box), one has a better chance of making accurate and relevant forecasts.

The first law of forecasting: Forecasting is very difficult, especially if it's about the future.

When presenting a forecast: Give them a number or give them a date, but never both.

A forecaster's best defense is a good offense, so: If you have to forecast, forecast often. But: If you're ever right, never let 'em forget it.

From Edgar R. Fiedler, "The Three Rs of Economic Forecasting—Irrational, Irrelevant and Irreverent," *Across the Board*, Vol. XIV, No. 6 (June 1977), pp. 62–63. © 1977 by The Conference Board.

Forecasting is nothing new to business, of course, but traditionally these activities have been limited to the economic and technological environments (Figure 7.3). Economic forecasting at the macro level includes projections of future gross national product, consumption and investment expenditures, productivity projections, inflation, and balance of payments. The purpose of this level of forecasting is to get some idea of the general economic conditions with which business will be faced in the immediate future. For this purpose, many corporations subscribe to one or more of the econometric models that are available, sometimes adapting them to their own purposes.

Economic forecasting at the micro level involves forecasting related to the specific markets in which the company sells products—either mature markets that have been in existence for some time, markets that are newly

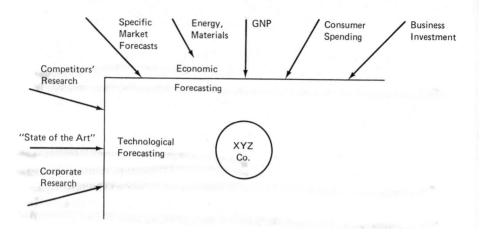

Figure 7.3
Traditional Environmental Forecasting

From Ian H. Wilson, "Socio-Political Forecasting: A New Dimension to Strategic Planning," *Michigan Business Review*, Vol. XXVI, No. 4 (July 1974), p. 19. Reprinted with permission.

developing, or potential markets the company may be considering. The purpose of this forecasting is to be more specific about the sales of particular products the company is already producing or considering. Micro forecasting also involves financial forecasts about the availability of money and credit to support the operations of the company.

Technological forecasting is concerned with state-of-the-art developments in products and processes. Forecasters try to predict where new technological breakthroughs that will significantly alter corporate planning are likely to happen. Forecasts of completion dates for company research and development projects are also a part of this area, as are attempts to assess competitors' technical competence and development activities.[11]

The traditional approach to environmental forecasting has been two-sided, concentrating on economic and technological environments. But the 1960s and 1970s taught many business organizations that the social and political environments were giving business the most trouble and affecting its profits and very survival. Ian Wilson, one of the early pioneers for a broader approach, proposed a four-sided model for environmental forecasting, including the political and social environments in addition to the economic and technological ones (Figure 7.4).[12]

Forecasting the political environment involves, in its broadest sense, some assessment of business-government relationship as a whole. A crucial question is whether the traditional adversarial relationship is likely to con-

[11] Ian H. Wilson "Reforming the Strategic Planning Process: Integration of Social Responsibility and Business Needs," *The Unstable Ground: Corporate Social Policy in a Dynamic Society*, S. Prakash Sethi, ed. (Los Angeles: Melville Publishing Co., 1974), p. 247.

[12] *Ibid.*, pp. 247–48.

tinue or whether business and government are tending more toward cooperation or, at least, a peaceful coexistence. The answer to this basic question has significant implications for the kind of political strategies a business adopts. More specific forecasting of the political environment involves keeping track of legislation being considered by Congress, the stage of the political process that legislation is in, what the likely outcome will be, and keeping aware of the various political pressures being applied by interest groups on issues of concern to the corporation.

Figure 7.4
The Four-Sided Model

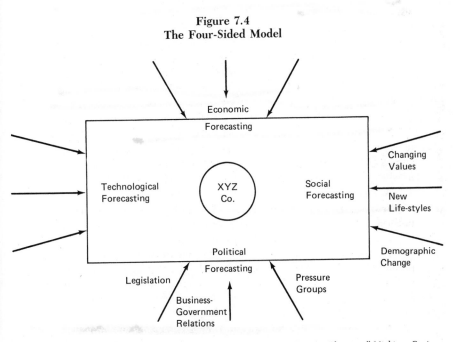

From Ian H. Wilson, "Socio-Political Forecasting: A New Dimension to Strategic Planning," *Michigan Business Review*, Vol. XXVI, No. 4 (July 1974), p. 20. Reprinted with permission.

The social environment is much more difficult to forecast. It is important, however, for business to attempt to predict major value changes in society that may give rise to new concerns and demands that will affect the corporation or the business system as a whole. Forecasting the social environment also means predicting whether current lifestyles are likely to continue or whether some major changes are probable. Finally, demographic trends are also important to follow, as shifts in population with respect to age or regional location can have major effects on the corporation.

An adequate forecasting system must include at least these four major environmental elements. It is not enough to focus on economic and technological aspects alone. Changes in government regulation and social expectations can affect profits as much as changes in technology or general economic conditions. Social and political forecasting is becoming more and more a part of the corporate scene.[13]

After developing the four-sided forecasting framework, Wilson goes on to describe the following principles that he believes should guide the forecasting—or scanning—effort:

1. It must be *holistic* in its approach to the business environment, i.e., it should view trends—social, economic, political, technological—as a piece, not piece-meal. Ecology and general systems theory both point to the maxim that "everything is related to everything else"; and Jay Forrester has demonstrated the dangers of applying linear, segmented thinking to analysis of any closed, complex system—a corporation, a city or a society—with its dynamic, interacting parts and constantly operating feedback-loops. The scanning system should, therefore, be comprehensive in its scope and integrative in its approach (cross-impact analyses and scenarios are remarkably useful techniques in this regard).

2. It must also be continuous, *iterative* in its operation. In a fast-changing world, it makes little sense to rely on one-shot, or even periodic, analyses of the environment. Only constant monitoring, feedback and modification of forecasts can be truly useful. Carrying on the radar analogy, I call this a "cybernetic pulsing through the future."

3. The system must be designed to deal with *alternative futures.* In an uncertain environment we can never truly know the future, no matter how much we may perfect our forecasting techniques. It is highly misleading, therefore, to claim (or believe) that an early warning system can predict the future. What it can do—and do effectively, if well designed—is to help us clarify our assumptions about the future, speculate systematically about alternative outcomes, assess probabilities, and make more rational choices.

4. It should lay heavy stress on the need for *contingency planning.* This is a necessary corollary to the preceding point. In fact, there is (or should be) a strong logical connection in our thinking among uncertainty, alternatives and contingencies; the three concepts are strongly bound together. In the final analysis, of course, after considering alternatives, we have to commit to a plan of action based on our assessment of the most probable future. But those lesser probabilities—even the "wild card" scenarios—should not be neglected, for they represent the contingencies for which we should also, in some degree, plan. A commitment to contingency planning is, it seems to me, the essence of a flexible strategy.

5. Most important, the environmental scanning system should be an *integral part of the decision-making system* of the corporation. Speculation about alternative futures makes no real contribution to corporate

---

[13] "Capitalizing on Social Change," pp. 105–6.

success if it results merely in interesting studies. To contribute, it must be issue-oriented and help make today's decisions with a better sense of futurity: but it can do this only if the planning and decision-making system is designed to include the requirements of such monitoring and early warning.[14]

In making an actual forecast, two concepts must be kept in mind— events and trends. Events can be defined as important specific occurrences in the social and political environments that may affect business. Such an event was the passage of legislation to raise the mandatory retirement age from sixty-five to seventy a few years ago, an event that took place very rapidly in the political environment. A trend, on the other hand, can be defined as a general tendency or course of events, that is, a whole series of events that seem to be leading in a certain direction. The aging of the population throughout the 1970s and worsening economic conditions are two trends in the social environment that built up pressure for changing the retirement age.

A forecasting system deals with both events and trends in some fashion. There are two approaches, according to Wilson, in developing a forecast of the future (see Figure 7.5). One can take scanning information and try to predict long-term trends—take a leap into the future, so to speak, and develop alternative scenarios. Then one can work backwards, through a process of deductive reasoning, to develop hypotheses on the implications of these various futures for the corporation in the immediate present. The other approach is to focus on the specific events themselves and continue to monitor them, and then, through a process of inductive reasoning, create a future five years hence based on these events.[15]

These two approaches should be seen as complements to each other rather than as alternative methods of forecasting. Environmental scanning can contribute to both long-term macro forecasts and short-term micro analyses. The purpose of either approach is to identify emerging issues in sufficient time to allow an intelligent response by the corporation. The more lead-time a corporation can have with respect to a given issue, the more options it has open to develop strategies to respond.

Evaluation of Issues

To be useful for planning purposes, the issues that have been identified as being of concern to the corporation must be ranked or prioritized. The corporation cannot concern itself with everything that has been discovered

[14] Ian H. Wilson, "Environmental Scanning and Strategic Planning," *Business Environment/Public Policy: 1979 Conference Papers*, Lee E. Preston, ed. (St. Louis, Mo.: AACSB, 1980), pp. 160–61. Quoted with permission.

[15] *Ibid.*, pp. 159–160.

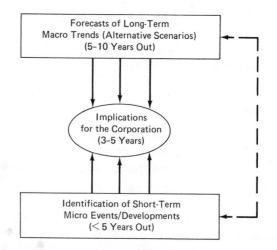

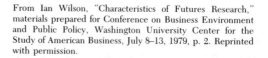

Figure 7.5
Approaches to Forecasting

From Ian Wilson, "Characteristics of Futures Research," materials prepared for Conference on Business Environment and Public Policy, Washington University Center for the Study of American Business, July 8–13, 1979, p. 2. Reprinted with permission.

in the scanning process and forecast as having an impact. It must focus its efforts on the issues that are likely to have the greatest impact.

One method of prioritizing issues is to lay out the issues in a matrix arrangement (Figure 7.6). The issues have to be analyzed by the forecasting group with the help of management. Decisions must be made about the probability of their occurrence, that they will be significant to large enough segments of society to be placed on the public agenda, and their potential impact on the specific company. Once placed in the appropriate cell of the matrix, the issues can then be categorized into high, medium, and low priority. Those issues falling into the top left-hand portion of the matrix should receive immediate management attention, those in the middle are not as crucial, but still need attention, and those falling in the lower right-hand corner can be put on the back burner for the time being. This assessment, however, must be done periodically, as conditions can change quite rapidly. The key to this method, of course, is a correct analysis of the issues according to the two dimensions of the matrix. For this analysis, techniques such as probability analysis, trend impact analysis, cross-impact analysis, and simulation modeling may be useful.

There are less sophisticated methods of prioritizing issues, of course, that use rather broad definitions of categories (see box). But regardless of the method used, the outcome should be some listing of issues in a priority scheme (Exhibit 7.6) that can be useful for planning. These priorities can then be factored into the planning process of the corporation to develop a position with respect to an issue and strategies that will be effective in implementing that position.

Figure 7.6
Issues Priority Matrix

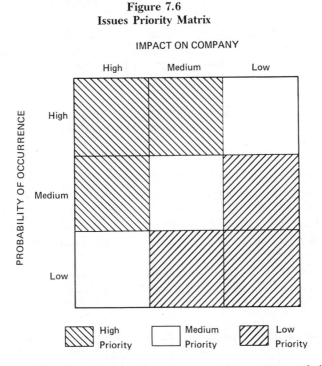

Adapted from James K. Brown, *This Business of Issues: Coping with the Company's Environments* (New York: The Conference Board, 1979) p. 32. Reprinted with permission.

THE PUBLIC AFFAIRS FUNCTION

The corporation relates to its external publics through the public affairs function as far as dealing with public issues is concerned. The old public relations functions typically performed two tasks: (1) publicizing the products of the company; and (2) building a positive image of the company in the minds of the public. These old tasks are today only a new small part of a much larger public affairs function.[16] The public affairs practitioner of today seeks to anticipate public problems, and on the basis of study and analysis, recommends the most responsible course of action to be taken by the company before these problems become key public issues that could adversely affect the organization. This new public affairs function typically includes the following responsibilities:

[16] George A. Steiner, "The New Class of Chief Executive Officer," *Long Range Planning*, vol. 14, no. 4 (1981), p. 16.

DEFINITIONS OF PRIORITIES FOR ISSUES; TWO COMPANY EXAMPLES

High priority—those issues on which we need to be well-informed in order to provide knowledgeable counsel or take specific action.

Nice to know—those issues which are interesting but neither critical nor urgent enough to warrant spending a disproportionate amount of time and resources on.

Questionable—those unidentified or unframed issues that will become important as soon as something happens or somebody elevates them.

—Xerox

Priority A: issue is of such critical impact on PPG as to warrant executive management action, including periodic review of the issue and personal participation in implementing plans to manage the issue.

Priority B: the issue is of such critical impact on PPG as to warrant division general manager or staff department executive involvement.

Priority C: the issue has potential impact so as to warrant government and public affairs department surveillance, assessment and reporting.

—PPG Industries

From: James K. Brown, *This Business of Issues: Coping With The Company's Environment* (New York: The Conference Board, 1979), p. 33. Reprinted with permission.

---

monitor the social and political environment to identify forces which may have a potential significant impact on company operations;

coordinate the analysis of environmental forces throughout the company;

identify the forces in the environment which are most likely to have the most important impact on the company and transmit that information to top management and other staff;

help top management in the selection of those public policy issues on which the company will concentrate attention;

prepare appropriate analyses of public policy issues which top management chooses to address;

contribute to and participate in the injection of social and political projections in the strategic planning processes;

develop communications programs aimed at various company publics of the enterprise and framed within policies of the company;

develop programs to advance the interests of the company in the political processes of federal, state and local governments;

EXHIBIT 7.6
Sears' Agenda of Public Issues

Issues with Direct Impact on the Company		
First Priority	*Second Priority*	*Third Priority*
Equal Employment Opportunity	Equal Pay	Postal Service
Social Security	Profit Sharing/Stock	Product Usage: Codes and Restrictions
Minimum Wage	Ownership/Capital Gains	Flame Retardency
Employee Health Care	Pensions	Raw Material Pricing and Access
Credit Income/Financing/ Interest Costs	Corporate Taxes	Environmental Protection
FTC Requirements	Worker's Compensation	Retirement Policies
Product Liability	Unemployment Compensation	OSHA
Warranty Requirements	Labor Law	Product Restrictions
	Transportation Regulations	Privacy
	International Trade Policy	Copyright Laws
	Product Safety	Disclosure
	Labeling and Packaging Specifications	Corporate Governance
	Product Specifications	Metric Changeover
	Energy Requirements	Sex/Violence on TV
	Franchise Regulations	
	Energy Costs	
	Electronic Funds Transfer	
	Electronic Communications Regulation	
	Credit Practice Regulations	
	Federal/State Legislative/ Regulatory Conflicts	
	Advertising Regulations	

Issues with Indirect Impact on the Company		
	Fourth Priority	
National Energy Program	Government Subsidy of Business/Cities	Food Policy
Full Employment	Housing Policy	Public Confidence in Institutions
Inflation	Immigrants	National Planning
Government Spending/ Deficit	Welfare Reform	Plaintiffs Access to the Courts
Monetary Policy	Water Conservation	White Collar and Corporate Crime

From Robert E. Barmeier, "The Role of Environmental Forecasting and Public Issues Analysis in Corporate Planning," *Business Environment/Public Policy: 1979 Conference Papers,* Lee E. Preston, ed. (St. Louis, Mo.: AACSB, 1980), p. 158. Reprinted with permission.

develop programs by means of which the company may respond appropriately to the interests of the people in the communities in which it
does business.[17]

Some companies distribute these tasks among different staff groups,
but in more and more companies, the organizational approach taken is to
integrate them in one public affairs department or have staff groups report to
one individual. The individual who heads public affairs is most likely a vice-
president, as shown in Table 7.4, who in turn has various reporting relationships including another vice-president, the chairman of the board, the
CEO, or the president of the company. Many of these senior public affairs
people came from outside the organization. The data for this table comes
from a survey of 401 firms conducted by the Public Affairs Research Group
in the School of Management at Boston University.[18]

Table 7.4
The Senior Public Affairs Officer

A. The title of the most senior full-time public affairs officer:		C. How long has this person held the senior public affairs position?	
Vice President	68.6%	Range	1 to 30 years
Director	20.3%	5 years or less:	61.7%
Manager	5.4%	10 years or less:	88.7%
Other	5.7%		
B. To whom does this person report?		D. How long has this person been with the company?	
Vice President	31.3%		
Chairman	25.6%	Range:	1 to 40 years
CEO	19.4%	5 years or less:	26.7%
President	16.5%	10 years or less:	46.8%
Other	7.2%		

Source: Public Affairs Research Group, School of Management, Boston University, "Public Affairs
Offices and Their Functions: Highlights of a National Survey," *Public Affairs Review*, Vol. II (1981),
p. 93.

There are various external publics to which the public affairs function
relates. Table 7.5 shows the importance of these publics based on the percentage of the 401 companies that have a particular activity. Community
relations and government relations are highly held as primary areas of responsibility. Because of the critical importance of government to corporations, governmental relations will be discussed separately.

[17] *Ibid.*

[18] Public Affairs Research Group, School of Management, Boston University, "Public
Affairs Offices and Their Functions: Highlights of a National Survey," *Public Affairs Review*,
Vol. II (1981), pp. 88–99. See also Public Affairs Research Group, *Public Affairs Offices and
Their Functions: Summary of Survey Responses* (Boston: Boston University School of
Management, 1981).

Table 7.5
Defining the Public Affairs Function

Activity	Percentage of Respondents	
	Yes	No
Community relations	84.9	15.1
Government relations	84.2	15.8
Corporate contributions	71.5	28.5
Media relations	70.0	30.0
Stockholder relations	48.5	51.5
Advertising	40.4	59.6
Consumer affairs	38.5	61.5
Graphics	33.5	66.5
Institutional investor relations	33.5	66.5
Customer relations	23.8	76.2
Other*	26.3	73.7

*Some firms included grass-roots lobbying and political action committees in this category, but most considered these a part of government relations.

Source: Public Affairs Research Group, School of Management, Boston University, "Public Affairs Offices and Their Functions: Highlights of a National Survey," *Public Affairs Review*, Vol. II (1981), p. 90.

It is interesting to note that stockholders ranked lower than the media, reflecting the importance of devoting time and effort to media relations. The media convey information about business and have a tremendous impact on public opinion, making it an important constituency.

The stockholders are an important constituency to some corporations as far as public issues are concerned. They can be mobilized to help implement a company's position on a public issue. For example, in 1976, Dart Industries requested support from stockholders on the issues of tax reform and oil company divestiture. The company conducted a random survey of 1,052 of the 8,591 stockholders who had been mailed letters to evaluate the effectiveness of the effort. Of the 146 people who responded to the survey, 55 said they had taken a position on both the tax reform and divestiture issue, 49 said they had taken a position on one of the issues, and 42 said they had acted on neither issue. These results were encouraging enough for the company to continue the program.[19]

The growth in the public affairs function is shown in Table 7.6 which indicates the years in which public affairs departments were created. The most dramatic growth of public affairs took place in the 1970s, as almost 60 percent of all public affairs departments in existence at the time of the survey

[19] Phyllis McGrath, *Action Plans for Public Affairs* (New York: The Conference Board, 1977), pp. 21–24.

were created in that time period. Nearly one third of all public affairs departments were created in the last five years of this period. This growth pattern is consistent with the increased importance of public policy to the modern business corporation.[20]

Table 7.6
Creation of Public Affairs Departments

Date of Creation	Number	Percentage	Cumulative Percentage
Before 1950	32	8.9	8.9
1950–1959	37	10.3	19.2
1960–1969	80	22.1	41.3
1970–1974	100	27.7	69.0
	212	58.7	
1975–1980	112	31.0	100.0
n =	361		

Source: Public Affairs Research Group, School of Management, Boston University, "Public Affairs Offices and Their Functions: Highlights of a National Survey," *Public Affairs Review*, Vol. II (1981), p. 91.

Thus the public affairs function has become of increasing importance to corporations. The field of public affairs is becoming professionalized as exemplified in a statement of ethical guidelines for public affairs professionals (see box). Increasing attention is being given to the training of people for the public affairs function.[21] There is a need for people with an in-depth understanding of the external environment and a knowledge of the public policy process so that public issues which emerge out of the external environment can be managed effectively.

GOVERNMENT RELATIONS   Because of its importance and growth, the government relations function deserves to be treated separately. The increased federal regulation in the 1970s contributed to a dramatic growth in efforts to systematically manage federal government relations. While relations with the federal government used to deal primarily with winning federal contracts, the responsibilities involved with governmental relations have increased significantly.

About 500 corporations today have offices in Washington compared with from 100 to 200 in the late 1960s. Along with this growth in numbers

[20] Public Affairs Research Group, "Public Affairs Offices," p. 91.

[21] See Rogene A. Buchholz, "Education for Public Issues Management: Key Insights from a Survey of Top Practitioners," *Public Affairs Review*, Vol. III (1982), pp. 65–76.

A STATEMENT OF ETHICAL GUIDELINES
FOR BUSINESS PUBLIC AFFAIRS PROFESSIONALS

A. The *Public Affairs Professional* maintains professional relationships based on honesty and reliable information, and therefore:
   1. Represents accurately his or her organization's policies on economic and political matters to government, employees, shareholders, community interests, and others.
   2. Serves always as a source of reliable information, discussing the varied aspects of complex public issues within the context and constraints of the advocacy role.
   3. Recognizes diverse viewpoints within the public policy process, knowing that disagreement on issues is both inevitable and healthy.
B. The *Public Affairs Professional* seeks to protect the integrity of the public policy process and the political system, and therefore:
   1. Publicly acknowledges his or her role as a legitimate participant in the public policy process and discloses whatever work-related information the law requires.
   2. Knows, respects and abides by federal and state laws that apply to lobbying and related public affairs activities.
   3. Knows and respects the laws governing campaign finance and other political activities, and abides by the letter and intent of those laws.
C. The *Public Affairs Professional* understands the interrelation of business interests with the larger public interests, and therefore:
   1. Endeavors to ensure that responsible and diverse external interests and views concerning the needs of society are considered within the corporate decision-making process.
   2. Bears the responsibility for management review of public policies which may bring corporate interests into conflict with other interests.
   3. Acknowledges dual obligations—to advocate the interests of his or her employer, and to preserve the openness and integrity of the democratic process.
   4. Presents to his or her employer an accurate assessment of the political and social realities that may affect corporate operations.

Public Affairs Council
Committee on Professionalism

Charles S. Mack, Chairman	Gordon D. MacKay
Richard A. Edwards	Horace E. Sheldon
Robert J. Grimm	F. Clifton White
	May 1979

From Charles S. Mack, "Ethics and Business Public Affairs," *Public Affairs Review* Vol. I (Washington, D.C.: Public Affairs Council, 1980), p. 28. Reprinted with permission.

there has been an expansion of responsibilities. The typical Washington office is a warning-post for a company to identify forces which should be dealt with. It is a center for communications about political activities. It provides services for visiting personnel. It is a source of expertise on who the CEO and others in the company should see, what should be presented, how to be persuasive, and so on. It represents the company among members of the Congress. It engages in analysis and research on public policy issues. And, of course, it engages in lobbying.[22]

Of the 401 companies that responded to the survey of the Public Affairs Research Group of Boston University, 73 percent said they maintained a significant involvement or presence in Washington. Table 7.7 shows the various forms this involvement took among the responding companies. Despite the recent growth in Washington offices, trade associations are still used most frequently to maintain a Washington presence. The amount of time senior executives spent on public affairs work ranged from 1–90 percent of the total time in this survey, while 53 percent of these senior executives spent 5–25 percent of their time in Washington alone.[23]

Table 7.7
Types of Washington Presence

Activity	Yes	No
Trade Association	67.8%	32.2%
Frequent visits to Washington by senior executives	58.4%	41.6%
Company office in Washington	42.7%	57.3%
Washington law firm (as needed or on retainer)	38.0%	62.0%
Washington-based government relations counsel	11.9%	88.1%
Washington public relations firm (as needed or on retainer)	8.6%	91.4%

Source: Public Affairs Research Group, School of Management, Boston University, "Public Affairs Offices and Their Functions: Highlights of a National Survey," *Public Affairs Review*, Vol. II (1981), p. 93.

Regarding the organization of the government relations function, of the 389 companies that participated in a 1979 Conference Board study, 73 percent had a separate unit dealing with government relations. The existence of these separate units depended on the size of the company. Only 53 percent of those companies reporting up to $250 million in sales had a government relations department. But among respondents with sales of $10 billion or more, 90 percent reported they had a separate department.[24]

[22] Steiner, "The New Class of Chief Executive Officer," p. 17.

[23] Public Affairs Research Group, "Public Affairs Offices," p. 93.

[24] Phyllis McGrath, *Redefining Corporate-Federal Relations* (New York: The Conference Board, 1979), p. 56.

The existence of these units by industry grouping was also studied. Industries that have been regulated for years by the old-style industry regulation (utilities, communications, transportation) head the list. But industries such as food, petroleum, chemicals, drugs, lumber, and paper, which have been affected by food safety and drug regulations, or energy and environment regulations, are also high on the list.

The government relations function can be physically positioned in either headquarters, at the Washington office of the company, or at both places. The Conference Board study showed that the headquarters location was most preferred by the 285 companies having a separate government relations function. The following list shows these preferred locations, including some that deviate from the more traditional pattern:

94 have only a headquarters unit

56 have only a Washington office

104 have both a headquarters unit and a Washington office

16 have a subunit in the general counsel's department

7 have a headquarters unit and a subunit in the general counsel's department

4 have a Washington office and a subunit in the general counsel's department

4 have some "other" organizational arrangement[25]

Reporting relationships and titles of unit heads vary with the location. When there is a headquarters unit only, the unit head usually reports directly to the CEO or president of the company. The most prevalent titles are vice-president, director, manager, or counsel. The same reporting relationship is most prevalent when there is a Washington office only—that is, the unit head reports directly to the CEO or president. The most prevalent title is vice-president, but director is also common, and there are a few managers.[26]

When units are located in both Washington and headquarters, the Washington office can report to the headquarters executive, the headquarters unit and the Washington office can report to the same executive, or each unit can report to a different executive. Titles differ, and sometimes vice-presidents report to vice-presidents, or vice-presidents report to directors, and so forth.

The background of the government relations executive is varied. Most of them are lawyers, public affairs or communications specialists, or have had experience in government. Other are academicians or people who have

---

[25] *Ibid.*, p. 57.

[26] *Ibid.*, pp. 60–61.

worked for trade associations, or people who have come up through the ranks of the company.[27]

DISCIPLINES REPRESENTED ON THE GOVERNMENT RELATIONS
STAFF (IN ORDER OF FREQUENCY)

Washington	*Headquarters*
Law	Law
Government Relations	Public Relations-
Business	Communications
Public Relations-	Government Relations-
Communications	Public Affairs
Technical	
Government	Political Science
Other (including marketing	Economics
and international)	Government

From Phyllis McGrath, *Redefining Corporate-Federal Relations* (New York: The Conference Board, 1979), p. 65. Reprinted with permission.

The type of person who heads the government relations unit reflects the company's government relations philosophy. For a communications-oriented company that views government relations as a means of getting the company's message across to legislators, the unit head is likely to have a communications background. Companies concerned more with regulatory matters are likely to have a lawyer in this position.[28] The staff of the government relations unit also reflects a variety of disciplines (see box), indicating that the function actually calls for a combination of talents.

The government relations function is concerned with three areas of government—legislative, executive, and regulatory—and involves activities at all of these levels. Strategies for legislative relations include Washington contact and grass-roots programs as well as political action committees. Maintaining contact with the executive branch requires someone with Washington experience who may still have contacts, or someone who has an interest in developing them. Working through organizations such as the Business Roundtable is a successful strategy for executive branch relations. Maintaining regulatory relations involves more legal work, but also increasingly involves technical people who are brought in from company

---

[27] *Ibid.*, p. 63.
[28] *Ibid.*

headquarters to provide detailed technical information for the regulators. This information can be critical to getting the kind of regulations that the company can live with and successfully incorporate into its operations.[29]

Contacting government officials, including lobbying and social contact, is an important activity. The government relations function, particularly a Washington office, assists other people in the company when they lobby and testify before Congress or regulatory agencies. Another set of activities relates to internal communications—keeping key people in the corporation informed about legislative and regulatory developments of interest to the company. One of the basic day-to-day responsibilities of government relations is to monitor public policy developments that may have an impact on the company's operations.[30]

Table 7.8 shows the range of activities the respondents to the Boston University study were regularly engaged in to communicate the company's policies, objectives, and positions at the federal level. The listing of regular correspondence at the top of the list is somewhat surprising, and shows the importance corporations attach to maintaining continual contact with their political representatives. The table also shows the importance of political action committees, which are a growing phenomena on the corporate scene. The effectiveness of government relations activities was also ranked by the respondents to this survey. Starting with the most effective activity, the ranking included: (1) serving as eyes and ears, (2) representing the company to regulatory agencies, (3) influencing proposed legislation, and (4) influenc-

Table 7.8
Federal Government Relations Activities

Activity	Yes	No
Regular correspondence	88.8%	11.2%
Lobbying	73.1%	26.9%
Political action committees	69.9%	30.1%
Employee newsletters	63.3%	36.7%
Plant visits	52.4%	41.1%
Economic education programs	33.9%	66.1%
Speakers' bureaus	29.3%	70.7%
Advertising	23.2%	76.8%

Source: Public Affairs Research Group, School of Management, Boston University, "Public Affairs Offices and Their Functions: Highlights of a National Survey," *Public Affairs Review*, Vol. II (1981), p. 94.

[29] *Ibid.*, pp. 5–7.
[30] *Ibid.*, pp. 10–24.

ing compliance with regulation. Note that the monitoring function was ranked above the influencing functions.[31]

While this discussion has focused on government relations on the federal level, government relations at the state and local level is also important to many corporations. Some companies have as part of the government relations function a subunit that deals with state and local government relations.[32]

There is some evidence to suggest that a trend toward less federal control over business activities could mean increased state regulations with all the related problems. Whether or not this is true, corporations cannot neglect state and local governments, because government at these levels can also affect business organizations.[33]

Finally, government relations is in some sense the job of everyone who is part of the corporation, not just that of the government relations unit. Because of the importance of public policy, there is a constant flow of corporate people into Washington to testify, meet with government officials, contact the staff of legislators or regulatory agencies, and attend meetings on governmental matters.[34]

The executive who plays the most critical role in the company's total government relations effort is, of course, the CEO. The CEO is the best person to meet with high-level government officials and help motivate staff, stockholders, and others by putting his or her stamp of approval on PACs, grass-roots programs, and similar strategies. Table 7.9 shows the different government relations activities of the CEO and the frequency of CEO involvement in these activities. The Conference Board study also indicates that CEO commitment and support of government relations is increasing, reflecting the increasing importance of public policy to corporations.[35] The Chairman of the Board for the Allstate Insurance Companies, has the following words to say about the role of the CEO in the public policy process:

> It is my belief that the chief executive in today's environment must do his utmost to see that his organization participates in the public policy process, acting in some cases as an informational agent and in other cases as a guide or advocate, when appropriate. In no case can he and his organization shirk their responsibilities in the national forum of public policy debates.[36]

[31] Public Affairs Research Group, "Public Affairs Offices," p. 96.

[32] McGrath, *Action Plans*, pp. 34–40.

[33] Kenneth W. Chilton, "Would 'New Federalism' Really Spark a Major Increase in State Rulemaking?" *Public Affairs Review*, vol. III (1982), pp. 104–11.

[34] McGrath, *Corporate-Federal Relations*, p. 70.

[35] *Ibid.*, pp. 74–77.

[36] Archie R. Boe, "Fitting the Corporation to the Future," *Public Relations* Quarterly, vol. 24, no. 4 (Winter, 1979), pp. 4–6.

Table 7.9
Government Relations Activities of the
Chief Executive Officer[1]

Activity	Number of Mentions
Spokesperson for the company	334
Active in peer group efforts	300
Personal contact with key legislators	277
Personal contact with executive branch	206
Spokesperson for the industry	195
Presents testimony	130
Personal contact with regulatory agencies	129
Other	82

[1]The list of activities in the survey was not an open-ended one, therefore the number of mentions is greater than the number of companies in the sample because respondents were permitted to check more than one activity.

Source: Phyllis McGrath, *Redefining Corporate-Federal Relations* (New York: The Conference Board, 1979), p. 76. Reprinted with permission.

EVALUATING PUBLIC ISSUES MANAGEMENT Evaluating the public issues management effort poses , as the Conference Board points out, a conundrum. Evaluation is important as a basis for future planning and budgeting regarding the effort. Yet using either a management-by-objectives approach or a results-oriented evaluation can be very frustrating, so much so that many companies simply abandon the evaluation effort entirely. There are no reliable yardsticks, many executives believe, with which a company can measure the effectiveness of its public issues management effort. Some even believe that there is no need to evaluate the effort, since it is a job that simply must be done regardless of the results.[37]

> As is the case with many other staff functions whose impact on corporate profits is not immediately evident, external relations does not readily lend itself to measurement. This general difficulty is compounded in the case of external relations by the multitude of influences outside of management's sphere of control that can and do affect the issues and publics that corporate external relations programs are aimed at. In most areas, "results achieved," whether good or bad, cannot be attributed to corporate actions alone.[38]

[37] Phyllis McGrath, *Managing Corporate External Relations: Changing Perspectives and Responses* (New York: The Conference Board, 1976), pp. 68–69.

[38] *Ibid.*, p. 64.

Yet a company must expect some payoffs from the activity or it will not be continued. There are a number of payoffs that may stem from a successful public issues management program (see box). The following anecdotal information indicates payoffs some companies have received with regard to specific issues.

The Whirlpool Corporation, through its technological monitoring efforts, was the first washing-machine manufacturer to recognize the significance of the development of permanent-press fabrics and so became the first, by a couple of years, to produce a machine capable of laundering garments made from them.

A major food processor, foreseeing that the food additive called Red Dye #2 would become controversial because of evidence of its association with untoward health effects, withdrew this additive from its products well before the predicted hue and cry about it materialized.

PPG Industries, responding to the glass industry's perception that the public was increasingly concerned about product safety, offered commercial safety glass for residential sliding doors and storm doors well before its competitors. And before the onset of the energy crisis, this company developed double-glazed reflective-surface glass that excludes heavy summer solar heat gain, thereby conserving energy.

At the Bank of America, a task force on credit discrimination, formed by the internal social policy committee, concluded that credit discrimination against women was a substantive issue. Among other things, the task force discovered that there was considerable subtle, if not overt, discrimination included in the bank's Standard Practice Manuals and that there was attitudinal discrimination on the part of lending officers in the branches. Thereupon, the social policy committee initiated a program of change, altering the credit-scoring mechanism, "talking turkey" to regional vice-presidents, and preparing training films and writing articles for employee publications inveighing against credit discrimination. Each of two subsequent shopping surveys, in which researchers from an outside agency posed as credit applicants, indicated the bank had made considerable progress in reducing such discrimination.

At Prudential Insurance Company, the public affairs staff and top management recognized that lack of consumer understanding about life insurance, the obscure language of insurance policies, and the lack of cost disclosure about policies were three issues of vital importance. This recognition led to a two-year advertising campaign aimed at educating consumers about the nature of life insurance and a continuing effort to make the language of policies simpler and clearer and to provide consumers with more information about costs.[39]

---

[39] James K. Brown, *Guidelines For Managing Corporate Issues Programs* (New York: The Conference Board, 1981), p. 33.

PAYOFFS FROM ISSUES PROGRAMS

(1) Competitive advantages—in marketing, products, corporate image.

(2) Salutary changes in corporate behavior.

(3) Avoidance of serious mistakes made in the absence of issues programs.

(4) Ability to detect issues and develop corporate responses to them while they are in an emerging stage, when a company has more options and will incur less cost in confronting them.

(5) Enhancement of the firm's credibility.

(6) Reduced vulnerability to "the slings and arrows of outrageous fortune."

(7) Indirect benefits—for example, greater management confidence in its decisions; improvements in planning; acceptance by management that the future will be different from the past.

From: James K. Brown, *Guidelines For Managing Corporate Issues Programs* (New York: The Conference Board, 1981), p. 33.

Corporations that do evaluate the effort on a more systematic basis generally use one of two approaches: (1) evaluation on the basis of set objectives, or (2) evaluation on the basis of activities carried out. Regarding the first approach, the two objectives of public issues management most frequently mentioned were to improve business credibility and develop a positive corporate image. The former is the most global objective, as the restoration of public trust usually refers to not just one company or even one industry, but to the total business community. The attainment of a positive corporate image relates to the degree of public acceptance of the company.[40] The following are among some of the results looked for in accomplishing this objective.

Accurate and objective coverage by the media.

The ability to conduct the regular business of the corporation without interference, and the continued growth of the company.

A sound environment for advancing the marketing and investment objectives of the company.

Some perceptible degree of change in external attitudes to the company.

Some degree of success in anticipating problems; a minimum of surprises from the company's publics.[41]

---

[40] McGrath, *External Relations*, p. 64.

[41] *Ibid.*, p. 65.

Judgment about attainment of these objectives is based on informal or formal feedback. Informal feedback includes the feedback a CEO gets when he or she comes into contact with business peers, from other people who are not part of the business community, and even from family and friends. Senior management also obtains feedback from employees, customers, educators, and government officials. The opinion survey is most frequently used to determine whether or not the company's message is reaching its targeted publics.[42] Some companies develop an elaborate procedure for the use of opinion surveys for evaluation (see box).

A major utility conducts a three-pronged approach to public opinion polling. First, the company subscribes to all of the available political and public opinion measuring services. Second, once a year, the public relations department conducts a public overview survey of its own. This survey measures customer satisfaction, asking a sampling of customers questions not only concerning the quality of the product, but whether or not the customer thinks the company is a good corporate citizen. At the same time, an internal survey is conducted to find out how employees perceive and react to messages from senior management. The third aspect consists of dozens of special studies done each year, relating to whatever issues or problems are topical. Because the unit operates with a small staff, most of this survey work is conducted by outside polling firms.

From: Phyllis McGrath, *Managing Corporate External Relations* (New York: The Conference Board, 1979), p.66.

Evaluation on the basis of activities focuses on what the public issues management group is doing. This evaluation can get as specific as measuring the number of contacts with legislators, the number of internal communications issued, or the number of people involved in the grass-roots lobbying program. Meeting budgeted forecasts is an activity measure used in some corporations.[43]

Basic to the problem of evaluation is the question of what constitutes success in public issues management. A study of success in external affairs based on information from external affairs executives showed that the level of perceived success was highest for customer and stockholder relations, two areas that organizations traditionally have monitored. Environmental affairs

[42] *Ibid.*, pp. 65–66.
[43] *Ibid.*, pp. 66–67.

was ranked lowest because it is a more recent concern for management and may also be more complex.[44]

The formulation of objectives and policies was found to have a positive correlation to perceived success in external affairs, even though only 57 percent of the respondents indicated their companies had established such policies and objectives. Over 72 percent of the firms had a formal evaluation mechanism, however, suggesting that many firms are evaluating their external affairs effort without formal objectives. Again, the existence of an evaluation procedure was linked to a higher level of perceived success.[45] Thus evaluation and setting of objectives may be important factors in the process, at least as far as perceived success of the public issues management effort is concerned.

Also important for the success of public issues management is its linkage with strategic planning, which can be defined as "that activity which specifies for a business a course of action that is designed to achieve long-term objectives in the light of all major external and internal factors, present and future."[46] Strategic planning must take into account social and political factors identified by the public issues management process to be of significance to the corporation in order to avoid the discontinuities and restraints that come from ignoring these factors.

SELECTED REFERENCES

AGUILAR, FRANCIS JOSEPH. *Scanning the Business Environment.* New York: Macmillan, 1967.

ANDREWS, K. *The Concept of Corporate Strategy.* Homewood, Ill.: Dow-Jones Irwin, 1971.

ANSOFF, H. I. *Corporate Strategy.* New York: McGraw-Hill, 1965.

BROWN, JAMES K. *This Business of Issues: Coping with the Company's Environments.* New York: The Conference Board, 1971.

LAWRENCE, P., AND J. LORSCH. *Organizations and Environment.* Cambridge, Mass.: Harvard University Press, 1967.

LORANGE, P., AND R. VANCIL. *Strategic Planning Systems.* Englewood Clifs, N.J.: Prentice-Hall, 1977.

---

[44] W. Harvey Hegarty, John C. Alpin, and Richard A. Cosier, "Achieving Corporate Success in External Affairs," *Business Horizons*, vol. 21, no. 5 (October 1978), p. 68.

[45] *Ibid.*, pp. 70–72.

[46] Wilson, "Reforming the Strategic Planning Process," p. 250.

McGrath, Phyllis. *Action Plans for Public Affairs.* New York: The Conference Board, 1977.

————. *Managing Corporate External Relations: Changing Perspectives and Responses.* New York: The Conference Board, 1976.

————. *Redefining Federal Corporate Relations.* New York: The Conference Board, 1979.

MacMillan, I. C. *Strategy Formulation: Political Concepts.* New York: West, 1978.

Pfeiffer, Jeffrey, and Gerald R. Aalancik. *The External Control of Organizations.* New York: Harper & Row, Pub., 1978.

Post, James E. *Corporate Behavior and Social Change.* Reston, Va.: Reston, 1976.

Rothschild, W. E. *Putting It All Together.* New York: American Management Association, 1976.

Steiner, G. A. *Top Management Planning.* New York: Macmillan, 1969.

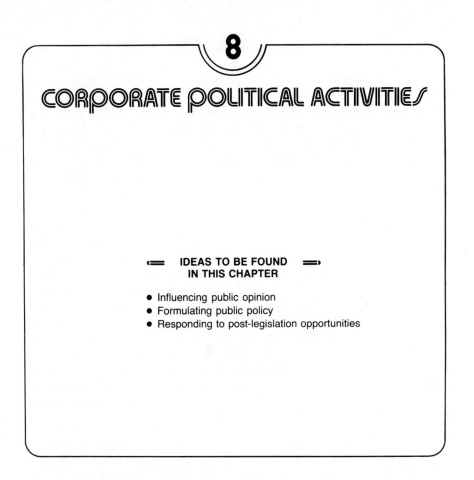

8

CORPORATE POLITICAL ACTIVITIE∫

⟸ **IDEAS TO BE FOUND** ⟹
IN THIS CHAPTER

- Influencing public opinion
- Formulating public policy
- Responding to post-legislation opportunities

Since public policy is formulated through a political process, corporations must be active in this process to have some influence on the outcome, just as they are active in the exchange process to determine the value of the goods and services they provide. Corporations have values with respect to public goods and services as well, and these values have to be registered through some kind of political activity in order to have an impact on public policy.

The methods that corporations have for participating in the public policy process will be discussed in a framework that corresponds with the various stages of the public policy process. The first stage concerns the formation of public opinion on specific issues that affect business or attitudes toward business in general. By helping to shape public opinion, corporations can exercise a broad influence in the society as a whole. The second stage is public policy formulation, a critical area when Congress or the executive branch is considering specific legislative proposals or holding hearings on issues of concern to business. The corporation has various ways by which it can participate in this stage of public policy formulation. The last stage occurs after legislation is passed, when regulations are being written and court decisions made on specific issues that affect business.

Obviously, these stages overlap—activities useful at one stage may also be effective at another—but certain activities seem more appropriate at one stage than another and will be discussed accordingly. The purpose of the public issues management system described in the previous chapter is to select the political activities or tactics that will be effective in accomplishing the overall strategy with respect to a public issue. Knowledge of the uses and limitations of the various political activities is essential in making this choice.

INFLUENCING PUBLIC OPINION

It is important for business to identify key issues in society that may affect business and to engage in a debate about these issues before they are picked up by the formal political system. At such an early stage, the options that business has to deal with an issue are broadest; involvement at this stage has the potential of being very effective. Some argue that when government gets involved with an issue, it is too late for business to have much effect on the outcome. Government is reactive, they believe, and when it does finally begin to consider an issue, such as hazardous waste disposal, society has already formulated opinions and the general outlines of policy on that issue have already been drawn. In any event, business has various methods at its disposal to participate at this stage in an attempt to influence public opinion.

Speaking Out on Issues

One such method is the attempt of business to get involved in speaking out on issues that concern the company's interests. Management at some companies spends a good deal of time taking advantage of opportunities to speak to civic groups, participate in conferences, speak to high school and college classes, write articles for business journals or newspapers, or meet with the media to get its viewpoint before the public. Some corporations have changed from a posture of keeping quiet on issues and working behind the scenes to one of raising their voices in public and becoming much more visible. This strategy not only involves top management at headquarters, but management at all levels in communities where company facilities are located. [1]

The success of this method of influencing public opinion depends a great deal on how well business has done its homework. The position that management takes on an issue must be factually correct and defensible. Those who "go public" can expect to be questioned, sometimes hostilely, by their audience. If the homework is done well, however, and the business people involved have communications skills to articulate a business position

[1] See Hugh D. Menzies, "Union Carbide Raises Its Voice," *Fortune*, September 25, 1978, pp. 86–89.

and engage in debate, this can be an effective way to influence public opinion and gain credibility with the public. Increased communications with the public can be a positive factor in shaping public opinion with respect to business and the business system. Instead of sending out a public relations representative who has neither the knowledge nor authority to say anything meaningful about corporate policies or operations, management itself gets involved in speaking to the public. The corporation is often better represented by someone who can respond confidently to unanticipated questions.

The leading role in this type of corporate advocacy is played by the chief executive officer of the company. The example of the top corporate officer sets the pattern for the total organizational effort. A Conference Board survey of 395 CEOs of major manufacturing, financial, and utility firms found that 26 percent of the CEOs described themselves as public communicators who spoke out widely on public issues. Another 21 percent were company spokespeople who took their views to the top levels of government and made them known to shareholders and customers, but did not beam their opinions at the general public.[2] Thus there is some evidence to suggest that a good many CEOs are taking this role of speaking out on issues seriously.

There are problems, however, with this approach. One problem is the speaker's credibility. For whom is the manager speaking? What group does his or her position represent? Who is the corporation? Agreement on a position may be reached by the management of a corporation, but is management alone the corporation? What about shareholders, customers, and employees? These constituencies, if indeed they are a legitimate part of the corporation, will undoubtedly have different views on an issue. How, then, can these diverse views be represented in a single "corporate" position?[3] A public issues management system can be useful in establishing the legitimacy of a particular viewpoint.

A second problem concerns the kinds of issues in which business gets involved. If these issues are only those in which the company has a significant stake, the company can be criticized as pursuing only its own narrow self-interest at the expense of the public interest. This may only contribute more to the credibility problem that business already has with the public. To gain credibility, it is argued, business must concern itself with broader interests rather than just its own self-interest. It must seek to understand the concerns of other groups in society outside the business community and

[2] "Study Classifies 40% of Chief Executives 'Political Activists,' " *The Wall Street Journal*, March 26, 1980, p. 12.

[3] Rogene A. Buchholz, *Business Environment/Public Policy: Corporate Executive Viewpoints and Educational Implications* (St. Louis: Washington University Center for the Study of American Business, 1980), p. 21.

[4] *Ibid.*, p. 20.

engage in debate about a broad range of issues that have a bearing on the quality of life.[4] The Conference Board survey mentioned earlier found that over half of the executives in the sample were prepared to go beyond issues directly affecting their companies and speak out on broad public policies affecting the society as a whole.[5]

Finally, there is a question of how much influence business can have on public opinion with this method no matter how credible the message or the speaker. Most managers have a recognition problem the same as many public officials. Who knows them? And worse yet, how many people seriously listen to their opinions? To overcome this problem, managers might direct their effort to the opinion leaders in society or in a community—those people who are influential in molding public opinion on an issue.[6]

Advocacy Advertising   This method has been defined as a form of advertising in which business takes a public position on controversial issues of public importance, aggressively stating and defending its viewpoint and criticizing those of opponents. Advocacy advertising is "concerned with the propagation of ideas and elucidation of controversial social issues of public importance in a manner that supports the position and interests of the sponsor while expressly denying the accuracy of facts and downgrading the sponsor's opponents."[7] Advocacy advertising can deal with specific issues, such as divestiture policy toward the oil companies (see Figure 8.1) or general issues, such as public attitudes toward free enterprise or capitalism (see Figure 8.2).

Advocacy advertising might be used for a number of reasons. One reason may be to counteract public hostility caused by ignorance or misinformation. Surveys indicate that the public has a grossly distorted view of after-tax profits, believing that business sometimes makes twenty-eight cents on a dollar of sales rather than the four cents average that business as a whole actually makes.[8] Such misperceptions, if allowed to continue unchecked, can lead to a great deal of public hostility towards business and contribute to the decline of the public's positive attitude towards business that has taken place in the last decade.[9] Advocacy advertising can attempt to counter this hos-

---

[5] "Political Activists," *The Wall Street Journal*, March 26, 1980, p. 12.

[6] Buchholz, *Corporate Executive Viewpoints*, p. 21.

[7] S. Prakash Sethi, "Advocacy Advertising as a Strategy of Corporate Response to Societal Pressures: The American Experience," *Business and Its Changing Environment*, proceedings of a conference held at UCLA, July 24–August 3, 1977, p. 56.

[8] See "America's Growing Antibusiness Mood," *Business Week*, June 17, 1972, pp. 100–103.

[9] See *Ibid.*; also Seymour Martin Lipset and William Schneider, "How's Business? What The Public Thinks," *Public Opinion* (July–August 1978), pp. 41–45; Daniel Yankelovich, "On the Legitimacy of Business," *Issues In Business and Society*, 2nd ed., George A. Steiner and John F. Steiner, eds. (New York: Random House, 1977), pp. 76–79.

IF THEY BREAK UP THE OIL COMPANIES, YOU'LL PAY THROUGH THE HOSE.

There are people who want to dismember America's integrated oil companies—those companies that do the whole job from exploration through marketing.

Today, more than 50 integrated oil companies compete for your business. Hundreds of firms compete in various phases of the industry—exploration, production, refining, transportation, and marketing.

What would happen if the oil companies were taken apart?

Ironically, prices would go *up*, not down. A so-called breakup would destroy the efficient integrated system and create a need for a new layer of costly and unnecessary "middlemen." Additionally, the chaos created by such a breakup would make it tougher for the industry to attract the capital it needs. Millions of Americans in oil and oil-related industries could lose their job security. Technical advances would be slowed down. Money needed to search for new supplies would dry up.

The result? *Less domestic oil would be available,* increasing our dependence on foreign oil. America could be weakened. You, the consumer, would be less certain of getting the oil—the automotive gasoline and home-heating fuel and other products you need—when you need it, *while paying more for what you get.*

Before it's decided to take apart the oil companies—let's find out just who would benefit. We firmly believe it wouldn't be *you.*

TEXACO

We're working to keep your trust.

Figure 8.1

From *Newsweek*, March 5, 1976. Reprinted with permission.

Capitalism: moving target

The list of things wrong with business in this country is almost endless. Nearly as long, in fact, as the list of what's right with it.

Perhaps the most frustrating thing about business, for those who keep trying to shoot it down, is this: Corporations are so tenacious that they will even do good in order to survive. This tenacity goes beyond the old maxim that man, in his greed for profit, often unavoidably serves the public interest. In times of crisis, business will even do good *consciously* and *deliberately*.

Nothing could be better calculated to confound business's critics than this underhanded tactic. The Marxist dialectic has it that capitalism must inevitably founder in its own inherent contradictions; that it contains the seeds of its own destruction. But business also contains the seeds of its own adaptation and survival.

Businessmen are pragmatists, and with their daily feedback from the marketplace, they readily abandon dogma whenever their survival instinct tells them to. It has become less and less a question of what they *want* to do or might *like* to do, but of what their common sense and survival instinct tell them they *have* to do.

Remember the Edsel? That was one of the fastest plebiscites in history. But it wasn't the American public that took the loss; it was the shareholders of Ford Motor Company. (Then, you'll recall, Ford changed course and bounced back with the Mustang, which quickly showed its tailpipe to the competition by breaking all sales records for a new make of car.)

Because it is keyed so closely to the marketplace and so responsive to it, private business is necessarily the most effective instrument of change. Some would call it revolutionary. Many of those who attack business fail to comprehend its constructive contributions to responsive change. And this sort of change is one of the basic reasons business manages to survive.

Not *all* businesses survive, of course. The record is replete with companies that expired because they didn't adapt rapidly enough to a new milieu.

While businessmen as a whole are not exactly social reformers, they do respond to criticism and to sustained social pressures. The alert businessman regards such pressures as a useful early warning system. The danger is that criticism can become a mindless reflex action that persists long after the basis for it has been dissipated.

Partly because of its ability to adapt—which is simply another word for responsive change—private business remains the most productive element in our society and on balance the best allocator of resources. If you decide to draw a bead on it, remember you're aiming at a moving target. Because, as we've said here before, business is bound to change.

Figure 8.2

tility by presenting businesses' side of the story in as factual and objective a manner as possible.[10]

Advocacy advertising can also be used to counteract the spread of misleading information by critics and fill the need for greater explication of complex issues. Business often believes that its critics oversimplify many issues, whether it is hazardous waste disposal or nuclear safety, thus creating false impressions in the minds of the public. Through advocacy advertising, business can present its side of the issue to counter-balance information given to the public by its opponents. In the process of presenting another side to an issue, the issue itself receives greater exposure than would otherwise be the case.[11]

Another use of advocacy advertising is to foster values of the free-enterprise system, which many businessmen believe have been eroded by the growth of a welfare state with "cradle-to-the-grave" security, and ever-expanding government regulation that saps industrial initiative and creativity. By reinforcing traditional values and beliefs, perhaps free-enterprise can be restored and the autonomy of business preserved.[12]

There are a great many problems with this role of advocacy advertising, however, not the least of which is a possible incongruity between the message and the reality. When business goes hat in hand to Washington and asks for protection from foreign competition or a loan guarantee for a failing business, it does not present an image of having confidence in the free enterprise philosophy it often espouses. There is more danger in this usage of advocacy advertising than perhaps any other. The public is quick to see through an ideological shell game.

Finally, advocacy advertising can be used to counteract inadequate access to and bias in the news media. There is widespread belief in the business community that an antibusiness bias exists among journalists and reporters that prevents business from getting fair and objective public exposure. This bias is believed to be particularly true of television news which is strongly distrusted compared with other media. A survey by Lou Harris and Associates of 600 high-level executives showed that 73 percent of the executives believed the business and financial coverage of television news is prejudiced against business.[13] Businessmen contend that their access to the television news media is inadequate when compared with the amount of time devoted to discussing the viewpoints of the opposition. Television shows such as *60 Minutes* came in for particular criticism. One company

---

[10] S. Prakash Sethi, "Advocacy Advertising and the Development of an Effective Corporate External Communications Program," *Private Enterprise and Public Purpose*, S. Prakash Sethi and Carl L. Swanson, eds. (New York: John Wiley, 1981), p. 400.

[11] *Ibid.*, pp. 404–6.

[12] *Ibid.*, pp. 406–7.

[13] "Business Thinks TV Distorts Its Image," *Business Week*, October 18, 1982, p. 26.

went to great lengths to create its own version in rebuttal of the *60 Minutes* program about the company, much of it footage that *60 Minutes* chose not to air to the public.[14] Thus the media is often seen as an adversary of business. According to Louis Banks, a former editor of *Fortune*:

> We are fed a daily diet of authoritative ignorance, most of which conveys a cheap-shot hostility to business and businessmen. Here is where the nation sees a persistently distorted image of its most productive and pervasive activity, business . . . The reporters and the editors in the general media are woefully ignorant of the complexities and ambiguities of corporate operations, and being so, are easy targets for politicians or pressure group partisans with special axes to grind at the expense of business.[15]

There is some evidence to suggest that media personnel are more liberal and Democratic than the public at large.[16] While basically supportive of private enterprise, they also show a strong preference for welfare capitalism, supporting assistance to the poor in the form of income redistribution and guaranteed employment. The media show a clear preference for post-bourgeois goals such as citizen participation and a humane society. Because of differences like this, questions have been raised about journalism's qualifications as an objective profession.

The key issue, however, according to Michael Jay Robinson, writing in *Public Opinion*, is whether this liberal bias which exists in the minds of media personnel finds its way into their news reporting. After analyzing more than 6,000 news stories and testing almost every dimension of press behavior in a media analysis project at George Washington University which focused on network and wire coverage of the 1980 national political campaign, Robinson stated that there was no liberal bias in the reporting of this campaign. His conclusion was that in "looking at domestic press content, it seems fairly clear that most hard news reporting, whatever its shortcomings, reflects the canons of objectivity more often than the political opinions of the newspeople themselves."[17]

Advocacy advertising can be used to counteract bias and distorted

---

[14] See "Illinois Power Pans '60 Mintues,' " *The Wall Street Journal*, June 27, 1980, p. 18.

[15] Louis Banks, "Media Responsibility for Economic Literacy," speech given at the Annual John Hancock Awards for Excellence in Business and Financial Journalism, "A Bicentennial Examination of the Free Market System," John Hancock Mutual Life Insurance Co., Boston, October 28, 1975, as quoted in Sethi, "Corporate External Communications," p. 407. See also Louis Banks, "Taking on the Hostile Media," *Harvard Business Review*, vol. 56, no. 2 (March–April, 1978), pp. 123–30.

[16] S. Robert Lichter and Stanley Rothman, "Media and Business Elites," *Public Opinion*, vol. 4, no. 5 (October–November, 1981), pp. 42–46.

[17] Michael J. Robinson, "Just How Liberal Is The News? 1980 Revisited," *Public Opinion*, vol. 6, no. 1 (February–March, 1983), p. 60.

presentation, to the extent it exists, and influence public opinion towards a more positive image of business. The corporation can offer its technical knowledge and experience on particular public issues to rebut false impressions created by the media. The net effect can be to broaden the debate about an issue by letting the public hear another side to the story in rebuttals to media charges.[18]

The right of corporations to speak out on public issues in this manner was upheld by the Supreme Court in a 1978 decision. This ruling struck down a Massachusetts law, upheld by a state court, that made it a criminal offense for any bank or business incorporated in the state to spend money to influence a vote on referendum proposals in the state other than those materially affecting the property, business, or assets of the corporation. The specific instance in the case concerned a referendum to win voter approval for a graduated, rather than a flat rate, income tax, which the law stated did not materially affect corporations. This law was challenged by a few banks and corporations in Massachusetts. The majority of the Supreme Court held that the type of speech the companies wanted to engage in was at the heart of the protection offered by the First Amendment to the Constitution, which was aimed at promoting a free discussion of public issues.[19]

The most important question concerning advocacy advertising may be the question of its effectiveness. A poll conducted by Yankelovich, Skelly, and White in 1978 showed that the advocacy advertisements of Mobil Oil Corporation had a high visibility among administration, congressional, and other government leaders, as 90 percent of the sample had read them. On the other hand, 66 percent of the government leaders said that the ads were of little or no use to them in understanding energy deregulation issues and did not have any influence on their opinion about policy matters. Only 33 percent found the ads useful in this regard, and 1 percent were unsure.[20]

As far as the public was concerned, only 6 percent considered public issue ads generally as "very credible" and as many as 53 percent said they were "not credible."[21] However, a Harris poll conducted in 1976 showed that Mobil in particular among the seven oil companies included in the survey ranked highest in public perception as a company that had consumer interests in mind, was helping to improve the quality of life, and was seriously concerned about the energy problem. Mobil was also viewed as being committed to free enterprise, working for good government, and being

---

[18] Sethi, "Corporate External Communications," pp. 407–10.

[19] *First National Bank of Boston v. Bellotti*, 435 U.S. 765. Rehearing denied 438 U.S. 907. See also "A Right-To-Speak Ruling Business May Regret," *Business Week*, May 15, 1978, p. 27; and "Corporation's Right to Disseminate View on Political Issues Backed by High Court," *The Wall Street Journal*, April 27, 1978, p. 4.

[20] "How Good Are Advocacy Ads?" *Dun's Review*, June 1978, p. 76.

[21] *Ibid.*

honest and direct in talking to consumers. The company believes that this reflects a real change in public attitudes.[22]

Some pitfalls in the use of advocacy advertising must be mentioned. First, a high level of intellectual integrity must be maintained if business expects community or government officials to give serious consideration to what is admittedly a partisan position. To help accomplish a positive impact, S. Prakash Sethi recommends that the sponsoring corporation should openly identify itself with the message and not hide behind such innocuous sounding names as the "Citizens Committee for Better Economic Environment."[23]

Second, there must be a congruence between the message of advocacy advertising and business performance.[24] If, for example, a corporation's advertising is directed toward promoting the values associated with free enterprise, competition, and laissez faire, and then is subsequently found guilty of price-fixing or making payments to government officials of a foreign country, its advertising efforts are very likely to be counter-productive and the company's credibility questioned even more severely. Corporations who use advocacy advertising must not only concentrate their fire on corporate critics, but must also speak out against abuses of power by corporations that adopt practices that are illegal or harm the broader public interest.

Then there is the matter of how advertising expenditures are treated with regard to taxation. The Internal Revenue Service prohibits writing off expenditures to influence public opinion about legislative matters. Pure image advertising (see next section) would seem to fall outside this ruling, but sometimes the distinction between image advertising and advocacy advertising is not altogether clear. Sethi recommends that the emphasis in a corporation should not be on what ad expenses can be squeezed into the deductibility area, but on what expenses must stay out because they fall into the gray area and therefore may become controversial.[25]

Finally, there is a possible danger of shareholder suits over wastage of corporate assets by using corporate resources to further views with which some shareholders might disagree. Minority shareholders, for example, might resort to lawsuits to challenge corporate expenditures made for improper purposes or merely to further management's own interests.

Abuses of advocacy advertising would probably lead to some form of regulation or forced disclosure of financial records to assess how much corporations spend to influence public opinion.[26] But properly used, advocacy advertising can serve the corporate objective of reducing public distrust of

[22] "Industry Fights Back," *Saturday Review*, January 21, 1978, p. 21.

[23] Sethi, "Advocacy Advertising as a Strategy," p. 77.

[24] *Ibid.*, p. 79.

[25] *Ibid.*, pp. 78–79.

[26] See A. F. Ehrbar, "The Backlash Against Business Advocacy," *Fortune*, August 28, 1978, pp. 62–68.

its actions and performance. Advocacy advertising can contribute to improved understanding on the part of the public as to what can reasonably be expected of business in fulfilling a society's expectations. To be successful, "advocacy advertising should be an integral part of the total corporate communication program and designed to communicate the firm's public policy positions. The communication must bear a close relationship to the activities of the corporation, the vision of society and its role that the corporation wishes to project, and societal expectations regarding corporate performance."[27]

Image Advertising   This type of advertising does not deal directly with public issues, but instead seeks to better the image of a particular company or industry by presenting it as being genuinely concerned about the environment, health and safety, or some other issue of social concern. The purpose of image advertising is to change the public's perception of business performance through information the public might not otherwise have available. The distinction between image ads and advocacy ads, as stated earlier, is not altogether clear in some cases. The real purpose of an oil company ad trumpeting its commitment to environmental cleanup might be to influence public opinion about the windfall profits tax rather than to sell gasoline.[28]

Examples of image ads are the American Forest Institute ads on forest conservation and the Chemical Facts of Life ads of Monsanto Corporation (see Figure 8.3). The purpose behind these ads is to better the image of the industry by educating the public about issues related to forestry and the use of chemicals in daily life. It is hoped that this information will have some positive influence on public opinion with respect to that industry in general and companies in the industry doing the advertising. Regarding the AFI ads, the Yankelovich poll found that 56 percent of the government leaders and 70 percent of the public said that the ads were useful in supplying them with information on forestry issues.[29] Monsanto spent $4.5 million on its ad campaign in 1977, and has since equaled or exceeded that amount each year seeking to improve the image of the company and the industry.[30]

Economic Education   This method of influencing public opinion is based on the assumption that much of the American public is economically illiterate. The credibility problem business has and the support given for regulation that adversely affects business performance is based on an ignorance of how business actu-

[27] S. Prakash Sethi, "Corporate Political Activism," *California Management Review*, Vol. XXIV, No. 3 (Spring 1982), p. 42.

[28] Ehrbar, "Backlash," p. 62.

[29] "How Good Are Advocacy Ads?" p. 77.

[30] "Cleansing the Chemical Image," *Business Week*, October 8, 1979, p. 73.

Without chemicals, life itself would be impossible.

Some people think anything "chemical" is bad and anything "natural" is good. Yet nature is chemical.

Plant life generates the oxygen we need through a chemical process called photosynthesis. When you breathe, your body absorbs that oxygen through a chemical reaction with your blood.

Life is chemical. And with chemicals, companies like Monsanto are working to help improve the quality of life.

Chemicals help you live longer. Rickets was a common childhood disease until a chemical called Vitamin D was added to milk and other foods.

Chemicals help you eat better. Chemical weed-killers have dramatically increased the supply and availability of our food.

But no chemical is totally safe, all the time, everywhere. In nature or in the laboratory. The real challenge is to use chemicals properly. To help make life a lot more livable.

For a free booklet explaining the risks and benefits of chemicals, mail to:
Monsanto, 800 N. Lindbergh Blvd., St. Louis, Mo. 63166. Dept. A3NA

Name _____

Address _____

City & state _____ Zip _____

Monsanto

Without chemicals,
life itself would be impossible.

Figure 8.3

From *Monsanto Speaks Up About Chemicals* (St. Louis, Mo.: Monsanto Company, 1977), p. 14. Reprinted with permission.

ally operates and how the economic system functions. Many people simply do not understand the role of profits; concepts such as efficiency and productivity have no meaning, and the way a market system allocates resources is poorly understood. Many of the problems business has with the public and with government thus stem from an ignorance about business and the economic system rather than hostility toward business or the system.

More and more companies are developing extensive educational programs directed at various segments of the public, including their own employees, educators, high school students, and shareholders.[31] These programs can include speakers dealing with various economic subjects, videotapes, and reading materials prepared by the company itself. According to a recent *Business Week* article, nearly three thousand corporations, including more than half the top five hundred, distribute educational materials to classrooms across the country.[32] In addition to corporate activities, there are "think tanks" around the country which try to make sure that both scholars and school children have a sound knowledge and appreciation of the free market system.[33]

The three major objectives of these programs are to (1) improve understanding of economic principles, (2) improve audience attitudes toward business in general, and (3) explain the free enterprise system.[34] Whether these objectives are actually attained, however, is difficult to ascertain since the impact of these programs is often measured subjectively, making the success claimed open to question.[35]

Paul Weaver, writing in *Fortune*, believes that most of the activities which go by the name of economic education have little to do with economics in the strict sense of the word.[36] They are programs of indirect corporate advocacy, according to Weaver, and their purpose is political persuasion. Yet there is no evidence to suggest that economic education has made any headway in changing the political character of a community or nation, because it rests on the false assumption that Americans are economically illiterate. According to Weaver:

> Opinion polls do not reveal any great economic illiteracy on the part of the American people. What they do show is that many Americans don't like the profit motive, job insecurity, or other features of a market

---

[31] Myron Emanuel, Curtis Snodgrass, Joyce Gildea, and Karn Rosenberg, *Corporate Economic Education Programs: An Evaluation and Appraisal* (New York: Financial Executives Research Foundation, 1979), p. xv.

[32] "Industry's Schoolhouse Clout," *Business Week*, October 13, 1980, pp. 156–57.

[33] See Trevor Armbrister, "Think Tanks With Clout," *Reader's Digest*, January, 1982, pp. 179–80.

[34] Emanuel, Snodgrass, Gildea, and Rosenberg, *Economic Education*, p. 338.

[35] *Ibid.*, p. xiv.

[36] Paul H. Weaver, "Corporations Are Defending Themselves With the Wrong Weapon," *Fortune*, June, 1977, pp. 186–96.

economy. Giving these people information isn't going to dispel their misgivings.[37]

Americans like private enterprise and the efficiency of big business. They have not lost confidence in the economic system of this country. But people do question the honesty, dependability, and integrity of business leadership. They believe that business serves its own self-interest by profiteering at the expense of the rest of society. They see businessmen as greedy and indifferent to the human consequences of their actions. In general, the public is bothered by the seemingly cynical, self-interested abuse of power by those at the summit of business.[38]

Thus there is a potential backlash in the use of educational materials. Some experts expect that the debate over industry-produced materials will emerge as a major antibusiness rallying point, going hand-in-hand with the debate over advertising aimed at children. Some observers believe the government must step in to protect the "captive audience" in the classroom from being exposed to what are admittedly biased educational materials.[39] The self-interested use of educational materials may only reinforce existing stereotypes of American businessmen and lead to further deterioration of the public's attitudes towards business. Educational materials are no substitute for sound business performance that is in line with the expectations of society.

FORMULATING PUBLIC POLICY

The foregoing techniques are useful for attempting to influence emerging issues—those that are currently being debated by a society which is in the process of forming opinions about a common course of action. The stage of formulating public policy deals more with current issues—those that are the subject of government action where there are already strongly held opinions about what needs to be done. Issues have become politicized. While some options may be closed to business at this stage, business must get involved in the political process to have some influence on the outcome of the legislative process and to engage in more formal public policy formulation. Because of the influence of government on business, it is important for managers to become students of public affairs and learn how to influence the political process appropriately. Various methods of policy formulation may be useful at this stage of the public policy process.

[37] *Ibid.*, p. 186.

[38] Yankelovich, "On the Legitimacy of Business," p. 78. See also Lipset and Schneider, "How's Business?" p. 47.

[39] "Industry's Schoolhouse Clout," *Business Week*, p. 157.

General Business Associations   There are several nationwide organizations that are composed of corporate members representing all or most industries in the country. These groups can organize the resources of many business organizations across the nation to get involved in public policy formulation. They can help business organizations to identify issues being considered in government, gather information about issues, assess the political climate, coordinate the strategies of the various companies that are concerned about a given issue, lobby on behalf of their membership, and perform other functions related to this stage of public policy formulation. Individual business organizations can use these general associations to pursue their interests at the level of the federal government. The most prominent organizations of this type are the National Association of Manufacturers (NAM), the Chamber of Commerce of the United States, and the Business Roundtable.

The NAM moved its headquarters to Washington, D.C. in 1974 and reorganized itself in the process. The organization is currently structured into four divisions covering various regions of the country. The functions of the NAM are to provide early information to its membership at the formative stages of legislative development and activate corporate grass roots programs. The NAM restructured its activities in Washington into fourteen policy committees, each of which is headed by a registered lobbyist who follows a major issue through all the branches of government. The organization also conducts meetings for member companies to bring together corporate executives with the legislators from their region of the country. The NAM's member firms account for 75 percent of the nation's industrial capacity.[40]

The United States Chamber of Commerce has a membership of 154,000, most of whom are corporations, but which also includes municipal and state chambers of commerce and trade associations. The membership relies on the Chamber's assistance in the legislative field in testifying before Congress on behalf of business, lobbying or talking with government leaders, going to court for business, keeping track of the legislative agenda, and speaking out for business whenever possible. This latter function is accomplished through a number of publications such as *Washington Report, Voice of Business,* and *Nation's Business.* The Chamber also conducts a far-reaching grass roots program to mobilize its constituency with respect to an issue. Finally, the Chamber engages in business education by holding legal workshops for corporate executives, conducting executive development programs, and offering a communications education program to teach executives how to use the media, especially television, effectively.[41]

---

[40] *NAM: Industry's Voice in Washington* (Washington, D.C.; NAM, undated).

[41] Phyllis S. McGrath, *Redefining Corporate-Federal Relations* (New York: The Conference Board, 1979), pp. 86–87.

The Business Roundtable was formed in 1972, but it has had a tremendous impact that in many ways has eclipsed the older organizations. The Roundtable was formed partly because many leaders of large business corporations believed their interests were not being adequately represented by the NAM or the Chamber because their membership was so diverse and consisted largely of smaller business corporations. The Roundtable's membership consists of heads of large companies. The organization presently has a membership of about 200 chief executive officers representing a wide diversity of industries and regions of the country.

The really unique feature of the Roundtable is the fact that the chief executive officer of a company is the person who is involved. These CEOs, of course, have direct personal access to the highest levels of government. The Roundtable has offices in New York and Washington, but these offices have very small staffs in comparison to the other general business associations. The Roundtable occasionally hires outside help for research and public relations efforts, but the bulk of its work is done through task forces that cover such issues as taxation, consumer interests, energy, environment, regulation, antitrust, and the like. Each task force is headed by the CEO of a member company (see Exhibit 8.1), who can draw on the research capabilities of his or her own company or the companies of the other task force members. This help is of no cost to the Roundtable itself.[42]

These task forces research issues in their domain and eventually draft a position paper. When the task force reaches a consensus, the issue then goes to a policy committee that works out any differences remaining on the issue and then formally releases a position paper to the media, government officials, and other interested parties.[43] The positions of the Roundtable do not always reflect the interests of its entire membership. The Roundtable, for example, opposed the government loan guarantee for Chrysler Corporation, and Chrysler subsequently canceled its membership.

These position papers form the basis for further lobbying efforts on the part of Roundtable membership. The CEOs of member corporations can use this research for their own speeches or in contacts with individual policymakers. Most of the Roundtable's efforts go into lobbying and related research efforts. The Roundtable also spends some of its resources promoting internal self-reform on the part of corporations as exemplified in its statement on boards of directors.[44] It also engaged in a one-shot campaign of advocacy advertising on behalf of the free-enterprise system.

[42] "Business' Most Powerful Lobby in Washington," *Business Week*, December 20, 1976, pp. 60–61.

[43] McGrath, *Corporate-Federal Relations*, p. 88.

[44] See *The Role and Composition of the Board of Directors of the Large Publicly Owned Corporation* (New York: The Business Roundtable, 1978).

The Business Roundtable has thus far been highly effective and its advice and counsel on a wide range of issues is sought by the administration and Congress alike. The enthusiasm of its membership is probably responsible for a large degree of its success, along with its resistance to becoming bureaucratized. This helps the organization to be flexible and respond to issues more quickly than larger organizations like the NAM and the Chamber, which have a great deal of organizational inertia to overcome.[45] Another reason for the Roundtable's success is its pragmatic and positive approach to problems and acceptance of government involvement. Two Roundtable guidelines are pivotal in this regard:

> A recognition that the adversarial relationship of business and government is exaggerated and counterproductive; that in most instances business and government seek the same ends; that the means to the end, not the end itself, is usually the principal concern; and that business and government must work together to find the best way to achieve agreed goals.

> A recognition that the Roundtable will receive better support for its views, and make a greater contribution to society, if it registers "positive ideas and objectives," and avoids the negative posture on important issues that critics of American capitalism often present as the stereotype stance of the business community.[46]

Industry and Trade Associations

Industry and trade associations perform many functions for their membership, including development of industry standards, conducting educational programs, and industry-wide advertising. Increasingly, politics is becoming the major focus of these organizations, which perform many of the same political functions for their membership as do the general business associations mentioned earlier.[47] Many members simply do not have enough strength of their own in Washington and must rely on their trade association for political activity. These political activities include testifying at congressional hearings on matters affecting the industry, appearing in proceedings before government agencies and regulatory bodies on issues of concern to the industry, contributing to precedent-setting cases before the courts, raising political contributions,

---

[45] Donald J. Watson, "The Changing Political Involvement of Business," paper presented at the Conference on Business and Its Changing Environment, UCLA, July 31, 1978, p. 16.

[46] *Ibid.*, p. 7.

[47] "For Trade Associations, Politics Is the New Focus," *Business Week*, April 17, 1978, pp. 107–15.

EXHIBIT 8.1
The Business Roundtable Task Forces, 1983

Accounting Principles	Roger B. Smith
	General Motors
Antitrust	John M. Richman
	Dart & Kraft
Construction Cost Effectiveness	John F. Bookout
	Shell Oil
Corporate Responsibility	Andrew C. Sigler
Employment Policy	Champion International
	James E. Burke
Energy Users	Johnson & Johnson
	Paul F. Oreffice
Environment	Dow Chemical
	David M. Roderick
Federal Budget	U.S. Steel
Government Regulation	Robert D. Kilpatrick
	CIGNA
International Trade and Investment	Warren M. Anderson
	Union Carbide
National Health	Lee L. Morgan
	Caterpillar Tractor
Product Liability	Richard D. Wood
	Eli Lilly
Social Security and Pensions	Robert H. Malott
	FMC
Taxation	Robert A. Beck
Tort Liability Issues	Prudential Insurance
	Theodore F. Brophy
	GTE
	John K. McKinley
	Texaco

From *The Business Roundtable*, June 1983. Reprinted with permission.

making industry information available to the courts, and serving on various advisory committees.

The nation's capital now contains 1,500 association headquarters with more to come. Many of these have recently moved their headquarters from New York City to Washington, reflecting the focus on politics.[48] The budgets and membership of some of these associations are large (Table 8.1) and managers of these associations can make up to $150,000 a year, reflecting

[48] *Ibid.*, p. 107.

their increasing importance. These industry and trade associations stand between business and government, interpreting the government's actions and attitudes to their business constituency and bringing the interests of business before government officials.

Table 8.1
Some Top Spenders among Trade Associations

Industry	Association	Annual Budget* (millions of dollars)	Corporate Membership
Energy	American Petroleum Institute	$30	350
	American Gas Assn.	30	300
Banking	American Bankers Assn.	20	13,254
Automotive	Motor Vehicle Manufacturers Assn.	11	11
	National Automobile Dealers Assn.	10	21,146
Housing	National Assn. of Home Builders	11	96,000
Utilities	Edison Electric Institute	11	200
Trucking	American Trucking Assn.	11	2,000
Steel	American Iron & Steel Institute	10	2,600
Beer	U.S. Brewers Assn.	8	37

*BW estimates

Source: "For Trade Associations, Politics Is the New Focus," Reprinted from the April 17, 1978 issue of *Business Week* by special permission, © 1978 by McGraw-Hill, Inc.

Lobbying   Lobbying by business has both an offensive and a defensive function. The offensive function consists of getting a company's views on pending legislation across to senators, members of the House of Representatives, their aides, and committee staff members. Of late, these efforts have been largely geared to opposing or at least amending the rising flow of federal legislation that results in greater government control over business decision-making. The defensive function of lobbying is geared to avoiding embarrassing investigations of and attacks on a company or industry. This function is accomplished by providing additional information and presenting the "other side of the story" at an early stage of a committee's deliberations.

The nature of lobbying has changed from what it was in the past. The job demands, as never before, homework on issues and legislators.[49] *Time* magazine reported: "Instead of cozying up to a few chairmen or a powerful speaker, the lobbyist must do tedious homework on the whims and leanings of all the legislators . . . Lobbying now demands, as never before, highly sophisticated techniques, a mastery of both the technicalities of legislation and the complexities of the legislator's backgrounds, and painstaking

---

[49] "The Swarming Lobbyists," *Time*, August 7, 1978, pp. 15–16.

effort."[50] Many yearn for the simpler, splashier days of the trade. As stated by one longtime corporate lobbyist: "My job used to be booze, broads, and golf at Burning Tree. Now it is organizing coalitions and keeping information flowing."[51]

The success of lobbying depends a great deal on finding where the real power lies in government.[52] In past years, this was not too difficult since powerful committee chairmen existed and a few key congressmen exercised great influence over their colleagues. But while power as a whole has become centralized in Washington, it has also become more diffused with the change in the committee structure of Congress, which has weakened the power of committee chairmen. Diffusion of power has also resulted from the election of independent-minded legislators who do not necessarily adhere to the party line, the increasing importance of congressional staffs in drafting legislation, and the growing regulatory bureaucracy that implements the legislation.

Constituency Building

Lobbying only in the nation's capital has its limitations. Corporations have turned increasingly to grass-roots lobbying on the assumption that rank and file legislators in this new political environment may be more sensitive to expressions of political sentiment from their home districts. Grass-roots lobbying takes place in the legislator's home district rather than in Washington, and involves building a constituency that will support corporate interests on a particular issue.

Many companies have instituted grass-roots lobbying programs throughout the company in response to this change. They are putting a good deal of money and energy into organizing employees and shareholders into a concerted voice powerful enough to capture the attention of legislators. Table 8.2 shows the prevalence of such grass roots programs by industry. Table 8.3 shows that most of these programs have been introduced in the last few years, indicating that for many companies this is a new effort.

A company gets into grass-roots programs because such efforts represent a force in the community that is largely untapped. A great deal of political power within the corporation itself potentially can be mobilized to influence government. The first task in mobilizing this political power is to identify a network of individuals who share the interests of the company—in other words, to build a constituency. Employees are a natural source of

---

[50] *Ibid.*, p. 16.

[51] "New Ways to Lobby a Recalcitrant Congress," *Business Week*, September 3, 1979, p. 148.

[52] See Dan H. Fenn, Jr., "Finding Where the Power Lies in Government," *Harvard Business Review*, vol. 57, no. 5 (September–October 1979), pp. 144–53.

Table 8.2
Prevalence of Grass-Roots Programs by Industry

Industry	Percent of Respondents
Food	56
Lumber and Paper	70
Chemicals and Drugs	48
Petroleum	70
Metals	63
Machinery	51
Transportation Equipment	71
Other Manufacturing	76
Total Manufacturing	60
Transportation	31
Utilities and Communication	64
Retail and Wholesale	52
Banks	32
Life Insurance	43
Diversified Financial	40
Total Nonmanufacturing	44

Source: Phyllis S. McGrath, *Redefining Corporate-Federal Relations* (New York: The Conference Board, 1979), p. 37. Reprinted with permission.

Table 8.3
Introduction of Grass-Roots Programs

Years	Percent of Programs*
1940–1969	12
1970–1974	26
1975–1978	61

*Will not total 100% because of rounding.

Source: Phyllis S. McGrath, *Redefining Corporate-Federal Relations* (New York: The Conference Board, 1979), p. 37. Reprinted with permission.

people who share company interests and at the same time vote locally and may even have personal relationships with local legislators. Shareholders constitute another source of people who identify with corporate interests and can be made part of the corporation's political constituency. There are about twenty-seven million shareholders; when spouses are added, the total is more than fifty million people. Some research has found that 96 percent of these shareholders voted in a recent election compared to 53 percent of the general public.[53]

Such numbers add up to a major political force to support corporate interests on public policy matters. Individual shareholders, who are usually the silent partners in big business, may become the political activists of the decade, according to Gerry Keim of Texas A & M University. In a survey of three thousand stockholders from five major corporations within the Fortune 500, the following interesting results were discovered:

> 84 percent felt corporate executives should continue to speak out on public policy issues; while 7 percent disagreed; and the remainder had no opinion
>
> 64 percent of the shareholders supported corporate positions on policy issues; 6 percent disagreed
>
> 90 percent wanted their companies to provide them with analysis of public policy issues; 10 percent disagreed
>
> 57 percent wanted companies to provide voting records of politicians; 22 percent disagreed[54]

These results suggest shareholders can be mobilized to support the political interests of business. If only a small percentage of these stockholders can be mobilized to become politically active, the public policy process, says Keim, would reflect more accurately the interests of business.[55]

Grass-roots programs vary among corporations, but some of the typical elements include the organization of political education or discussion groups for employees and stockholders, presentation of management's views on issues that concern the company, and mailings of political information along with the company's position on certain legislative issues to employees and stockholders (see Figure 8.4). Once a network of people is developed that will support company interests, it needs to be kept informed about public policy developments. It can then readily be mobilized when necessary to respond to an issue by contacting its local elected officials and making their views heard.

Not all potential constituents can be motivated, however, to be politically active, nor are they necessarily interested in the same issues. According to Keim and Baysinger, "effective constituency building efforts must thus identify the politically active subset of constituents and must utilize appropriate members of this group on the basis of the relevance of a par-

---

[53] Gerald Keim, "Firms Silent Partners May Turn Political Activists," *Dallas Morning News,* July 5, 1981, p. 2H.

[54] *Ibid.*

[55] *Ibid.*

ticular issue."[56] Shareholders, for example, may be more interested in issues that affect capital formation, while employees may be more interested in equal employment or job safety issues.

Lobbying efforts at both the Washington and grass-roots levels are believed to be effective and perform a useful function in the formulation of public policy by government. The professional lobbyist in Washington can supply a practical knowledge that is vital in the writing of workable legislation. Potential consequences of certain provisions in the law can be pointed out that may otherwise be overlooked. The lobbyists in Washington are eager to point out such hazards and do so at no public expense. Grass-roots lobbying lets a congressional representative know what his or her immediate constituencies believe about an issue, and makes for a closer link of accountability between elected officials and the people they represent.

Campaign Contributions   Another way to exercise influence at the stage of public policy formulation is to contribute money to candidates for political office. This can be done to help elect people who will be favorable to business interests or who will then owe business some favors because of the help given them in their campaigns. Society has been concerned about this kind of involvement since the beginning of the century, and has passed legislation to limit the financial participation of business in the election process.

The Tillman Act of 1907 made it illegal for business to make contributions to campaigns involving the election of federal officials. The objectives of this act were to (1) destroy business influence over elections, (2) protect stockholders from the use of corporate funds for political purposes to which they had not given their assent, and (3) protect the freedom of the individual's vote. The Corrupt Practices Act of 1925 broadened this concept by defining corporate contributions to include not only monetary contributions, but anything of value, a definition which markedly affected future contributions activities. The Labor-Management Relations Act of 1957 extended these same restrictions to labor unions.[57] Finally, in 1972, Congress passed the Federal Election Campaign Practices Act, which requires that candidates for federal office and their potential committees must make public the names and addresses of their supporters who contribute more than $100 to the campaign. The act also limits the contributions an individual can make to all candidates for federal office to $25 thousand per year and $3 thousand per candidate per campaign ($1 thousand each in primaries, runoffs, and general elections).

[56] Gerald D. Keim and Barry D. Baysinger, "Corporate Political Strategies Examined: Constituency-Building May Be The Best," *Public Affairs Review*, Vol. III (1982), p. 85.

[57] Keith Davis and Robert Blomstrom, *Business and Society: Environment and Responsibility*, 3rd ed. (New York: McGraw-Hill, 1975), p. 210.

Legislative news for International Agricultural Equipment Dealers

ILLINOIS BULLETIN

Unemployment insurance bill passage urgently needed to avoid penalty

October, 1977

Private employers in Illinois face the imposition of a $175 per employe penalty if the Illinois Legislature does not approve House Bill 236.

This legislation will put Illinois unemployment insurance law into compliance with the federal U.I. law and thereby avoid the imposition of penalties on Illinois businesses. If the Legislature fails to pass H.B. 236, the U.S. Department of Labor has indicated private employers will lose the 2.7 percent credit they are now allowed toward their federal unemployment insurance tax rate. This credit—or federal offset—is granted to only those employers contributing to a state unemployment insurance system that is in compliance with federal law. If H.B. 236 passes, Illinois law will be in compliance and employers will be permitted to continue to take the credit.

Further, a quirk in the loan payback requirements the state faces for its U.I. trust fund would also raise 1977 taxes already paid, if the state law does not comply with federal statutes. This additional non-compliance penalty amounts to a retroactive .3 percent surtax on the 1977 payroll wage base.

Some experts have estimated the per employee cost of non-compliance penalties to be $174.60 per employee. To determine your own cost, use the following formula:

Number of Employees $\times$ $6000 $\times$ .027 = _____

Number of Employees $\times$ $4200 $\times$ .003 = +_____
Approximate total of penalties
for non-compliance _____

Utilizing that formula, it has been estimated a small firm with 25 employees would be facing a penalty of $4,365 each year the state unemployment insurance law is not in compliance with federal law.

Figure 8.4

Public Affairs Dateline: International Harvester

From Phyllis S. McGrath, *Redefining Corporate-Federal Relations* (New York: The Conference Board, 1979), p. 36. Reprinted with permission.

Thus both business and labor unions are prohibited from making contributions to federal political campaigns from company or union funds. Some states also prohibit contributions to state elections. These laws, however, do not prevent such contributions from being made from time to time. During the Watergate era it was disclosed that a number of corporations had made illegal contributions to the campaigns of people in both parties. Most of the money, however, went to the Committee to Reelect the President (CREEP), with some companies alleged to have given as much as $100 thousand to Nixon's campaign.

The new phenomenon that has appeared in recent years with respect to campaign contributions is the development of Political Action Committees (PACs). The labor movement had already initiated something called political action committees in the 1930s, which utilized voluntary contributions from union members for campaign contributions rather than union funds. In 1955, the AFL-CIO formed a Committee on Political Education (COPE) to administer these funds which became the model for more formal committees. The legal status of these committees was unclear, however, and unions favored formal legislation permitting the formation of PACs using separate funds for campaign purposes. Thus an amendment was added to the Federal Election Campaign Act of 1971 that institutionalized PACs and established their legality for not only labor unions, but for business corporations and trade-professional associations as well.[58]

In subsequent years, the role of PACs was clarified and strengthened through a series of legislative, judicial, and regulatory decisions. Because of ambiguities in language of the 1971 Act, the Sun Oil Company sought an advisory opinion from the Federal Election Commission as to whether the right to operate a PAC included the right to use general treasury funds to pay PAC operating expenses.[59]

In response to this request, the Federal Election Commission issued an historic advisory opinion, now called the SUNPAC Decision, upholding the right of a corporation to establish and administer a separate, segregated fund out of which political contributions could be made. This opinion set forth rules and limitations for such funds, including the following:

1. General treasury funds can be expended for establishment, administration and solicitation of contributions to the PAC—if it is maintained as a separate segregated fund.
2. A company can make political contributions in a federal election, if made solely from PAC funds which are obtained voluntarily.

---

[58] Carl L. Swanson, "Corporations and Electoral Activities: The Legal, Political, and Managerial Implications of PACS," *Private Enterprise and Public Purpose*, S. Prakash Sethi and Carl L. Swanson, eds. (New York: Wiley, 1981), pp. 359–362.

[59] *Ibid.*, p. 363.

3. A company can control disbursement of funds from a separate segregated fund.

4. A company can solicit contributions from its shareholders and employees.

5. A company can accept contributions to its PAC from any source that would not otherwise be unlawful.[60]

In 1976, the Supreme Court in Buckley vs. Valeo basically upheld the Federal Election Campaign laws ruling that limitations on contributions, record keeping requirements, and public financing of presidential elections were constitutional. But it also ruled that expenditure limitations were unconstitutional, except in presidential elections, ruling that both candidates and citizens acting independently can spend as much as they wish. The court also ruled that the Federal Election Commission was unconstitutional because of the manner in which the commission was appointed.[61]

This action necessitated amendments to the Federal Election Campaign law to reconstitute the Federal Election Commission. With regard to PACs, the 1976 amendments specifically provided for: (1) "crossover," where hourly employees may be solicited twice a year only, in writing at their residence, provided there is confidentiality of contributions of $50 or less; (2) solicitation of executive and administrative personnel and shareholders without limitations; (3) a cloudy definition of executive or administrative personnel; (4) solicitation guidelines, requiring corporations to inform solicitees of the political nature of the particular action and the solicitees' right to refuse without reprisal; and (5) anti-proliferation rules stating that political committees which are established, administered or controlled by a single organization will be treated as a single political committee and there will be an aggregation of their contributions.[62]

These developments, in a sense, opened the door for PAC growth. From 1974 to 1979, the number of PACs tripled from 608 to 1,900. In 1980, there were 2,551 PACs, and by 1982, the number had grown to 3,149, a fivefold increase in eight years. In 1980, PACs gave $55.2 million to House and Senate campaigns; in 1974, by way of contrast, PACs then in existence contributed only $12.5 million. Estimated total contributions of PACs in the 1982 races reached a staggering $240 million. These figures include PACs not only from business, but also from industry and trade associations and similar organizations. Regarding business PACs alone, in 1974 there were only 89 corporate PACs in the country—by 1976 there were 433, by 1979 there were 812, and by 1980, there were 1,251 corporate PACs.[63] There

[60] *Business' Political Awakening: PAC Overview* (Washington, D.C.: Fraser/Associates, 1979), p. 6.

[61] Swanson, "Corporations and Electoral Activities," pp. 362–3.

[62] *Business' Political Awakening*, p. 7.

[63] *Ibid.*, p. i; Federal Election Commission, Press Release, February 21, 1982, p. 1.

were names such as Back Pac, Peace Pac, and Cigar Pac. Beer distributors had a committee named Six Pac and Whataburger called its PAC, most appropriately, Whata Pac.[64]

These PACs solicit money from individuals including employees, stockholders, and others. This is different from using corporate funds for contributions. A company, however, must not use coercion to solicit these contributions. An individual is not to be penalized for refusing to contribute or rewarded for participating. Should such incidents occur, the chairman and treasurer of the PAC would be subject to criminal prosecution. The operation of a PAC is usually monitored by the company's legal counsel.[65] The following methods are generally used to solicit contributions from employees:

Letters from the CEO or PAC chairman

Individual contacts

Solicitation meetings

Solicitation brochures

Management newsletter[66]

The legal definition of a PAC is a fund that receives political contributions from more than fifty people and receives or spends more than $1 thousand a year. Such organizations must file regular reports with the Federal Election Commission. The maximum annual contribution that an individual can make to a PAC is $5 thousand per election. The ceiling on the contribution a PAC can make to any one candidate for federal office is also $5 thousand per election. Such relatively small amounts are not likely to buy a candidate's vote for any corporation, but they can open the door to future corporate influence.

The typical PAC organization is shown in Figure 8.5. The law permits a company to pay the costs of administering the PAC, including expenses for salaries, rent, postage, and the like. Contributions to candidates, however, must be made out of the voluntary contributions of individuals. Each PAC is required to have a chairman and treasurer, and a number have set up contributions committees. The officers of the PAC on these contributions committees must often decide where the money will go, but some companies allow the contributors to designate the party they wish their money to reach and most are open to suggestions from contributors.[67]

In 1980, corporate PACs contributed a total of $31.4 million to political campaigns, ahead of labor's $25.1 million. Trade association PACs reported

---

[64] "Running With The Pacs," *Time*, October 25, 1982, p. 20.

[65] McGrath, *Corporate-Federal Relations*, p. 49.

[66] *Ibid.*

[67] *Ibid.*, pp. 50–51.

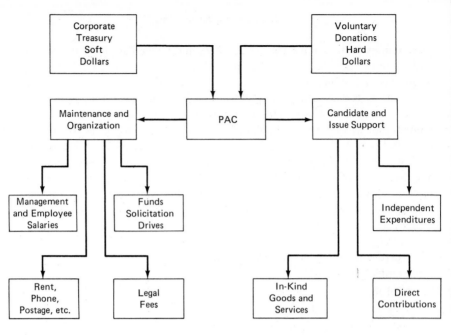

Figure 8.5

Typical PAC Organization

From *Business' Political Awakening: PAC Overview* (Washington, D.C.: Fraser/Associates, 1979), p. 16. Reprinted with permission.

$32.0 million, while PACs organized by other groups contributed $2.7 million. Nonconnected organizations contributed the highest total, $38.6 million to the 1980 campaign.[68] The top ten corporate and association contributors are shown in Exhibits 8.2 and 8.3. These figures show that the amount given by the top ten associations far outweighs the top ten corporate contributors.

During the first few years of contributions by business PACs, it was clear that more money was being given to Democratic candidates than Republican candidates, a surprising development for many corporate leaders. The reason for this development seems to be that PACs were supporting incumbents more than challengers, and there simply were many more Democrats in that position.[69] In 1977, for example, business favored incumbents over challengers by a nine-to-one ratio.[70] The data for 1980 show a slight change in that trend (Table 8.4) as business and professional PAC contributions began to be weighted in favor of Republicans, indicating a shift to more ideologically supported efforts. Still, the labor PACs gave a significantly

[68] Federal Election Commission, p. 3.

[69] McGrath, *Corporate-Federal Relations*, p. 54.

[70] *Business' Political Awakening*, p. 64.

EXHIBIT 8.2
Leading Corporate PAC Contributors to the 1980 Elections

Sunbelt Good Gov't Cmte. of Winn Dixie Stores, Inc. (Winn-Dixie Stores, Inc.)	$251,350
Dart & Kraft Inc. Political Action Committee (Dart & Kraft Inc.)	$226,229
Tenneco Employees Good Government Fund (Tenneco Inc.)	$203,850
Amoco Political Action Committee (AMOCO PAC) (Standard Oil of Indiana)	$193,575
Litton Industries Inc. Employees Pol. Assistance Cmte. (Litton Industries Inc.)	$190,510
American Family Political Action Committee (AF-PAC) (American Family Corporation)	$187,200
Flour Corp. Public Affairs Committee (Flour PAC) (Flour Corporation)	$186,528
Grumman Political Action Committee (Grumman Corporation)	$172,180
Voluntary Contributors for Better Government (International Paper Co.)	$163,750
Harris Corporation-Federal Political Action Cmte. (Harris Corporation)	$160,400

Source: Federal Election Commission, press release, February 21, 1982, p. 5.

higher proportion of their money to Democratic candidates than business PACs did to Republican candidates. Even if a challenger is more closely aligned ideologically with a company's position, it is a fact of political life that incumbents win most elections.

There has been a good deal of concern in government about the growth and impact of PACs, especially those of business and professional organizations. The House voted to prevent any PAC from giving a House candidate more than $6 thousand; the previous limit was $10 thousand. The House also voted to bar any House candidate from accepting more than $70 thousand from PACs in any two-year period between elections. The House measure also provides that candidates who dip into their own pockets to finance their campaign cannot later reimburse themselves from PAC funds for any more than $35 thousand. Formal legislation has been introduced to place a limit on the amount of PAC contributions a candidate for either the House or Senate may accept.

PACs have been widely criticized for distorting the political process in favor of special interests. They have further weakened party discipline, be-

EXHIBIT 8.3
Leading Trade/Membership/Health
PAC Contributors to the 1978 Elections

Realtors Political Action Committee (National Association of Realtors)	$1,536,573
American Medical Political Action Committee (American Medical Association)	$1,348,985
Automobile and Truck Dealers Election Action Committee (National Automobile Dealers Association)	$1,035,276
National Association of Life Underwriters PAC (National Association of Life Underwriters)	$652,112
American Dental Political Action Committee (American Dental Association)	$647,875
American Bankers Association BANKPAC (American Bankers Association)	$592,960
NRA Political Victory Fund (National Rifle Association of America)	$434,603
Build Political Action Committee of the N.A.H.B. (Nat'l Association of Home Builders)	$379,391
Associated General Contractors Political Action Cmte. (Associated General Contractors of America)	$361,627
Attorneys Congressional Campaign Trust of the A.T.L.A. (Association of Trial Lawyers of America)	$360,125

Source: Federal Election Commission, press release, February 21, 1982, p. 8.

cause Democrats and Republicans alike have become more dependent on PAC funds and less dependent on party support. In the 1980 election, for example, it was estimated that 43 percent of a winning candidate's spending in a House race came from PAC contributions.[71] The PACs who contribute money to politicians clearly want something in return; they don't give money out of generosity. They are buying influence in the political process, making politicians beholden to them rather than to the party. There is some evidence to suggest that the PACs are successful in this effort. *The Wall Street Journal*, for example, reported the following circumstantial evidence regarding the influence of PACs on the political process.

> Physicians, dentists and optometrists whose PACs have contributed more than $2 million to lawmakers over the past three years are seeking legislation to exempt these professionals from the Federal Trade Com-

[71] Brooks, Jackson, "The Problem With PACS," *The Wall Street Journal*, November 17, 1982, p. 28.

Table 8.4
Committee Contributions to Federal Candidates
(In Millions of Dollars)

Types of Committees	Number of Active Committees	Number Making Contributions to Federal Candidates	Contributions to Federal Candidates	Senate	House	Democrat	Republican	Other	Incumbents	Challengers	Open Seats
Corporations	1251	1101	19.2	6.9	12.3	6.9	12.3	.002	10.9	5.9	2.4
Labor Organizations	331	240	13.2	3.8	9.4	12.4	.8	.001	9.4	2.2	1.6
Non-Connected	471	243	4.9	1.8	3.1	1.5	3.4	.004	1.5	2.4	.9
Trade/Membership/Health	635	490	15.8	4.1	11.7	7.0	8.8	.002	10.2	3.6	2.0
Cooperatives	36	31	1.4	.4	1.0	.9	.5	0	1.1	.09	.2
Corporations w/o Capital Stock	61	50	.6	.2	.4	.3	.3	.0009	.4	.2	.07

Source: Federal Election Commission, press release, February 21, 1982, p. 3.

mission's antitrust and consumer-protection regulations. FTC Chairman James Miller, a Reagan appointee and ardent foe of most government regulation, calls this proposal "bad law, bad economics, and bad politics." But it has cleared the Senate Commerce Committee and has 192 cosponsors in the House. Of the House sponsors, the American Medical Association PAC has contributed to 186 or 97% of them.

Used-car dealers have persuaded both houses, by better than 2-to-1 margins to overturn an FTC regulation requiring them to place stickers on cars listing known defects. The National Automobile Dealers Association, which runs the used-car salesmen's PAC, has dished out more than $840,000 over the past three years to more than 300 representatives and senators. About 85% of the recipients voted against the FTC's disclosure rule. Last year, 16 members agreed to cosponsor the resolution of disapproval within 10 days of getting campaign contributions from the car dealers.

The dairy interests have escaped most of the sharp budget cutbacks in this Congress. The three major dairy PACs contributed $1.2 million to candidates in the 1980 congressional elections. And in the key vote last year, the House rejected an effort to cut dairy subsidies $600 million over four years. Supporting the dairy industry was Democratic Rep. Fred Richmond, who got $11,500 from the dairy PACs. He represents a Brooklyn district not over populated with cows.

The National Education Association, which sponsors one of the more liberal labor PACs, has set a goal this year of defeating pro-Reaganomics lawmakers. But the NEA PAC contributed $1,000 a few months ago to Republican Sen. William Roth of Delaware, the main Senate sponsor of the huge tax cuts enacted in 1981. Sen. Roth is the chairman of the Senate Government Operations Committee, which has jurisdiction over any legislation to dismantle the Department of Education, something the NEA wants to avoid.

The PAC run by the National Association of Home Builders is expected to swell this year to more than $2 million, an astonishing 60 times the amount of four years ago. Build-PAC made it clear early this year that campaign support would hinge on such issues as the proposal for a mortgage-interest subsidy to bolster the slumping housing market. The PAC managers did pretty well. Of the 18 senators getting campaign contributions from Build-PAC, 16 voted for the measure; of the 153 House members receiving donations from the builders, 136 voted for the legislation.[72]

Besides making it appear that Congress is up for sale, PACs are also

[72] Albert R. Hunt, "Special-Interest Money Increasingly Influences What Congress Enacts," *The Wall Street Journal*, July 26, 1982, p. 1. Reprinted by permission of *The Wall Street Journal*, © Dow Jones & Company, Inc., 1982. All rights reserved.

accused of driving up the cost of campaigning. The desire to buy more and more television time, because PAC money is available, only increases PAC dependency. Candidates become hooked on lavish campaign expenditures just as people become hooked on drugs. In 1974 the average cost of campaigning for the House was $50 thousand; in 1980, the average was $150 thousand; and in 1982, races costing $500 thousand were not uncommon. The availability of PAC money is believed to be largely responsible for this increase.[73]

PACs are not only operative at the federal level. Much attention was devoted to the state level in the 1982 elections as deregulation and federalism gained favor in Washington, pushing the economic stakes at the state level higher and higher. The number of PACs in Texas, for example, rose to fourteen hundred in 1982 from one thousand two years previously, and PACs contributed $2.8 million to the 1982 primaries. In California, PACs tripled in number from 1976 to 1982, and gave $17.7 million to candidates for state office in 1982 representing two-thirds of total campaign gifts in the state.[74]

A study conducted by the Center for Research in Business and Social Policy at the University of Texas at Dallas showed that the public generally perceived PACs to be a "bad" thing by a 2.5 to 1 ratio. The study was based on a sample of 1,007 people representing a scientifically selected and statistically valid cross section of the U.S. population. Data were collected by the Roper organization in face-to-face interviews conducted in respondent's homes.[75]

When people perceived PACs as having a great deal of influence on the outcome of the elections, they considered PACs to be a "bad" thing by a margin of 4.4 to 1 in almost all demographic and socio-economic characteristics. Even business executives, who might be expected to be supporters of PACs, held attitudes towards PACs consistent with the rest of the population. There was also no relationship between a person's political philosophy and his or her attitudes toward PACs. It did not matter whether a person was conservative or liberal, Democratic or Republican, PACs were generally perceived negatively.[76]

Despite these attitudes towards PACs, however, a Lou Harris poll of 600 business leaders showed that 213 of them believed that business is much better organized now than five years ago to deal with politics. In many cases,

---

[73] "Running With The PACS," p. 21.

[74] "Corporate PACS Turning Attention to the State as Deregulation Gains," *The Wall Street Journal*, October 28, 1982, p. 31.

[75] S. Prakash Sethi and Nobuaki Namiki, *Public Perception of and Attitude Toward Political Action Committees* (Dallas: University of Texas Center for Research in Business and Social Policy, 1982), p. 1.

[76] *Ibid.*, pp. 7–15.

this favorable reaction resulted from the formation of a PAC organized by the company to assist in the election of candidates who favored the company's interest. Some 44 percent of these executives believed that, compared with five years ago, business is generally getting its money's worth out of political campaign contributions. In distributing PAC money, 87 percent of the executives polled said they gave money to candidates who agreed with the views of the company, whether they were Republican or Democrat.[77]

RESPONDING TO POSTLEGISLATION OPPORTUNITIES

There is not much to say about corporate involvement at this stage of the public policy process compared with the other stages, because many options for business are closed after formal legislation is passed. During this stage, regulations are written to implement the statutes passed by Congress, and disputes are adjudicated through the court system. It is important for business to continue involvement at this stage of the public policy process. Business may get a bill passed they believe they can live with, only to see it modified beyond recognition as it is finally implemented by a government agency that issues regulations. Disputes over implementation of the law can be resolved through the courts, thus business must be active here also to give shape to the specific requirements of a public policy measure.

Contact with Regulatory Agencies

Continual contact with government agencies is important. Industry has much of the technical information needed if reasonable and workable regulations are to be developed. Experts in environmental affairs, for example, need to work with EPA professionals to reach realistic compromises on pollution standards, timetables, and the kind of pollution control equipment the company has to install to be in compliance. These relationships between corporate and regulatory staffs are difficult to keep in balance. Because of its dependence on information from companies, an agency can be criticized as being captured by the industry it is supposed to regulate. Further complications arise when government officials leave the federal service for higher-paying jobs in industry. Both parties need to remember that they operate in a fishbowl, and thus need to be circumspect and aboveboard in their relationships.

Much of the work at this level is done through advisory committees. There are thousands of businesspeople, who at the government's request, provide data and advice to help shape public policy. Many of these committees are created by Congress to perform a specific task, such as the Federal

---

[77] "How Business Is Getting Through to Washington," *Business Week*, October 4, 1982, p. 16.

Paperwork Commission created in 1977 to prepare recommendations for easing the burden imposed by government reports. Others are set up by Congress to see how well legislation is being implemented. Agencies themselves can set up committees to maintain objectivity and take the heat off the agency on a controversial issue. Finally, other committees are established by presidential order to advise the President on public policy matters.[78] Service on any of these advisory committees can be seen as a way of influencing public policy.

Some agencies have encouraged companies and industries to make counterproposals to the regulations they have proposed, recognizing that managers and engineers probably know better than rule writers how to meet requirements in specific situations. Managers know that no one regulation will exactly fit their situation. A regulation, once issued, is often too inflexible to allow managers much leeway in meeting the requirements in ways that make sense for their operations. Thus the EPA has introduced the concept of "controlled trading" which encourages managers to take the initiative in proposing new ways to meet pollution standards. Instead of writing rules and enforcing them, controlled trading makes it possible for business to propose smarter alternatives before government moves on to enforcement. Thus if business doesn't like an EPA regulation, it can make a counterproposal, which will probably be accepted if it meets the same standards.[79]

It is generally believed that business will have greater success in working with an agency if someone in the company has some familiarity with the agency and its staff. Business is well-advised to undertake long-range programs to establish a dialogue with regulators. Business should understand the mission of the agency as well as the provisions of the Administrative Procedures Act that apply to its actions. Beyond these, other suggestions have been offered to help establish and maintain agency contacts.

> As a general rule, contacts should be initiated and developed at the working-staff level. Subsequent contacts with higher-echelon staff may be necessary, but it is essential to start at the working level. Ideally, initial contact and development of a working relationship should occur when there is no immediate problem to solve.
>
> Cultivating contacts with key working-staff people is crucial in establishing a mutually beneficial and effective liaison. An effective liaison means a continuous informational and working relationship on relevant matters. It does not mean continuous contact at times when there is nothing truly relevant to discuss.

[78] "Advisory Committees: The Invisible Branch of Government," *Industry Week*, February 23, 1976, p. 44.

[79] William Drayton, "Getting Smarter About Regulation," *Harvard Business Review*, vol. 59, no. 4 (July–August, 1981), pp. 38–52.

Avoid "leapfrogging" within an agency or department. In this respect, it is probably advisable to follow excessive protocol rather than to alienate helpful contacts and possibly damage future working relationships. However, if the lower-echelon executives cannot be of adequate assistance, move on. This must be done tactfully to ensure that the liaison at the working level is kept intact. It is important to remember that top officials often refer a matter back to the working level. Make sure that the lower-echelon executives are aware of the particulars and are prepared in advance. Such assistance aids the staff in performing well for its superiors.

Know who does what. It is important to identify the appropriate department or agency and staff person with whom to get in touch on a specific problem. This may require research. Consider these approaches: (1) Obtain the necessary information from existing staff contacts. (2) Some agency or department contacts are obvious; there are divisions or bureaus that are identified with and concentrate on specific industry problems. (3) Telephone directories of specific agencies or departments often provide information on staff and areas of responsibilities. There are also specialized publications which will furnish this information.

It is recommended and generally advisable that concerned business executives work with their associations in establishing contacts with an agency or a department. However, it must be remembered that an association represents the views of an entire industry and cannot appear to be going to bat for a single member.

Once rule making has begun in an agency, it is useful to generate pressure from other sources by mailing or presenting copies of the relevant comments to other key Washington people. Besides getting in touch with the agency, it is essential that your senators and representatives be copied in. The Regulatory Analysis Review Group, the White House's regulatory watchdog, should also be informed.

In writing comments, keep the following thoughts in mind:

1. Regulations are usually more technical than legislative. Product safety standards, environmental technology specifications, and many other regulations are intricate. If you have scientists or engineers on your staff, enlist their assistance in writing comments.
2. Regulators do not respond to some of the arguments to which politicians do. They are not elected to their positions and consequently do not respond to emotionalism. Try to use statistics or other supporting facts for your arguments.
3. Try to quantify what a proposed regulation will mean to your business in terms of staff time and money spent to conform to the substance of the regulation and to meet paperwork requirements.
4. If keeping up with regulatory requirements will cause you to lay off

employees or otherwise reduce your productive capacity, try to quantify these problems.

5. Ask your trade association for information. On major regulatory issues, associations and organizations like the United Stages Chamber frequently form working groups to pinpoint problem areas in proposed regulations and outline arguments.[80]

Use of Judicial Procedures

Business can try to block regulatory requirements in court or contest enforcement activities of government agencies. In some cases, business first has to take its case to a special court, such as the Occupational Safety and Health Review Commission, in order to contest an enforcement action. Most such cases can be taken directly to the regular court system. Many of the standards proposed by OSHA have been the subject of court proceedings. Some of these, such as the benzene standard and the cotton dust standard, have gone all the way to the Supreme Court for a final ruling.

Business has a number of grounds on which it can challenge a standard. Business can challenge the way a rule was made, claiming that a rule was promulgated without sufficient notice and opportunity for comment, as required by the APA, or that an agency did not follow procedural requirements specifically contained in the statute it is implementing. Before a product can be banned by the Consumer Product Safety Commission, for example, it must present facts showing that the product presents an unreasonable risk of injury.[81]

The substance of a rule can also be challenged by questioning the agency's authority to regulate a particular kind of activity, or by trying to prove that a rule is not based on substantial evidence, thereby making it arbitrary and unreasonable. Business may also challenge the application of a regulation, claiming that its activities are not covered by the regulation. If the regulation as written does not clearly refer to the situation at hand in the charged violation, it may not apply.[82]

Regulations must also be enforced in a reasonable manner. If a regulation does not prescribe a particular method for implementing a standard, the agency may not impose an impractical or unfeasible manner of achieving the required result if a business is reaching the desired standard of performance with another method of control. Finally, business can insist upon fair and unbiased agency adjudications, which involves adequate notice and a fair

[80] Jeffry H. Joseph, "Lobbying the Agencies on Rule Making," *Conquering Government Regulations: A Business Guide*, McNeill Stokes, ed. (New York: McGraw-Hill, 1982), pp. 96–97. Reproduced with permission.

[81] McNeill Stokes, "Fighting Agency Enforcement," *Conquering Government Regulations: A Business Guide*, McNeill Stokes, ed. (New York: McGraw-Hill, 1982), pp. 147–53.

[82] *Ibid.*, pp. 153–59.

hearing with unbiased administrative law judges. Unreasonable delay in holding a hearing may prejudice the party against whom an agency action is brought. Witnesses may no longer be available or evidence may have been destroyed in the normal course of business if the delay is too lengthy. The case may be set aside if adjudicatory procedures are not appropriate.[83]

Recently, business has adopted another strategy in regard to judicial procedures. It has begun to file friend of the court briefs with the Supreme Court, an activity which is a relatively new approach for business. These friend of the court briefs are nothing new to some groups, as labor unions and civil rights groups have for years been telling the court how they believe issues ought to be resolved. There were more such briefs filed in the Bakke civil rights case, for example, than for any case in history.

Yet business's purpose in filing such briefs is different from these groups. Traditionally, such briefs are filed after the Supreme Court has agreed to hear a case, presenting a particular point of view on the case for the Court to consider. Business, however, places more emphasis on calling attention to cases before the Court has decided to hear them. The objective is to argue that a particular case is of greater importance to business than the justices might realize. Business believes that early briefs of this nature will increase the chances of the case being heard. Increased activity of this sort stems from an awareness of the importance of the Supreme Court in adjudicating disputes affecting business interests.[84]

SETTING GUIDELINES FOR INVOLVEMENT

Business has many ways to participate in the political process to influence public policy. The Public Affairs Research Group at Boston University asked a question in its survey of public affairs officers related to the importance of various activities in influencing federal legislation (Table 8.5). It is interesting to note that attempts to influence the legislative processes directly are ranked highest in importance, while attempts to influence public opinion (issue advertising, economic education, speaker's bureaus) are ranked lowest.

Certain guidelines for managerial involvement in political activities may be useful at this point. Such a set of guidelines has been suggested by Donald J. Watson, formerly Director of Public Policy Research for General Electric Company and presently a Distinguished Lecturer at the University of South Florida.[85] The first guideline mentioned by Watson is that management must be *proactive rather than reactive*. Anticipation of future issues,

[83] *Ibid.*, pp. 159–70.

[84] "Business Starts Pushing More at High Court," *The Wall Street Journal*, April 23, 1982, p. 33.

[85] Watson, "The Changing Political Involvement of Business," pp. 5–10. Quoted with permission.

Table 8.5
Influence on Federal Legislation

Activity	Mean Rank	Activity	Mean Rank
Lobbying	4.4	Plant visits	3.2
Regular correspondence	3.9	Issue advertising	3.1
Political action committees	3.7	Economic education programs	2.9
Employee newsletters	3.3	Speakers' bureaus	2.8

Source: Public Affairs Research Group, School of Management, Boston University, "Public Affairs Offices and Their Functions: Highlights of a National Survey," *Public Affairs Review*, Vol II (1981), p. 95.

says Watson, buys lead time and encourages a more positive approach to issues. It gives' business time to choose among a variety of options rather than being placed in a position where it can only react to events beyond its control. With a reasonably accurate agenda of future legislative initiatives, business can have time to analyze the elements of an issue and come up with constructive alternatives.

The second principle of management involvement is to be *constructive rather than destructive.* Business in the past has all too often simply opposed all legislation that affected it without proposing any constructive alternatives to help solve the problem the legislation was addressing. The problems, however, do not disappear. Society wants some kind of solution, and if government responds, however inefficiently, it at least looks like a good guy rather than a narrow-minded reactionary. A constructive approach to public policy problems might go a long way toward working out compromises that are acceptable to business and also helpful to society.

Third, Watson advocates a *nonpartisan approach* to political activity. There is only one President and one Congress at any point in time. It is in the best interests of business, says Watson, to work with them in bringing about constructive legislation and regulation regardless of their political make-up. To refuse to do on partisan grounds may reduce business' role to that of spectator, where it again can only react to events.

The fourth principle or guideline is to limit political activity to areas in which management has *competence and credibility.* With so many issues on the public agenda, business must limit itself to those it can speak about with experience and knowledge. The manager must do his or her homework and be accurate so a legislator can use the manager's material with confidence. Competent staff work on a limited number of issues is crucial to maintain the credibility of business in the political process.

Finally, the chief executive officer must be *committed and involved* for corporate political activity to be successful. The CEO sets the tone for the entire organization, and without that commitment, the whole effort is much less likely to succeed. The success of the Business Roundtable can be attributed to the direct involvement of the top management of member corporations. This commitment and involvement is a must, according to Watson, for corporate political activity to be effective.

SELECTED REFERENCES

BLUMBERG, A. *The Scales of Justice.* Chicago: Aldine-Transaction Books, 1970.

BUCHHOLZ, ROGENE A. *Business Environment/Public Policy: Corporate Executive Viewpoints and Educational Implications.* St. Louis: Washington University Center for the Study of American Business, 1980.

Business' Political Awakening: PAC Overview. Washington, D.C.: Fraser/Associates, 1979

CHRISTOFFEL, TOM, DAVID FINKELHOR, DAN GILBARG. *Up Against the American Myth.* New York: Holt, Rinehart and Winston, 1970.

EDWARDS, RICHARD C., MICHAEL REICH, AND THOMAS E. WEISSHOPF. *The Capitalist System: A Radical Analysis of American Society.* Englewood Cliffs, N.J.: Prentice-Hall, 1972.

EMANUEL, MYRON, CURTIS SNODGRASS, JOYCE GILDEA, AND KARN ROSENBERG. *Corporate Economic Education Programs: An Evaluation and Appraisal.* New York: Financial Executives Research Foundation, 1979.

EPSTEIN, EDWIN M. *The Corporation in American Politics.* Englewood Cliffs, N.J.: Prentice-Hall, 1969.

HACKER, ANDREW. *The Corporation Take-Over.* New York: Harper & Row Pub., 1964.

McGRATH, PHYLLIS. *Redefining Corporate-Federal Relations.* New York: The Conference Board, 1979.

MINTZ, MORTON, AND JERRY S. COHEN. *America, Inc.: Who Owns and Operates the United States?* New York: Dial Press, 1971.

NADER, RALPH, AND MARK J. GREEN. *Corporate Power in America.* New York: Grossman Publishers, 1973.

RAYMOND, A., POOL, ITHIEL DE SOLA, AND LEWIS ANTHONY DEXTER. *American Business and Public Policy: The Politics of Foreign Trade.* Chicago: Aldine, 1972.

ROSE, ARNOLD M. *The Power Structure: Political Process in American Society.* New York: Oxford University Press, 1967.

SCHUMPETER, JOSEPH A. *Capitalism, Socialism, and Democracy.* New York: Harper & Row Pub., 1947.

SETHI, S. PRAKASH. *Advocacy Advertising and Large Corporations.* Lexington, Mass.: Lexington Books, 1977.

TRUMAN, DAVID. *The Governmental Process.* New York: Knopf, 1951.

9

THE FUTURE OF PUBLIC POLICY AS A NEW DIMENSION OF MANAGEMENT

⇐ **IDEAS TO BE FOUND** ⇒
IN THIS CHAPTER

- Guidelines for Public Policy Involvement
- The Future of Business and Public Policy

Some generalizations can be drawn from all the preceding chapters that can serve as guidelines for managerial involvement in the public policy process. What lessons are there to be learned from reading this book that apply to managers in general, not just top management? What principles underlie this new dimension of management?

GUIDELINES FOR PUBLIC POLICY INVOLVEMENT The first guideline is that management must get involved in public policy formulation in some fashion, because the environment in which business functions is shaped by public policy whether formal or informal. Management has no choice but to deal with public policy; the only question is whether it will do so in an intelligent fashion with some awareness of the stakes involved, or whether it will do so in a largely reactive mode. In the long-run, the latter is not likely to work in the interest of either business or society. Management must understand what changes are taking place in its environment, and how these changes are going to affect business in general and their company in particular. Management must take the lead in exploring the implications and ramifications of this new dimension of management and how their particular segment of the business is affected.

Getting involved, however, requires an understanding that goes beyond a mere mechanical knowledge of how the public policy process works and who the major actors happen to be at any point in time. Management must develop some solid theoretical and conceptual foundations about public policy. Without being consciously aware of the fact, most managers undoubtedly have a conceptual knowledge of the market system that informs their behavior in a competitive context. They share the values of that system and have a working knowledge of its important elements. These foundations are important in developing policy that is likely to work in the corporation's best interests when it comes to developing new product lines or expanding existing facilities.

The same kind of foundations must be developed when it comes to working within the public policy process. There must be an understanding of the values and important elements that are part of the process, how issues get raised, what problems exist in allocating resources through the public policy process, and the advantages and limitations of the process. Without this kind of foundation, management is likely to flounder around, taking a very short-run view of what can be accomplished. Management must come to appreciate that public policy is not always a needless intrusion into the market economy that is politically motivated. Expediency and immediate self-interest as guidelines may win some battles along the way, but the war is likely to be lost in the process.

Acquiring an historical perspective to the development of public policy is a valuable aid in developing these conceptual foundations. A careful study of history helps us understand how we got where we are today, and may help us understand where we are heading tomorrow. History can help management understand that real problems have been dealt with through the public policy process that were not being addressed by private enterprise very effectively. In our society government most often responds to these problems, not necessarily because politicians want more power, but because they are attempting to be responsive to the needs of their constituencies. These needs are often not able to be addressed in any other way, and a study of history can develop that kind of understanding.

A study of history will help management understand how issues originate in our society—how various forces and influences come to bear in propelling an issue through its life cycle. It is important for management to understand this concept of a life cycle, so that appropriate policies can be developed that will work in the corporation's and in society's best interests. An issue does not develop mechanically, however, and management must develop the political and social sensibility to make intelligent judgments about issues and their potential impact on the corporation.

Knowledge of how the formal public process operates is also essential. The government is not an easy institution to understand and policy is not made according to organizational charts or flow charts tracing the flow of a bill through Congress. Knowledge of government requires constant study of changes in the process of policy making as well as changes in personnel. This knowledge is essential if business is to be influential in the process and not waste its time chasing after fruitless pursuits. Management must be aware that there are many strategies that it can pursue to influence public policy. Choice of these strategies depends on an accurate assessment of where the power lies with respect to a given issue, and what can realistically be done to influence those power centers.

The extent of one's influence also depends on having facts and figures in hand—on having done some hard analysis rather than relying on ideology or mutual self-interest. Management must develop a useful framework that can be used to analyze the impacts a given policy will make on the corporation. This is vitally important given the stake corporations have in the maintenance of a healthy environment that is conducive to the free enterprise that business espouses.

Most important in this regard is the fact that business is in a position to ascertain the economic impacts of public policy better than anyone else in society. Government does not seem interested in many cases in imposing an economic discipline on itself. Most of the legislation passed in the 1960s and 1970s contains no provision for agencies to assess the economic impact of the regulations they issue. President Reagan's effort to impose an economic discipline on the regulatory process through benefit-cost analysis does not affect all regulatory agencies. Even a conservative government dedicated to curtailing the size of government has been unable to do so, as federal deficits swelled to historic proportions.

The public often does not know the impact public policy makes on their lives. Before studies were completed on the compliance costs of federal regulation, the public was largely unaware that such costs existed. This situation leaves business with an important role to play in imposing an economic discipline on the public policy process. Business simply must, as part of its public responsibility, support economic impact studies on proposed public policy measures, and bring these costs to the attention of policy-makers as well as the general public. The government itself is not going to do this job, it has no incentive to impose economic limitations on itself as long as its taxing power remains unaffected. Business organizations, however, can play a unique role in this regard. They must devote some resources to studying the economic impacts of public policy measures, using appropriate methodologies that are as objective and unbiased as possible. This information must then be disseminated to the rest of society. It is obviously in the self-interest of business to do these cost studies. It is also in the public interest, as a society must consider the economic costs of what it is doing through the public policy process.

All of the foregoing tasks present a formidable agenda for the modern manager. It should be clear that the public policy dimension of management requires considerable staff work to be successful. Management must develop the in-house capability to perform the tasks associated with what has come to be called public issues management. Those corporations that are too small to develop their own capability can rely on general business and trade associations. Good staff work is important in this process, and good staff work calls for well-trained specialists in public policy and governmental affairs.

Finally, management must learn to integrate these public policy concerns with traditional business concerns in developing corporate strategy. Management must strike a balance between minding the store and its involvement in the public policy process. There is no magic formula for making this integration. It requires all the sensibilities that have been mentioned previously to make informed judgments about where an issue is going and how public policy is likely to affect markets, capital expenditures, and all other business concerns.

The goal of management's involvement must be to strengthen but not dominate the public policy process. The latter can be self-defeating, as business may learn if PACs continue to grow and be relied on as a major way to buy influence in the process. Business already has a credibility problem, and should not contribute to that problem by appearing to dominate the policy process, acting out of unmitigated self-interest in accomplishing its objectives. Again, the public policy process must be appreciated as a way to resolve very difficult problems that require the development of a common course of action. The purpose of public policy is not simply to complicate the management task and make things difficult for business. The purpose most often is to resolve problems, benefiting business and society.

THE FUTURE OF BUSINESS AND PUBLIC POLICY

These last comments on objectives in the public policy process raise a most critical issue with respect to the legitimacy of corporate involvement in the public policy process. There are many critics of business who would like to severely limit any kind of political activity of business. They believe business can wield too much political power and shape public policy in its own favor much more than other institutions and individuals in society. The economic power of the large corporation can readily be transferred into political power, it is believed, because of the money business has available for lobbying purposes and the huge sums it can raise for political contributions through the PAC mechanism. It is feared that the public policy process will come to be dominated by business interests if its political activity is allowed to expand without limits, and business values will largely shape public policies to the detriment of society as a whole.

It is also argued that business managers lack political legitimacy to participate in the public policy process beyond the participation open to an ordinary citizen. These executives are not duly elected representatives of the public, and to have them play a dominant role in public policy formulation is to make a mockery of representative democracy. Their competence in the public policy arena is also questioned.

There is some evidence to suggest that society or the public holds a rather negative view of business political activity. Such is the conclusion of a Harvard Business Review study which states that while business has become better organized and more skillful at employing the political process, society has shown substantial distaste for corporations' growing political muscle.[1] An in-depth survey of executives and a national consumer opinion poll provided the data for this conclusion.

The perceived propriety of various political activities, especially those that involve direct business to politician contact, is on a discernible downward trend as far as the public is concerned.[2] Where only 37 percent of the executives rate past corporate political activity as "extensive," 70 percent of the public thinks of past corporate political activity in these terms. And while 71 percent of executives want future corporate political activity to be "extensive," only 14 percent of the public sample shares this view.[3] Thus there is a clear divergence between executives and the general public regarding past and future corporate political participation. Society does not seem to share business leaders' confidence in the benefits resulting from corporate political activities, and the gap between society and the executive viewpoints should be a cause of concern for business.

> Perhaps the most significant finding, the single result which business managers should not overlook, is that business and society have different views of corporate political activity. The former group believes it is necessary and proper for its view to be effectively and forcefully supported in the governmental process. The public seems less sure of and certainly less comfortable with corporate political activity. This divergent view has boiled down to the question of whether organized business involvement in the political process is legitimate participation or illegitimate infiltration.[4]

[1] Steven N. Brenner, "Business and Politics—An Update," *Harvard Business Review*, vol. 57, no. 6 (November–December, 1979), p. 149.

[2] *Ibid.*, p. 152.

[3] *Ibid.*, p. 154.

[4] Reprinted by permission of the *Harvard Business Review*. Excerpt from "Business and Politics—An Update," by Steven N. Brenner (November–December, 1979), p. 162. Copyright © 1979 by the President and Fellows of Harvard College; all rights reserved.

The arguments in favor of political participation are based on the view that such participation is inevitable given the nature of our highly diverse and yet interdependent society where collective action on many issues is necessary for them to be successfully resolved. Corporations have legitimate political concerns in such a society because they are affected by this collective action. Corporate interests should be placed on a par with other interests and corporate institutions should be recognized as legitimate participants in the public policy process. Thus political participation by management and other employees of the corporation is not only inevitable, but as legitimate as any other form of representation within a pluralistic decision-making process.

> Our conclusions with respect to managerial participation in the public policy process, therefore, come down to a few very simple points. Such participation is inevitable and legitimate; and, as public policy becomes an increasingly important consideration in the process of management, such participation can be expected to become widespread and significant. Our caveat is that such participation should be acknowledged for what it is . . . both with respect to source and with respect to purpose . . . and that it not be conducted in such a fashion as to exclude other views and interests from equal participation in the process itself.[5]

For this view to prevail, however, means that corporations must take the public interest seriously and make a legitimate attempt to define their involvement in these terms. If corporations' participation in the public policy process is rationalized in terms of either blatant or disguised self-interest, the legitimacy of their participation will continue to be in question and will no doubt be limited. This presents a serious challenge to corporations that has been defined as follows:

> The style and substance of corporate political involvement and the contributions of business to the public interest will largely determine the degree of public acceptance of the corporation as a political participant and whether or not the corporation becomes a positive influence for social change . . . Any inconsistencies in current corporate behavior and rhetoric, or the perception that the corporation is not acting in the public interest, will have a disproportionate impact on the future political role of the corporation and reinforce the negative perceptions created in the past.[6]

[5] Lee E. Preston and James E. Post, *Private Management and Public Policy*, © 1975, p. 147. Reprinted by permission of Prentice-Hall, Inc., Englewood Cliffs, N.J.

[6] S. Prakash Sethi, "Corporate Political Activism," *California Management Review*, vol. XXIV, no. 3 (Spring 1982), p. 33. © by the Regents of the University of California. Reprinted by permission of the Regents.

This challenge brings us full circle to the unanswered questions posed in the first chapter. The concept of public policy, which at first glance seemed to eliminate many of the dilemmas and problems with social responsibility and social responsiveness, actually fares no better on closer examination. As business becomes more politically involved in writing the rules of the game or preventing new ones from being written, the question of principles for managerial behavior again becomes relevant. What criteria, other than pure self-interest, are relevant to guide the corporation in its development of a position on a given public issue? What candidates should a corporate political action committee support—only those who are judged to have the company's best interests in mind and share traditional business values? Shall corporate political strategies be judged solely on their short-term effectiveness, say, in helping to defeat a certain bill that business doesn't like? Again, the nagging question of defining social betterment or of defining the public interest reappears.

Regarding the institutional context, there is the question of the appropriate role for government to play in shaping business behavior. Should government continue with a command and control system of regulation to accomplish social objectives, or should it adopt other incentive mechanisms more consistent with market behavior? Can the market really be used to accomplish social objectives? On the other side of the coin, what is the appropriate role for business to play in the political process?

Lobbying activities, advocacy advertising, and particularly political action committees, represent potential time bombs for business. If business is perceived as too influential in the political process and threatening to the pluralistic nature of American society, and if its behavior is perceived as being too self-serving and not cognizant of the broader public interest, adverse public reaction can be expected.

And finally, the absence of a clear moral underpinning for public policy involvement still presents a problem. Does the proactive approach, which is popular today, simply mean that business attempts to minimize the impact of social change on itself? Does not business have more of an obligation to society than is evident in self-serving attempts to manipulate the political environment? Does not business have a moral obligation that goes beyond obeying the law and complying with government regulations? If business does have social and political responsibilities as well as economic responsibilities, what is the basis of these responsibilities?

These questions are difficult because they are fundamentally ethical questions having to do with a definition of the good life, the meaning of human welfare, the meaning and purpose of existence, the nature of a human community, and similar questions that are basic to human existence. These questions cannot be answered by appeal to an economic calculus such as profit and loss or benefit-cost analysis.

Ethics is concerned with actions directed to improving "the welfare of people." Ethicists explore, in a wide variety of ways, the concepts and language used to direct such actions. Some are primarily concerned with the justification of this concern itself, others with the delineation or justification of principles that specify appropriate welfare-meeting conduct, and others with the relationship between these principles and the rules or character traits that guide people toward specific behavior to achieve human welfare. In essence ethics is concerned with clarifying what constitutes human welfare and the kind of conduct necessary to promote it.[7]

For business to be effective in responding to the social and political environments, it must be motivated to look beyond its own immediate economic self-interest and recognize the ethical and value dimensions of the issues being raised. Thus far business has gotten by on largely economic grounds by raising questions about the cost of regulations, the impact of regulation on economic growth, the economic constraints of being socially responsible, and similar arguments. It is unlikely that this strategy will be enough for business involvement in the future. Public policy issues involve questions of justice, rights, fairness, equity, goodness and purpose—all ethical concepts. For business to participate meaningfully in the resolution of public policy issues, it must learn ethical language and concepts and deal explicitly with the ethical and moral dimensions of these arguments. Otherwise, business may lose the battle by default.

Executives today are living "between the times"—that is, they are caught between the time when there was a strong social consensus that the market mechanism was the best way to control business activity, and some possible future time when society has a clear consensus about just how business institutions ought to advance human welfare. We are now searching for a new consensus: economic language, which has in the past often provided the sole rationale for corporate decisions, no longer, in itself, strikes a note of legitimacy for the American public. While corporate critics speak in ethical language employing terms such as fairness, justice, rights, and so on, corporate leadership often responds solely in economic language of profit and loss. Such discussion generates much heat but little light, and the disputing parties pass like ships in the night.[8]

What can emerge from ethical discourse and ethical analysis is a set of ethical principles that will guide management involvement in the public

---

[7] Charles W. Powers and David Vogel, *Ethics in the Education of Business Managers* (New York: The Hastings Center, 1980), p. 1.

[8] Oliver F. Williams and John W. Houck, eds., *The Judeo-Christian Vision and the Modern Corporation* (Notre Dame, Indiana: University of Notre Dame Press, 1982), pp. 2–3.

policy process—principles that relate to both the ends and means of involvement. Corporations must be able to develop a cogent view of the public interest and then develop positions on public issues that embody this notion. In doing this, companies must think about how their products and processes contribute to the betterment of life, what cultural and social role their products and services play, and what difference they make in terms of human welfare and the attainment of personal objectives. The corporate interest must then emanate from and be consistent with the broader public interest.

> The public interest must not be perceived, prescribed, or acted upon by the corporate community as if it were the secondary effect of corporate actions whose degree and magnitude depend on the extent to which corporate self-interest can conveniently accommodate the general interests of society.[9]

Business must also adopt political strategies that are supportive of the democratic process, that do not undermine our pluralistic structure, and that allow for maximum participation of all members of the corporate community who may have diverse views of a given public issue. Business must not pursue worthy objectives by means that are regarded as unethical and illegitimate. Both ends and means must conform to ethical principles that are accepted by society at large in order for business to attain legitimacy in the public policy process.

There are many public issues either on the current public policy agenda or that will make their way to that agenda that will affect business in one way or another. The resolution of these issues needs business participation. It is in society's interests to have business input, because of the technical and managerial expertise that business possesses. We would have better public policies today if more business input had been provided. But for business to participate meaningfully and legitimately, management must transcend its immediate self-interest and develop a habit of thinking and a broader capacity to think in terms of the public interest. Business must get beyond its bottom line orientation and think in terms of the larger interests of society as a whole. To do so, requires ethics, as ethics and politics are ultimately linked.

Ethical issues with respect to corporate performance are important on at least three levels. At the first level, there is a concern about personal and professional behavior in the context of the market system. The focus is on standards of managerial conduct (honesty, truthfulness, promise-keeping, trust) that are necessary for the market to function effectively. The second level concerns corporate policy decisions that involve questions of social

---

[9] Sethi, "Corporate Political Activism," p. 34. © by the Regents of the University of California. Reprinted by permission of the Regents.

justice. At this level, questions about equal opportunity, plant closings, pollution control, and workplace safety and health are relevant. The third level deals with the moral dimensions of the overall system in which corporations function. Ethical questions at this level include corporate governance, the role of profits, the nature of competition, and the role of private property.

Critics of business also have an obligation to engage in serious ethical discourse with regard to public issues. There is a great danger that ethics will become merely another moral catchword to harass business, and that critics will take the moral high ground and criticize business behavior they don't like from this lofty perspective. If this happens, the opportunity to discuss key ethical questions will have been lost to the entire society.

The public policy concept thus provides business with exciting challenges to contribute more to the betterment of society than it has in the past with a narrow focus on economic impacts and outputs. Through positive political strategies based on a broad concept of the public interest, business can become an initiator of public policy through identifying issues that will become agenda items, and develop positions that reflect public as well as corporate interests in creating a just and prosperous society. The initiator role is a new one, as business has not to date done much more than react to public policy at various stages of development. An initiator role stems from defining the business mission in both economic and social terms, and seeing these as co-equal in terms of importance. Business initiates new products it thinks will make a profit; it can also initiate public policy that it believes will benefit society.

If business assumes this role of initiator, it will have earned a legitimacy it does not now possess. To do so requires an adherence to ethical guidelines in public policy formulation that has heretofore been lacking. The most important task at present is for business managers to learn the language of ethics and engage in ethical discussion, developing principles to guide managerial participation in the public policy process.

SELECTED REFERENCES

The Changing Expectations of Society in the Next Thirty Years. Washington, D.C.: AACSB/EFMD, 1979.

Commission on Population Growth and the American Future. *Population and the American Future.* Washington, D.C.: U.S. Government Printing Office, 1972.

EWALD, WILLIAM R., JR., ED. *Environment and Change: The Next Fifty Years.* Bloomington: Indiana University Press, 1968.

KAHN, HERMAN. *The Future of the Corporation.* New York: Mason & Lipscomb, 1974.

269

KAHN, HERMAN, AND B. BRUCE-BRIGGS. *Things to Come: Thinking about the Seventies and Eighties.* New York: Macmillan, 1972.

————, AND A. WIENER. *The Year 2000.* New York: Macmillan, 1967.

Management in the XXI Century. Washington, D.C.: AACSB/EFMD, 1979.

MORRIS, DUBOIS S., JR., ED. *Perspective for the 70's and 80's: Tomorrow's Problems Confronting Today's Management.* New York: National Industrial Conference Board, 1970.

PERLOFF, HARVEY S., ED. *The Future of the U.S. Government: Toward the Year 2000.* Englewood Cliffs, N.J.: Prentice-Hall, 1971.

THEOBALD, ROBERT. *An Alternative Future for America Two: Essays and Speeches.* Chicago: Swallow, 1968.

————. *Futures Conditional.* New York: Bobbs-Merrill, 1971.

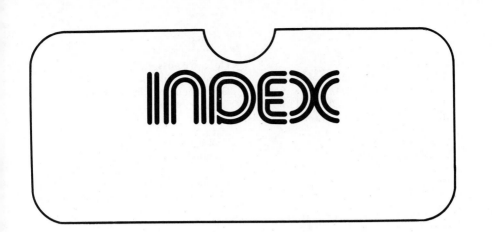

INDEX

271